BEYOND THE MOUNTAINS OF THE MOON

Mpuga

Beyond the Mountains of the Moon

The Lives of Four Africans

EDWARD H. WINTER

University of Illinois Press, Urbana, 1965

Originally published in a clothbound edition, 1959.

Copyright 1959 by the Board of Trustees of the University of Illinois. Manufactured in the United States of America. Library of Congress Catalog Card No. 59-13237.

At Bundibugyo, [Bwamba] you might have slipped back twenty years. This is Africa as it used to be, its people remote, uncivilised, riddled, no doubt, with horrible diseases and cruel superstitions, cooped up in their narrow world, ignorant of spiritual values: nevertheless, for reasons which remain obscure, infinitely more given to laughter and the joy of life than the generation that is superseding them.

The Sorcerer's Apprentice, Elspeth Huxley (1948)

CONTENTS

ILLUSTRATIONS

ACKNOWLEDGEMENTS

Field work among the Amba was made possible by a grant from the Colonial Social Science Research Council. In Uganda my investigations were greatly facilitated by the co-operation and help which I received from various officers of the Protectorate Government and from the East African Institute of Social Research, which at that time was under the direction of Dr. Audrey Richards.

Prof. David Aberle was the person who first aroused my interest in the collection of life histories and who showed me their relevance to problems of social structure as opposed to those of psychology.

As far as the life histories themselves are concerned my primary debt of course is owed to Mpuga, Kihara, Lugangi and Koke. The assistance of Mr. Felix Rwambarali was invaluable. Without his linguistic ability and tact the material, at least in its present form, could not have been gathered. My wife, Elizabeth Winter, recorded many of the interviews.

A grant from the Graduate Research Board of the University of Illinois made it possible to prepare the manuscript for publication. Mr. Thomas Beidelman did much of the actual work.

In addition to Mr. Beidelman the manuscript was read by Dr. Victor Barnouw, Mrs. E. M. Chilver and Prof. Aidan Southall.

I wish to express my gratitude of all of the above individuals and organizations for their assistance.

E. H. WINTER

Urbana, Illinois
March 1959

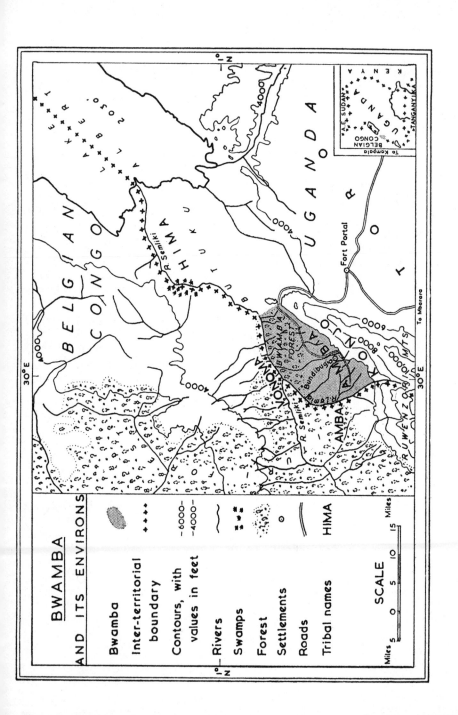

BWAMBA

AND ITS ENVIRONS

Bwamba

Inter-territorial
boundary

Contours, with
values in feet

Rivers

Swamps

Forest

Settlements

Roads

HIMA   Tribal names

SCALE

Miles 5   0   5   10   15   Miles

INTRODUCTION

The life histories presented here were collected in the course of anthropological field work in Uganda during the years 1950–1952. The four people—two men, Kihara and Mpuga, and two women, Lubangi and Kike, the wives of Mpuga—with whose lives we are concerned, are members of a group known as the Amba who live behind a great range of mountains on the western borders of Uganda.

When one first enters their universe it is as though one had walked through the looking glass. Their lives differ from those of the people with whom most of us are familiar in at least two important respects.

The situation in which they find themselves is different; different things happen to them and different things are expected of them. Over and above this they perceive situations and events in a way which is foreign to us. This different way of looking at things is most difficult for the student of primitive peoples to communicate to others. I believe, however, that in life histories of this sort the people themselves are able to convey some understanding of it.

For much of our knowledge of African peoples we are dependent upon the work of the social anthropologists. Broadly speaking, the task of the anthropologist, as it has been conceived by those who have worked in Africa, has been to observe the actions of the people in the societies which they have studied and to interpret these actions with the help of a slowly developing body of theory. In recent years the concept of social system, or social structure, has gained recognition as the organizing framework into which much of this data should be placed and interpreted. The result has been a magnificent series of studies which have immeasurably deepened our understanding of various African societies. Yet there have been complaints that these monographs which describe the highly complex anatomy of social groupings and the equally complex processes which operate within them fail to give their readers an immediate understanding of life in these societies. In rebuttal of this criticism, anthropologists can and do say that it is not their job to produce a photograph of African life; it is rather to go behind external appearances in order to understand the underlying mechanisms at work. Social anthropology has made progress in this direction only by becoming increasingly abstract and

1

analytical. Nevertheless, there is something to be said for the other viewpoint.

In western society to gain the type of awareness which has been mentioned, to get an intuitive grasp of the full complexity of social life, one goes to the works of the novelists rather than to those of sociologists or anthropologists.

In time we shall see the emergence of literature created by Africans. Although there are signs of it already, particularly in South and West Africa, it is very small indeed in quantity. Furthermore, Africa is changing very rapidly and, when such a literature does develop, the situation will be very different and the people who will write it will not have had the experiences of people now living. There are, of course, a number of fictional interpretations of African life by Europeans. Joyce Cary's *Mr. Johnson* is an excellent example. But the reader of the future will never be sure how realistic the interpretation is, how valid is the insight into the minds of the people who are portrayed, or how much it is based upon unwarranted projections of the author's attitudes to them.

In other words, it is all too often the case that if the anthropologist does not meet this need no one else will. Life histories, of which we as yet possess very few from Africa, would go far to fill this gap. Since they are narrated by the people themselves they avoid the risks inherent in a fictional interpretation made by a person from an alien society. To judge from my own experience, they can be recommended, too, as extremely useful supplements to the data collected by standard anthropological procedures.

The four life histories, plus the diary of events recorded over a period of several months by Mpuga, will, I hope, give the reader some understanding of what it means to be an Amba, some knowledge of the kind of experiences he has and the problems which he faces during the course of his life. In the following sections a certain amount of information is given about the Amba and their way of life in order to provide a background for the life histories themselves.

The Country

Bwamba, the area in which these people live, lies a few miles north of the equator in western Uganda on the border of the Belgian Congo. It is separated from the rest of Uganda by a great range of mountains known as the Ruwenzori or, sometimes, as the Mountains of the Moon. The highest peaks, which are perpetually covered with snow, rise to well over sixteen thousand feet. Bwamba occupies a small section of the floor of the western Rift Valley which at this point is a great depression in the earth's surface some twenty-five miles wide. For most of its length the valley is bounded by sheer escarpments rising to plateau lands, but here the Ruwenzori Mountains form its eastern wall. In the past, in order to reach Bwamba from the east, from Fort Portal for instance, one was forced to walk over the mountains. Today the area may be entered by a road which runs from Fort Portal and descends the escarpment after it has skirted the northern end of the Ruwenzori.

The total area of Bwamba is only one hundred and sixty-four square miles. Of this, half falls within the boundaries of the Bwamba Forest, an area which was closed to human habitation some thirty years ago as a result of an outbreak of sleeping-sickness. The area actually inhabited is a very small one indeed; consequently none of the places in Bwamba which are mentioned in the accounts are very far from one another. Another village may be reached within a few hours on foot; in many cases it is only a few minutes away.

The area is very atypical of Uganda as a whole. The altitude is very low; the majority of the Amba live at altitudes of less than three thousand feet. As a result the climate is hot and humid and quite unlike the pleasant conditions which prevail in most parts of the Protectorate. Again, this is a forest area, which is very unusual in Uganda, indeed in the whole of British East Africa. Bwamba is the easternmost limit of the great Ituri, which is famous as the home of the pygmies and of the okapi. Although a large river, the Semliki, which flows northward through the centre of the valley at this point connecting Lake Edward with Lake Albert, is one of the major sources of the Nile, the main connections of the area are with the Congo Basin. The watershed dividing the basins of the Congo and the Nile is in most places only a few miles to the west of the western escarpment of the valley.

The topography of Bwamba is characterized by a series of ridges which are separated from one another by valleys cut by the streams which flow from the mountains towards the Semliki. Very often the descent from the ridge top to the valley floor, a matter of a couple of hundred feet, is very steep. The Amba, for the most part, live on the rather level land found on the top of the ridges. Where the forest has been felled, as it has been in much of the inhabited area to make way for agriculture, and where the land is not actually under cultivation, the scene is dominated by elephant grass which grows to well over ten feet.

Rainfall, which is plentiful, amounting to some sixty inches a year, is distributed within the two rainy seasons which are separated by a fairly dry period. The soil and climatic conditions combine to give the Amba excellent returns for their agricultural labours.

Adjacent Areas and their Inhabitants

To the north, east and west the boundaries of Bwamba are very distinct. To the east the mountains rise with astonishing abruptness. The mountain slopes are inhabited by the Konjo, of whom there are some seventy thousand in Uganda. Great numbers of them are also to be found within the boundaries of the Belgian Congo. They are very sharply distinguished from the Amba both by their culture and by their appearance. Further to the east, beyond the mountains, live the Toro, of whom there are over one hundred and forty-five thousand. The Toro, who in their turn are readily distinguishable from both the Amba and the Konjo, form one branch of the great Inter-Lacustrine group of people who inhabit much of southern and western Uganda, north-eastern Tanganyika and Ruanda-Urundi. Their chief claim to fame lies in the fact that at the time they were discovered by Europeans many of them were organized into large and complex kingdoms. In Uganda today there are four such kingdoms; Buganda on the northern shores of Lake Victoria, which is now by far the largest and most important of them, and Bunyoro, Toro and Ankole in the west.

To the north the forest country of Bwamba suddenly gives way to open grasslands. This savanna area, known as Butuku or the Semliki Flats, stretches all the way to the shores of Lake Albert. It is very sparsely populated by a group of purely pastoral people who are known as Batuku, but who are really a local branch of the Toro. There are also a few fishermen, who live along the banks of the Semliki. The southern boundary of Bwamba, on the other hand, is not an obvious one in either ethnic or geographic terms. The boundary is formed by the Lamia, one of the small streams which descend from the mountains. The Lamia marks the international boundary between Uganda and the Belgian Congo. There are no frontier posts or guards, and one may easily wade across the stream. The Amba move back and forth across the border with complete freedom.

The Semliki River forms the western boundary of both Bwamba and Uganda. The people living on the western bank, although they are not called Amba, are very closely related in culture to the people living in Bwamba. Today, the Amba are separated from the Semliki by the Bwamba Forest, the borders of which at all points lie several miles to the east of the river. Although it is illegal to enter the forest, the Amba do travel through it to the banks of the Semliki, where they are ferried across the river, whenever they wish to visit the Congo.

The Amba have always had a certain amount of contact with neighbouring peoples. In pre-European days they received iron and salt from Toro. This trade, with the Konjo acting as intermediaries, has disappeared, but the traditional trade of vegetable produce for meat and fish with the people of Butuku continues unabated. Markets are held in Butuku twice a week. On the days preceding the markets it is very common to see groups of Amba women walking along the road towards Butuku, bent under the weight of great bundles which they carry by means of head-straps, while the men walk unencumbered. Markets are also held in Bwamba several times a week. The Konjo bring vegetable produce, principally cassava flour, to these markets. Great quantities are purchased by the Amba principally for the trade with Butuku. Those markets, which are often attended by thousands of people, are very important social occasions for the Amba themselves.

Personal contact between men in Bwamba and members of these other groups is often maintained by ties of blood-brotherhood. Blood-brotherhood is often a disguise for a purely commercial arrangement, but in addition it provides a man with a house at which he can expect hospitality in an area where he has no relatives and where there is nothing comparable to a hotel. Also, the man has someone upon whom he can depend for aid when he encounters difficulties in a strange environment. Ideally a man should have at least one blood-brother in Toro near Fort Portal, one in Butuku, one in the Congo and perhaps one among the Konjo.

The Population of Bwamba and the Linguistic Situation

Bwamba is inhabited by some thirty thousand people, the great majority of whom I classify as Amba. Except for differences brought about by modern conditions, all of these people share a common way of life. Despite this uniformity, the linguistic situation is extremely complex. The principal languages are Lubwezi and Kwamba or Lubulibuli. These two languages have very little in common. The language which is most closely related to Kwamba is that spoken by the Bira who live in the Congo. Lubwezi, on the other hand, is related to the language spoken by the Toro. One cannot say, for instance, that southern Bwamba is Kwamba-speaking while northern Bwamba is Lubwezi-speaking. Instead, one finds that one village will be Lubwezi-speaking while the next will be Kwamba-speaking. Two other minor languages are spoken in the area—Mvuba, a Sudanic language, and Vonoma. The majority of the speakers of both of these languages live in the Congo to the west of the Semliki. To complete the linguistic picture it should be mentioned that Toro is now the official language of the government and is the medium of instruction in the schools. On the Belgian side of the border Swahili is the official language.

In addition to the people who, despite their linguistic differences, may all be considered as Amba, the area has always been inhabited by small bands of pygmies, who are physically very distinct and who practise a purely hunting and gathering economy.

The Economy

The economy of the Amba themselves is based upon agriculture. The plantain was the most important food crop until a few years ago, when the groves were severely damaged by a weevil. Although plantains, which are utilized for beer-making as well as for food, have by no means disappeared from the scene, the damage done to them has forced the Amba to place greater reliance upon sweet potatoes and cassava. The Amba do not have cattle. Goats, sheep and fowls, however, are to be found in almost every house. Although many men never hunt, a few devote a certain amount of time to it. They use spears or bows and arrows, and sometimes they are aided by dogs. Hunting is almost entirely a sport, as the amount of meat which is produced as a result of it is minute in terms of the effort expended. In the past hunting was a more important activity, but it always played a minor part in the subsistence economy.

The Amba are now fully involved in a cash economy. The principal cash crop is coffee, followed in importance by cotton. In some years rice is exported in considerable quantity. In general the Amba are in a very fortunate position economically. They have favourable soil and climatic conditions and an adequate supply of land.

The Village

The Amba live in a large number of villages. In the aboriginal period all the inhabitants of the village lived in one compact settlement, their houses being aligned with precision along both sides of a wide street. In the centre was a thatched open-sided structure with a fire in the middle which served as a gathering place for men. Conditions rather like these still exist in a few places in Bwamba, but in most areas these compact settlements have broken up and the people live scattered in small groups of houses throughout the village area. This is the situation in Bundinyama, where the people with whose lives we shall be concerned live.[1] A village has clearly demarcated

[1] The place name is Bundinyama. Members of the lineage are known as Bandinyama, while one of them is referred to as a Mundinyama. As at September 1950 there were thirty-one adult Bandinyama who with their wives and children came to a total of a hundred and thirty-nine people. Of the adult men seven lived elsewhere, in other villages in Bwamba or in Buganda. Five men of other lineages with their families lived with the Bandinyama.

boundaries. In a typical case the village consists of a segment of one of the ridges with the streams on either side forming two of the boundaries. Bundinyama, however, does not straddle a ridge in this manner. Instead, the road which marks the centre of the ridge forms one of its boundaries and another village lies on the other side of it.

A village does not consist of a random collection of people. The village men are related to one another in a patrilineal line. That is, they all claim descent from a common ancestor. Thus all of the Bandinyama men claim descent from Nyama, an ancestor who lived in the distant past. A lineage, as a group of this type is called, is not an undifferentiated unit. Two men who have a common father consider themselves more closely related to one another than they do to men with whom they share a common grandfather. The unity of the lineage group as a whole, however, is seen in the extension given to kinship terms. A man uses the term 'brother' not only for another son of his father but also for any man of his own generation within the lineage. Thus, from the point of view of any given individual, all of the other men within the lineage may be called either grandfather, father, brother, son or grandson, depending upon their generational position. The same thing applies to women. While the men of the lineage should remain in the village throughout their lives, the female members of the lineage at marriage go to the homes of their husbands in other villages. A village, then, consists of the adult male core of the patrilineage plus the wives and children of these men. In addition, a village usually contains other people. Men who are not members of the lineage but who nevertheless have kinship ties with the men of the lineage may come and live in the village. A man who is a son of one of the women of the lineage may come and live with his 'mother's brothers' or a man may come and live beside his brother-in-law. Again, a woman who marries into the village may bring with her children by a previous marriage.

Until a few decades ago, each of these tiny villages, which today have populations varying from about fifty to three or four hundred people, was an independent political unit. The village did, however, have allies, because the lineage about which it was organized was grouped with other similar lineages to form a clan or exogamous group. Despite this system of alliances, which was more complex than I have indicated, Bwamba as a whole did not form a political unit any more than does South America. But leaving aside this matter of interlineage alliance, it must be understood that the village was not and is not a closed unit. As a result of the rules of exogamy a man may not marry a woman who is a member of his own lineage. This means that normally a man must obtain his wife from another village. This, in turn, means the creation of affinal ties with the relatives of the woman. Furthermore, a child who comes into being as a result of the union has consanguineal ties with the lineage of its mother. The mother's male relatives, collectively referred to as the 'mother's brothers', are very important to the individual in Bwamba. To a certain extent his mother's village represented a second home to him. Although a man should live in his own village, he does in many cases leave it and goes to live elsewhere. Should this occur it is very likely that he will move to the village of his mother's brothers. From the standpoint of the society as a whole the fact that marriage can only occur between individuals belonging to different lineages means that all of the people of Bwamba are tied together by a very complex network of kinship bonds.

The village itself has no leader and in the past there was no one who occupied a position comparable to that of a chief in other African societies. Joint action was only possible on the basis of the consent of all the adult men. Until it was finally suppressed a little more than thirty years ago, warfare was the most important collective action undertaken by the village. Warfare was regulated according to the rules of the feud. In brief, this means that if a man of lineage A was killed by a man of lineage B, the men of lineage A tried to kill a member of lineage B. Because of the operation of the feud, small-scale warfare between the various villages was endemic.

Internally the village was able to settle disputes between its members peacefully. Two people with a dispute had judgment passed upon their acts by one or more men living in the village. Very often all of the villagers came together to hear such a dispute. Although warfare has disappeared from the scene, the judicial system continues to operate in a vigorous manner. Whereas in the past disputes with members of other villages were able to be settled only by the threat of or the actual use of force, such disputes can now be settled through the government courts. This question of the new government courts leads us to a discussion of the recent political history of the area.

History

The territory to the east of the Ruwenzori Mountains is, as has been noted, the area of the great Inter-Lacustrine kingdoms. Until the earlier part of the nineteenth century the area immediately to the east of the mountains was under the control of the King of Bunyoro, according to legend the most ancient of all the kingdoms. Then Toro broke away to form a separate kingdom. Later in the century, however, under the famous warrior-king Kabarega, Bunyoro reconquered Toro from the north. When the British arrived in present-day

Uganda, Kabarega opposed them. In the course of their operations against him in the last decade of the nineteenth century the British once more freed Toro and placed a member of its royal house upon the throne. Subsequently the British signed an agreement with him which, among other things, delimited the area of the Kingdom of Toro.

Until this time Bunyoro, and Toro, in its turn, had never tried to administer Bwamba, although they had sent raiding parties into it from time to time. When the British established control throughout the Protectorate, the Toro claimed Bwamba as an integral part of their kingdom. At about the turn of the century the Toro sent chiefs accompanied by police armed with rifles into Bwamba and began to administer the area as part of the kingdom. A few local men were appointed sub-chiefs. However, the status of Bwamba remained rather anomalous until agreement had been reached between the British and the Belgians concerning the western boundary of Uganda. Until 1908, when agreement was finally secured, Bwamba remained a sort of 'no-man's land' as far as the two European powers were concerned. During the first world war the area came under full administration and shortly after the war the poll tax was levied for the first time on every able-bodied male.

During the 1920's the British government took in hand the problem of the economic development of Bwamba and introduced the cultivation of coffee. In the 'thirties cotton was introduced as a secondary cash crop. An event of major importance occurred in 1938 with the completion of a road from Fort Portal in Toro to Bwamba. This road, which serves only Bwamba, as it ends there, finally opened Bwamba to the outside world. Previously Bwamba was very inaccessible and was visited by very few people from the outside world, either Europeans or Africans.

In recent years one family of Indians has established a shop at Bundibugyo. No Europeans reside in the area. The only Europeans who have lived in Bwamba have been the Yellow Fever Research workers. For several years until 1949, one, and sometimes two, worked at the research station in Bwamba. A European Catholic priest based at Fort Portal is in residence in Bwamba for a week or so each month.

The road, however, has brought a large number of new African residents from other parts of Uganda. Most of them have come from Toro.

The great majority of the Toro have come into Bwamba in order to acquire coffee plantations. They have purchased established groves from Amba and have then expanded them. They work the coffee groves with local labour. Many of these Toro maintain their homes near Fort Portal and make journeys of inspection to Bwamba from time to time. Some of them, though, have established residence in Bwamba and live there permanently. With the rise in coffee prices this movement has accelerated in recent years. Now almost all of the houses directly adjacent to the road for some three miles north of Bundibugyo are occupied by non-Amba people, principally Toro. Living near the road is an important consideration to people who make frequent journeys to Fort Portal, because making the journey very often depends upon whether or not the person can hail a lorry which will take him to Toro. The fact that the roadside is now occupied by Toro is important in the present context because Mpuga and Kihara live very near the road and are in constant contact with the Toro and other foreign people who live near it. These immigrants have recently become a major influence in the development of Bwamba and they are important agents of social change.

New Settlements in Bwamba and their Relation to the Towns of Uganda

In recent years two small settlements, inhabited for the most part by non-indigenous people, have come into being. One of them, Nyahuku, in the southern part of Bwamba at the end of the road is purely a trading centre and consists of a dozen or so African shops. The other, Bundibugyo, in addition to being a trading centre with a small number of shops (which are often merely ordinary houses with one room set aside for commercial purposes), is also the administrative centre of Bwamba and contains the residence of the country chief, a courthouse, a jail and a dispensary. The two churches, while not in Bundibugyo itself, are nearby.

Bundibugyo and Nyahuku are very small places indeed. In fact, on first arrival in Bwamba it is quite possible to pass through Bundibugyo without realizing that one has done so. The nearest town is Fort Portal in Toro, which is some forty-seven miles by road (although a much shorter distance by foot across the mountains—less than a day's journey away). Fort Portal, in 1950, consisted of a few rather unimpressive government buildings, including a hospital, and a few houses occupied by a handful of European officials and their families. The well-kept lawns and the trees, particularly the jacaranda trees, lend it much charm. Nearby are a small number of Indian-owned shops lining both sides of its short, but wide, dirt street. The town also has a hotel which caters for travelling Europeans. Near Fort Portal are the large Catholic and Anglican Church stations, each with an imposing church and a hospital as well as other buildings. The Catholic station also includes a secondary school. Another secondary school, under government auspices, lies a few miles from the town. Fort Portal is also the seat of the Toro kingdom, or the Toro Native Authority, as it is officially known. The king's palace is situated on the top of a hill a few hundred yards from the Indian shops.

The main and, in fact, only city in Uganda, Kampala, lies two hundred miles to the east of Fort Portal in the kingdom of Buganda. The Protectorate capital, Entebbe, which lies on the shores of Lake Victoria some twenty miles from Kampala, is purely an administrative centre. In general terms, Buganda, with Kampala as its centre, is the sophisticated modern area of Uganda. Fort Portal and Toro are provincial, and Bwamba is very much a backwoods area.

Modern Political Organization

Uganda is divided into four provinces. The Western Province consists of four districts of which Toro is one. It is at this level that British Administration comes into direct contact with the local people. All of the European officials reside in Fort Portal, although they spend a great deal of time touring the district. A District Commissioner is in charge of the area. He is assisted by three junior administrative officers. In addition there are other European officials, each one of whom supervises the activities of his technical department throughout the district. For example, in Fort Portal are to be found the agricultural officer and the medical officer. Although both of them do come into direct contact with the people (the medical officer, for instance, treating people at the hospital), the bulk of their work consists in the supervision of their African staffs. The medical officer is in charge of a number of dispensaries which are manned by an African dispenser and a dresser, who are capable of carrying out routine diagnosis and treatment. The agricultural officer has a senior instructor and three junior assistants, who are responsible for most of the extension work carried out in Bwamba.

On the purely political side, the actual day-to-day administration is carried out by a hierarchy of chiefs. Toro is a classic example of the system of indirect rule. In Fort Portal are the king and the officials of the central government. Below this level Toro is divided into seven counties, of which one is known as Bwamba, although the county of this name, in addition to Bwamba proper, includes the area inhabited by the Konjo on the western slopes of the mountains and Butuku with its pastoral population.

The county (*Saza*) chief is the highest official permanently stationed in Bwamba and resides in Bundibugyo in a rather imposing brick house with a corrugated-iron roof. Nearby are the court-house and the jail and the living quarters for his staff, consisting of clerks,

11

messengers and policemen. During the last year I was in Bwamba, the county chief bought an automobile, which gives an indication of the difference between his standard of living and that of the local people.

The county in turn is divided into sub-county (*Gombolola*) areas. Bwamba county is divided into five such units, although only three fall into the area here referred to as Bwamba. Each of the sub-county chiefs has his own headquarters. They are less elaborate copies, minus the jail, of the county chief's headquarters. Each sub-county chief has a clerk and two policemen serving on his staff.

A sub-county is divided into five to seven smaller units (*Muruka*). Each of these units is headed by a chief who is known in the literature as a 'parish chief'—an unsatisfactory term. The parish is the smallest administrative unit. The headquarters of the parish chief is often little more than a shed. He has no official residence nor does he have a clerical assistant. He has no policeman. He is, however, assisted by one or two sub-parish (*mukungu*) chiefs. The sub-parish chiefs may in their turn have one or more unofficial assistants. Balikengo, whom we shall meet in the pages which follow, is a sub-parish chief, and Kihara served in this capacity at one time.

It can be seen that directives from above pass through a very complicated hierarchy before they finally reach the individuals concerned. To a certain extent this description of the system makes the European administrative officers unrealistically remote. In the course of touring the district they come into contact with chiefs on the lower levels. The administrative officers make a point of visiting the sub-county chiefs and this may be said to be the lowest level at which administration is effective on a personal basis. The District Commissioner, for instance, is well acquainted with each of the sub-county chiefs throughout the district, but, while he has met all of the parish chiefs, he is not really acquainted with them.

The chiefs also serve as judicial officials. The sub-parish chiefs do not hold court, but the parish chief has an unofficial court. He may hear the cases and render judgment, but he has no power to enforce such judgments. The first court of record is that of the sub-county chief. The whole system is very complex, in that people may initiate a case at the parish level and then take it to the sub-county level, appeal to the county, appeal to the central court at Fort Portal, appeal from there to the District Commissioner and appeal from his court to still higher courts within the Protectorate. Again, certain types of cases may only be introduced at particular levels. Cases involving a sum of money beyond a certain amount may be introduced only at the county level. Cases of manslaughter may not be dealt with by any of the native authority courts, but must go directly to the district level, where the judicial official is a European. The chiefs are also responsible for the collection of the poll tax. Each adult male must pay twenty-two shillings a year.

There is, and this is important to remember, a rather sharp line dividing the chiefs of sub-county rank and above from those below this level. Today a well-educated young man in Toro with political ambitions enters the system at the level of the sub-county. The distinction between these two types of chiefs is rather comparable to that between commissioned and non-commissioned officers in a European army. All of the Bwamba chiefs in recent decades at the sub-county level and above (with one exception) have been Toro, while the chiefs on the parish and sub-parish level are almost invariably Amba.

By this point it should be apparent that this is no simple colonial situation in which a group of European officials exercise control over a homogeneous native population. Here we have a hierarchy of European officials, exercising control over a complex African kingdom which, in turn, exercises control over the Amba. The overlords of the Amba, the Toro, consider the Amba to be very inferior human beings. English-speaking Toro use the word 'savage' to describe them. They view many of the customs of the Amba with horror and disgust and some of them go so far as to doubt the full humanity of the Amba.

The Missions

Missionary activity in Bwamba is carried out by members of two denominations, the Roman Catholic and the Anglican, as is the case in most of Uganda. Both of these have been at work in Bwamba since the early years of the century, but it has been only in the last quarter of the century that really serious efforts have been made in Bwamba, and it has been only recently that they have achieved marked success, at least in terms of the number of converts. At the present time there seems but little doubt that in the near future most of the Amba will be converted to one or the other of these two forms of Christianity. Each group maintains a large central church near Bundibugyo. Each group also has a number of chapels spread throughout the area, which serve as centres for proselytization. Each of these is staffed by a salaried catechist. The Catholics require the candidates for baptism to go to the central church and live there for several months under close supervision while they receive intensified instruction, but this is not so with the Anglicans. In addition to their purely religious work both churches maintain schools. Each has one large school which caters to children up to standard six (the end of the Primary course) and each has a number of small schools with two or three grades scattered about the countryside.

In many parts of Uganda, as in Buganda and Toro, the heroic days of missionary activity are over, and the local churches are well established and operate as they do in European countries. In such areas the word 'mission' is no longer appropriate. However, in Bwamba, where less than ten per cent of the people have been converted to Christianity, basic work is still in progress. The Anglican activities in Bwamba are directed by an African clergyman. Shortly before I came to Bwamba, this post was filled for the first time by an Amba. Catholic activities are directed by a European priest, who is only able to spend a part of each month in Bwamba. Neither church has ever had a European missionary permanently stationed in the country.

Employment Opportunities and Cash Crops

There are a certain number of employment opportunities for the Amba in Bwamba itself. The Government employs a number of people in various posts such as chiefs, policemen, labourers on the road, etc. Also the Amba are now able to work for the Toro on their coffee plantations. However, these opportunities to work for wages are limited in number. If he wishes to leave Bwamba, an Amba may easily find employment in other parts of the Protectorate. Near Fort Portal there are a few European-owned tea plantations. This is one of the few areas in the Protectorate in which such plantations are to be found. Looking further afield, there are many employment opportunities in Buganda. A small number of Amba are employed at the headquarters of the Virus Research Institute in Buganda as a result of the Institute's work in Bwamba. Mpuga's brother is employed there, as is one of Kihara's sons.

Today an Amba who wishes to acquire wealth is well advised to remain at home and cultivate the cash crops—coffee and cotton. In fact, although a certain number of Amba men do leave the area every year in order to seek their fortunes elsewhere, the main trend is the immigration into Bwamba of people from other parts of the Protectorate, particularly Toro, as has already been mentioned. This trend will continue as long as coffee and cotton, particularly coffee, maintain their present price levels.

The cash crops, of course, form a crucially important aspect of the contact of the Amba with the outside world. In so far as the marketing of the crops is concerned it suffices to say that the individual grower takes his coffee or cotton to a central depot, a large corrugated-iron structure, where his produce is purchased by Indian agents who then transport the produce out of Bwamba by lorry. The price and actual conditions of sale are closely supervised by the Government.

Marriage

Marriage forms a central theme in the pages which follow. The Amba maintain that they have always had two methods by which marriage might be contracted: the payment of bridewealth by the man to the girl's father or her brother, and the method of sister exchange, by which each man marries a sister of the other. Until relatively recently exchange marriage was the dominant form. Today, bridewealth is used in the majority of marriages, and a few years ago sister exchange was declared to be illegal. In spite of the ban, it continues to be practised, and, of course, many marriages now in existence were contracted under its rules before it was declared illegal. Sister exchange, incidentally, is another trait which links the Amba with the adjacent peoples of the Congo, for this system is unknown in the remainder of British East Africa. The Toro and all the other people of Uganda use bridewealth when contracting marriage. In Bwamba bridewealth traditionally has been paid in the form of goats and sheep, the only important transferable items of wealth to be found among the Amba until recently. At the present time, and in an increasing number of cases, cash is substituted for livestock in whole or in part. Bridewealth is not fixed in amount; it is a matter of negotiation between the two parties. Such negotiations are usually conducted through an intermediary.

When a woman goes to a man's house with the intention of becoming his wife, she cooks a meal on the fourth day after her arrival. She also carries out certain symbolic acts, such as gathering firewood and bringing water from the nearby stream under the guidance of one of the women resident in the man's group. Speeches are made advising the couple to treat one another properly. This ceremony on the fourth day is not the significant act in the creation of the marriage bond, however; the crucial act is the payment of bridewealth by the husband to the woman's brother or to her father, or the presentation of a woman to one of these men. In the case of bridewealth marriage, when, for example, ten goats have been agreed upon as the number to be paid by the man to the woman's relatives, if the man pays them but one as an initial payment and this is accepted by them, the marriage bond comes into effect. Until payment has been made, even though a man and woman live together, the woman is not considered the man's wife in a full, jural sense. The man has no right to control her activities. But it should be noted that, contrary to the regulations to

15

be found in the majority of the patrilineal societies in Africa, a child belongs to its genitor, its biological father. This means that any children who are born as a result of a union between a man and a woman belong to the man, irrespective of whether he has compensated the male relatives of the woman.

The proper way for a man to enter into marriage is to negotiate with the woman's male relatives either directly or through an intermediary. After having obtained their consent to the union and having reached agreement with them on the type and amount of the marriage payment to be made, he should deliver the goats or his sister, as the case may be, to them. Then he may remove his wife from her father's home. On the other hand, it is considered much more dashing and exciting to 'capture' a woman. In such cases the man induces the woman to elope with him. As the Amba say, anyone can obtain a wife by paying bridewealth to her father, but not everyone can convince a woman that she should elope with him. From the point of view of the woman's lineage the man has committed a theft. The lineage has lost its daughter and sister and has received nothing in return. In many cases the woman's relatives may go to great lengths to recapture her. On the other hand, they may decide to open negotiations with the man. In that case, the woman's brother, or father, goes to the homestead of the man and kills seven of his chickens. Once this act of aggression has taken place, the way is open for the parties concerned to begin marriage payment negotiations. The fowls, it should be noted, do not form part of the bridewealth nor does their slaughter commit the woman's brother or father to accept bridewealth and thus lend his support to the union. By killing the fowls the woman's male relative merely signifies that he is willing to discuss the matter.

When a suitor approaches a woman's father and brothers, the latter are in a very strong position. When an elopement has occurred they are in a very weak position indeed. The man may keep the woman as long as she is willing to remain with him. Furthermore, should she become pregnant, the child will be his even though she subsequently leaves him and returns to her father's home. Even worse from the standpoint of her relatives is the fact that once the woman has become pregnant no bridewealth may be paid for her until she has given birth, for to do so it is thought would endanger her life. In fact, impregnating the woman before he has given bridewealth for her is considered to be a great coup on the part of the Amba man. If she is living at her parents' home when her condition is discovered, the man may obtain her merely by taking a goat to her parents' home and going through a ceremony of purification.

When a man pays bridewealth to the relatives of the woman or when he gives them his sister he obtains many rights over her. For instance, the obedience which she formerly owed to her father she now owes to her husband. She should not even leave the village without his permission. However, this by no means implies that her ties with the men of her lineage are severed or that they lose all rights over her. After her marriage they maintain their interest in her affairs. They are responsible for making certain that the husband fulfils his obligations and that the woman is well treated at her husband's home. A woman who believes that her husband is not acting properly toward her may always run away to her father's home. When the husband follows her to bring her back, he must account to her relatives for his actions. On the other hand, should the woman act improperly, the husband or his male relatives may impose a fine on her of, say, a fowl. This fine must be paid by her relatives. If conditions become intolerable for the woman at the home of her husband, she expects her relatives to return the bridewealth to her husband and thus permit her to obtain a divorce.

When a marriage payment is made, all of the woman's relatives become affinal relatives to the man. Her father is no longer merely her father; now he becomes the father-in-law of the man. As far as observable behaviour is concerned, the most striking alteration is caused by the fact that the woman's mother is now his mother-in-law. The Amba practice mother-in-law avoidance. This means that the man and his mother-in-law should have no direct contact with one another. If a man walking along a path sees his mother-in-law approaching from the opposite direction, he should step from the path and hide until she has passed. However, they do remain in contact with one another, and, in the pages which follow, accounts will be noted of conversations between a man and his mother-in-law. Although a man must hide himself in the house when his mother-in-law approaches his home, it is quite permissible for her to sit near the wall of the house and talk to him while ostensibly directing her remarks to some third person. He may direct his remarks to another person inside the house or even in some cases think out loud. The man should give his mother-in-law presents from time to time, and today when bridewealth is paid an additional goat intended for the mother-in-law should be added to the number. Very often, when a man wishes to marry a girl, he makes particular efforts to gain the sympathy of her mother, and it is not uncommon for her to be deeply involved in the elopement of the young couple, although, if she is wise, she will do everything she can to avoid arousing in her husband any suspicion of her complicity.

A marriage, as has already been indicated, may be terminated by divorce. To dissolve the marriage bonds the woman's relatives must return the bridewealth to her husband or, in the case of an exchange marriage, they must return his sister to him. Divorce, as well becomes readily apparent, is a very common occurrence in Bwamba.

Should a man die, his widow may be taken in marriage by any man who is a member of his patrilineage, even by his son, if another woman gave birth to him. This is not an obligatory matter. If the woman wishes, she may return to her parental home. If she decides to remain with the lineage, she is at liberty to select her own husband. A special ceremony is carried out, the main purpose of which is to inform the spirit of the dead man of the new state of affairs. No payment is made to her lineage on this occasion, because it is considered that her first husband obtained her not for himself alone but for his lineage as a whole. This form of marriage is known as widow inheritance; it is not the levirate. That is, the children of the second union are considered to be children of the second husband; they are not counted as descendants of the dead man as is the case when the leviratic rule is practised.

Life Cycle

When a child is born, it is kept in the house for the first four days. Then it is brought into the courtyard and given its name in a brief ceremony. Should the child cry for any prolonged period after this, it is suspected that an ancestor is causing the trouble, and the father consults a diviner to discover whether or not this is the case. When the identity of the ancestor has been discovered by divination, the child is given his name.

In the ideal case the child should grow to maturity in the home of his parents, but the divorce of the parents often interferes with this. When divorce occurs, the woman has no right to the child in this strongly patrilineal society. However, if the child is very young, the father should allow the mother to take the infant with her for the child's own welfare. Furthermore, a woman may take a child of any age with her if she has her ex-husband's permission and if her new husband allows her to bring the child into his home. If a child is brought up in the house of such a man, the father of the child must subsequently pay him a fee for having 'grown' the child.

The Amba practise circumcision. In 1953, a year after I left Bwamba, circumcision ceremonies were held throughout the area for the first time in twenty years. Each village conducted its own ceremony, and all boys within the village above the age of five or six were circumcised. Although twenty years was an unusually long period to have elapsed between ceremonies, it appears that in the past they were never held at intervals of less than fourteen years. Since the ages of the participants may vary from five or six to twenty-four or twenty-five years, circumcision cannot be considered a puberty ceremony. Circumcision is not linked with any system of age grading, nor is it a prerequisite for marriage. Both Kigara and Mpuga were married before they were circumcised. Nothing similar to circumcision occurs in the life of a girl.

Marriage is the goal of everyone in Bwamba. A man is not considered to be fully adult until he has a wife and a house of his own. A woman, in addition to being married, must give birth to a child before she is accorded full adult status. Although many men do not marry for the first time until they are over twenty, girls are normally married shortly after they reach puberty, although, particularly in the past when sister exchange was the predominant form of marriage, girls were sometimes given in marriage before they reached puberty.

A woman should give birth to her first child at her husband's home. She need not be married in the full jural sense, with bridewealth having been paid for her, when she becomes pregnant. Trouble occurs only when she is unmarried and becomes pregnant while at her father's home.

In the normal course of events a child's birth occurs quite unobtrusively, the woman being attended perhaps only by another woman in her husband's group. However, when difficulties occur a great deal of tension develops. Midwives and diviners are brought to the house and a great number of people congregate. The husband may kill a goat and serve a meal to those present in the belief that this will satisfy the witches among them who are attempting to kill the woman. Death during childbirth appears to be common among the Amba.

Death sets in motion much group activity. The person is buried on the same or the succeeding day. On the fourth day after the burial a ceremony is held which is invariably attended by a great number of people. Many relatives of the deceased from outside the village come to it and many people are attracted by the intrinsic interest of the proceedings, since these death ceremonies are almost inevitably exciting. A man representing the lineage of the dead man or, in the case of a woman, the dead woman's husband, stands up and gives a long account of the events leading up to the death and the probable causes of it. If possible, he tries to point out the person or persons who are suspected of having bewitched the deceased. It is not a hereditary post or one conferring any authority. It is merely assigned to someone who is an able speaker. When a man has died, a goat is given to the men of his mother's lineage. If a woman has died the goat is given to her patrilineage. The object of the speech is to try to satisfy the mother's brother's lineage or the woman's own lineage, as the case may be, as to the causes of the death.

A second ceremony is held some three months later. On this occasion a man's widows are released from their mourning obligations and are now free to take another husband by the terms of widow inheritance or to return to their own homes.

The Family

The basic unit, the elementary family, is brought into being by the marriage of a man and woman and the subsequent birth of children. This unit is often embedded in larger and more complex groups. A man may have two or more wives, and they and their children and the man himself form a polygamous family. The man often lives with his father and his brothers and their families in an extended family grouping. Upon his death, the father's property is divided among his sons, while one of them, usually but not necessarily the eldest, is chosen to be his successor. For example, Mpuga is the successor of his father, while Kihara, although he expected to take his father's place upon the latter's death, was passed over in favour of a younger half-brother, Batigwa. The degree of authority possessed by the successor varies a great deal from case to case, depending upon such factors as whether or not the sons are full or half-brothers, their relative ages, etc., but it is always much less effective than the authority possessed by the father. When the sons in their turn die, no one among the grandsons is chosen to lead the group as a whole. Instead, each son has his own successor.

Despite the fact that the unit consisting of an elderly man, his wife, his sons, and their wives and children considers itself a group, most activities are carried out on a very low level of organization, on the level of the elementary family. For example, the extended family does not farm as a unit. Each woman has her own plots; if a man has three wives, then each wife will have her own sweet potato garden, plantain grove, cotton plot, etc.

A man is responsible among other things for providing his wives with housing, clothing and meat or fish. In the agricultural sphere the man is responsible for clearing the land of trees or elephant grass. The woman is responsible for the bulk of the work involved in cultivation. The hoe is her most important tool, in contrast to the axe and the knife of the man. She is also responsible for the bulk of the work connected with the house, such as the preparation of food, child care and the collection of firewood and water.

In the past the man obtained meat either by hunting or by trade with the people of Butuku. Today meat is usually obtained by using cash obtained from the sale of the cash crops, although this may occur in a rather roundabout way, as when a man buys cassava from the Konjo for cash and has it transported to Butuku, where it is traded for meat and fish. In order to keep his wives contented a man must give them liberal supplies of meat and fish.

Traditionally the Amba, both men and women, wore merely a simple loincloth made of bark cloth manufactured by the men. In 1950 the majority of the Amba still dressed in this fashion. However, the use of cotton cloth in the form of shapeless cotton dresses for the women and shirts and shorts for the men was becoming increasingly common. Two years later, the majority of people, at least when they left their homes, wore cotton clothing. The cotton cloth is purchased at the few shops in Bwamba or at shops in the Congo. This too must be purchased with money earned by the man.

Each woman should have her own house. If a man has three wives he should have three houses. The man should live in them in rotation. If he spends one night in the house of one of his wives, he must spend the next two nights in the houses of the other wives. Similarly, if he spends one week in the house of the first wife, he must stay a week in the house of each of the other wives. In Bwamba the house is the woman's castle. She and her children live in it. It is where she prepares meals and stores her tools, utensils and food supplies. The man may keep his personal possessions in which ever house he wishes. Very often such things as knives, spears, extra clothing, etc., are kept either in the house of his mother, if she is alive, or in the house of the senior wife. Livestock, goats and sheep are distributed among the houses. This is rather important since, should the man die, livestock kept in the house of any particular woman are inherited only by her children.

In the past, the Amba house was of a simple beehive construction. In the front was a doorway; a windscreen separated the entrance from the rest of the house. In the centre was a fireplace and around the sides were the beds, storage spaces, and platforms on which the goat and sheep were placed at night. Such houses are now comparatively rare in Bwamba. The modern house is rectangular rather than circular. Instead of the single entrance of the older type, it usually contains both a front and rear entrance and may contain windows. Instead of having the thatch reach the ground all the way around the house, the modern house has walls constructed of mud and wattle six to ten feet in height. The roof, which continues to be made of thatch, projects outward and creates a verandah around the house. The interior of the house is divided into a number of small rooms.

The new cash crops by the sale of which the man obtains money to carry out his traditional obligations to supply his wife or wives with meat, fish and clothing are seen as being the primary responsibility of the man, in contrast to the food crops for which the women

C   21

are primarily responsible. Although the case of cotton is more complex, as far as coffee, the main cash crop, is concerned, the men do the bulk of the work, with the exception of the weeding between the rows, which is the work of the women. Even under modern conditions when the men are more active in the agricultural sphere as a result of the cultivation of these new crops, the men actually do very little work. The women, although they do work longer hours in the fields than do the men, do not work excessively long hours in the agricultural sphere by comparative standards. But their household duties, duties from which the men are largely free, occupy them for long periods during the day. Thus the men have much more freedom of action.

The Supernatural: Religion and Witchcraft

The Amba believe in the existence of a very large number of supernatural beings. Many of these beings are thought to be able to influence people in their daily lives. The ancestors who live in a world below this one, a world which is very much like Bwamba, should be offered sacrifices from time to time in order to prevent them from causing trouble or bringing misfortune. At times, ancestors, particularly parents, speak to the living directly during dreams.

Although men sometimes have hunting spirits for which they build small miniature houses where they make sacrifices after a successful day's hunt, the most important spirits are those which 'catch' women when they are away from home collecting firewood or water. These spirits must be brought into the house and 'put upon the head' of the women, for unless this is done, the woman will become ill and may die, and various misfortunes may afflict other members of the family. Senior priestesses are brought to the house and they conduct an elaborate week-long ceremony which involves much drumming, dancing and singing. Very often during the course of these ceremonies the priestesses and the 'patient' go into trance states, either genuine or feigned, during the course of which the spirits speak through them. If a woman divorces a man and remarries, she is often required to conduct an additional ceremony to install the spirit in her new home. When a woman dies, her spirit leaves the house. Mpuga's mother, however, had a special type of spirit 'on her head', the goddess Nyakala, who does not return to her wild haunts but who instead seeks to possess one of the daughters-in-law of the deceased.

Generally speaking, misfortunes, as far as the Amba are concerned, do not merely occur. Almost always a casual agent is thought to be involved. Sometimes misfortunes are caused by ancestors; sometimes they are caused by other types of supernatural entities.

22

However, the vast majority of them are thought to occur as a result of witchcraft activities by someone, or some group of people, with whom the person is in contact.

The true witches are said to be cannibals. They kill people in order to devour them. Very often, it is thought, they seize a person at night when he is asleep. They drag him out of his hut, open his abdomen and remove his intestines. They then close the incision in a magical manner so that it is not visible. The victim survives a short time, perhaps a day or two, and then dies. After the death and burial, the witches return, disinter the corpse and eat it. It is believed that in each village a certain number of people who are cannibals of this type act as a group. A particularly sinister feature of their activity is the fact that a given group preys only upon members of its own village. Such a group does, however, co-operate with witches in other villages, in that they invite neighbouring groups of witches to the village to share the feast with them. Such favours should be reciprocated as nearly as possible in the same form. Thus, if the witches of Bundinyama have been invited to share in a feast of a young unmarried boy in Bundito-kwe, the witches of Bundinyama are obligated at a later date to serve a meal consisting of a similar young unmarried boy. They should not, for instance, serve a married woman in return. There is thought to be a group of such witches in the village with which we are concerned to which men, women and even children belong. However, no one can be absolutely certain of the identity of these people. Not even the most powerful diviner seems able to give a definitive list. Only occasionally, it is thought, do such witches give hints as to their identity, for instance by being observed standing on their heads, or going about naked or dressed in plantain leaves at night. In the past it was often possible to identify a witch among a number of suspects by administering the poison ordeal to them. The innocent vomited, while the guilty were unable to do so.

Some witches are said to have the ability to turn into leopards at will, while others have leopards which, at their command, will hunt down human beings for them.

In addition, each village is believed to contain a group of witches who specialize in the destruction of gardens by magical means. These people are, of course, not considered nearly so dangerous as the others, although, should a person come upon them at night while they are conducting their rites, dancing and singing, the Amba say that they might kill him in order to preserve their anonymity.

Ordinary people, who are not witches in the above sense, may practise sorcery. The Amba think that anyone may obtain medicines, sometimes accompanied by spells, which have lethal powers by buying them from a specialist. The basic principle is to bring medicine

23

into contact with the intended victim. An obvious way is to administer it to him in his food. It is possible, therefore, that death may sometimes occur in Bwamba as a result of genuine poisoning but if such cases do actually exist, and I am rather sceptical of their occurrence, they are certainly rare. In most instances the poison is thought to be placed in the victim's house or buried in a path which he uses every day, or even blown in his direction from a distance. While most medicines are said to be made from plants of various types, human flesh is considered equally dangerous when administered, for instance, in a soup. In addition to purchasing medicines of this sort there are certain methods which anyone may utilize; a man may strike a sleeping child with his penis and the child will die, or a person may defecate in a garden with a withering effect on the plants growing in it. Sometimes it is thought that people are able to inject foreign bodies, such as arrowheads, bits of bark cloth, etc., into their victims by shooting them into their bodies by magical means. Although a certain amount of actual sorcery undoubtedly occurs, that is, sometimes people do actually try to harm others by magical means, this is a relatively minor matter. What is vastly more important for an understanding of the Amba is the fact that they constantly suspect that they are being bewitched or that they may be in the immediate future.

When the Amba talk about witchcraft and sorcery in the abstract they speak as though it were effective at any distance. In actual fact, they behave on the assumption that witchcraft in any particular case emanates from someone in the immediate vicinity of the person who is ill. Thus, when a person is seriously ill, he is very often removed secretly from his house at night and carried, perhaps, several miles to the house of a relative in order to save him from further attacks.

Diviners

Living in Bwamba are a large number of men whom I refer to variously as diviners or doctors. Whenever an Amba is worried about something he may consult one of these men for a small fee. Usually they are consulted in cases of illness. The diviners use a variety of techniques, going into trance states, looking into a bowl full of water, watching the pattern of beans as they fall upon the ground, etc. They are not so much fortune-tellers as diagnosticians, analysing the causes of the client's present difficulties. An Amba prefers to consult diviners who live at some distance from his home, because he is suspicious of those who live nearby, since they know so much about him that it is not possible for him to evaluate their power properly.

In addition to their diagnostic activities most of these men are prepared to undertake a variety of other tasks. They may remove witchcraft substances from the body of a sufferer by sucking them out with a horn; they may 'smell out' witchcraft substances which have been planted near the house of a man; they may concoct a love potion, etc. In general they are prepared to put their hand to almost any work in the supernatural realm.

Whereas the doctors' medicines always have something magical about them, in that the doctor imparts to them some power above and beyond the powers which are innate in them, other people know herbal remedies which are treated in a purely utilitarian manner. Thus Mpuga knows herbal remedies for certain types of ailments, and he is prepared to sell them to anyone who wishes to use them. However, he is not considered a doctor, since the power is supposed to be innate in the herbs.

The Subjects of the Life Histories

Under aboriginal conditions Amba society was relatively homogeneous: any two people of the same sex had the same set of roles and had very similar types of experiences in the course of their lives. From the sociological point of view two men or two women were identical persons. Of course, no society is completely homogeneous in this sense; even in the past some men were diviners and others were not. Today, the degree of heterogeneity has greatly increased. Some people have been to school while others have not; many individuals have become Christians while others have remained pagan; one man works as a chief while his brother has worked on a European plantation in Toro. In view of this I shall try in a few words to give some indication of the positions held by the people with whom we are concerned in terms of present-day Amba society.

Kihara, Mpuga and Mpuga's wives all represent individuals who have been influenced by the new forces now impinging upon the Amba. All of them have had a good deal more personal contact with the Toro and members of other tribes than is usual among the Amba. Leaving aside other things, such as the experiences Mpuga has had in various jobs, there is the important fact of their geographical position. As I have mentioned, the houses along the road for some three miles to the north of Bundibugyo are occupied almost entirely by members of other tribes, principally Toro. On the accompanying rough sketch map it will be noted that Mpuga and Kihara live very near to the road, some two miles from Bundibugyo. Three houses, two occupied by Toro and one by a Ganda, are indicated on the map. Mpuga and Kihara and their families are in constant contact with the people living in these houses and with other people living near the

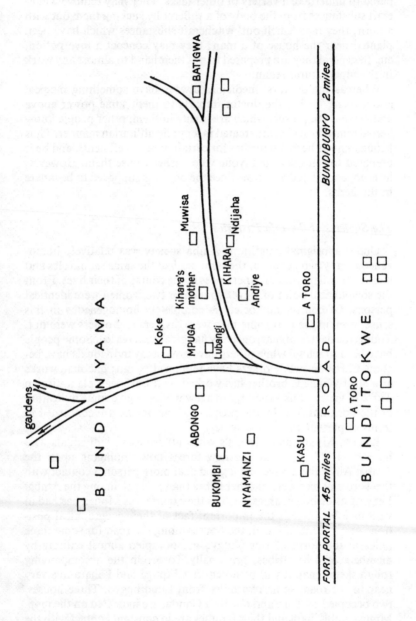

road. Such people are personifications of the modern world as far as the Amba are concerned. They are centres for the dissemination of new ideas, and the Amba model their conduct upon them. Only a few Amba live in such close proximity to people of this sort.

In 1950 all four of the people whose life histories are presented wore cotton clothes. Furthermore they considered clothing of this type a necessity, a mark of their station in life. Had cotton clothes been unavailable to them for some reason and had they been forced to wear the traditional bark cloth, they would have been ashamed and embittered. At the time, the majority of the Amba still wore clothing made of bark cloth.

In spite of the fact that they all consider themselves more sophisticated, in terms of the new world in which they live, than the average Amba, there is considerable variation among them. Koke and, especially, Kihara are closer to the traditional type than are Mpuga and Lubangi. The last two have taken a much more positive attitude toward the new situation: Mpuga and Lubangi have reached out and eagerly tried to assimilate new ideas and attitudes. They have accepted Christianity. By becoming Christians Mpuga and Lubangi believe that they have become people of a new type with ideals and standards radically different from those of the Amba of the past. Mpuga depends to a very large extent for his living upon wages and he actively seeks out opportunities for employment. Although Kihara has held such positions, he has never been interested in them to the same degree. The fact that Mpuga and Lubangi are Christians means that they belong to a small minority in a society as yet predominately pagan. Since it appears very likely that in the near future the majority of the Amba will become Christians, this implies that in terms of their religious orientation they represent an emerging type.

As far as age is concerned, Kihara is quite a bit older than the others. He is probably about fifty years old, while Mpuga is about thirty-five. Lubangi and Koke are even younger. Lubangi is probably about thirty and Koke is about twenty-five. Mpuga's third wife Kijungu is in her early twenties. In terms of the material presented in the life histories, this means that Kihara is able to recount events which occurred in the period before the area came under full British administration.

In regard to the earlier years it should be understood that Kihara's father, Gambeki, held an unusual position. He became a sub-chief in the new Toro administration when it was imposed upon the Amba at the turn of the century. As such he acquired a great deal of power, in fact an unprecedented amount in this previously chiefless society. It is quite clear that he was not adequately supervised, with the result that he was extremely arbitrary in the use of his power. Also, he used the position to further his own ends, and he became very wealthy and acquired a large number of wives. However, near the end of the first world war he fell from power.

Both Kihara and Mpuga have cash incomes which are considerably larger than those earned by most Amba. In 1950 I estimated that the average annual cash income of the Amba family was a little over a hundred and thirty shillings. By contrast in the same year Kihara earned roughly two hundred and fifty shillings, derived principally from the sale of coffee and cotton. Mpuga had an income of about three hundred and fifty shillings, most of it representing his salary for the year, with smaller amounts being earned by the sale of coffee and cotton.

Kihara's household consists of himself, his mother, the three women who are his current wives, Ndijaha, Muwisa and Andiye. Living with them are his children, both by his current wives and by former wives who have either divorced him or have died. He has three adult sons, Ngilani, Babogera and Kalisa. Ngilani is working in Entebbe for the Virus Research Institute. Shortly before the recording of the life histories Babogera quarrelled with Kihara and went to live with one of Kihara's half-brothers, Atube. Of his three adult daughters, two, Nyansegya and Nyabantuki, live elsewhere with their husbands. The third adult daughter, Mukundi, has been married, but recently she obtained a divorce from her husband and is now living with her father. However, a new marriage had been arranged for her, and she went to the home of her husband shortly after Kihara's life history was recorded. In addition, a young girl of eleven or twelve, Mugasaki, a daughter of Muwisa by a previous marriage, lives here with her mother.

The people in the other houses form a more complex grouping. Essentially they represent Mosumba's family. Mosumba died a few years ago, and Mpuga succeeded him as head of the family grouping. Two of Mosumba's sons, the twins Sengi and Atoku, left Bwamba several years before the death of their father. They appear to have settled permanently in Buganda. The other sons maintain houses here. First, there is Mpuga and his three wives, Lubangi, Koke and Kijungu. Living with them are Mpuga's children by Lubangi (two boys, Nkuba and Sogosa) and Koke (a boy, Bakatwika). In addition there are his sons Muganga, whose mother died several years ago, and Kisasi, whose mother is divorced from Mpuga. Kisasi's mother has married again, and he has spent most of his time with her. Recently Mpuga brought him to his home. During the period in which I knew them Kisasi went to his mother's home for several extended visits. Mpuga's three young daughters all live elsewhere. His younger brother, Bukombi, also maintains a house here. However, he is now employed with the Virus Research Institute in Buganda, and his first wife lives with him there. Mpuga has placed his third wife, Kijungu, in Bukombi's house in order to avoid having to build another one. Mpuga's half-brother, Abongo, and his wife and their infant also live here. Mpuga's three sisters are married and live elsewhere.

Mpuga and Kihara claim descent from a common grandfather and thus call one another brother.

BIBLIOGRAPHY

Winter, E. H. (1955) *Bwamba Economy: The Development of a Primitive Subsistence Economy in Uganda.* E.A.I.S.R., Kampala

(1956) *Bwamba: A Structural-Functional Analysis of a Patrilineal Society.* Heffer & Sons, Cambridge

(1959) 'The Aboriginal Political Structure of Bwamba' in *Tribes Without Rulers.* Middleton, J., and Tait, D. (eds.). Routledge & Kegan Paul, London

MPUGA

My mother was married the first time by a Musaru whose name was Kusaalia Tina. At his home she gave birth to my eldest sister who is called Kamanga. Then she had my eldest brother, Kuongo, and after that she had my second brother, Semugono.[1] Then she had a boy, Babongia, who died when he was two years old. About the time he died, war broke out between the Basaru and the Bandimanga. My mother's husband was killed in that war, and she returned to her first home in Bumati and stayed there for a year without a husband. Then Balikabona, a brother of her late husband, married her. This man got her with child and, when she was eight months pregnant, the same war broke out again. In this war the second husband was killed. A month later my mother had a daughter whose name was Batigwa. Then she stayed unmarried for one year waiting for the end of the mourning period. By that time she was disgusted with that lineage, so she left it and back to her old home at Bumati. The Bamati paid back the brideprice to the lineage. Six months after she had returned home, her child Batigwa died.

After one year my mother was married to my father, Mosumba. She was married by capture, and the Bamati did not want goats for her, but wanted a girl in exchange. My father gave them Nyakala, a daughter of his brother. My grandfather, the Mumati, had some sons and, when he received this girl who was very young, he did not want to marry her himself, so he presented her to one of his sons. This son was at that time living in a small hut in the garden trying to keep pigs away from the crops. He took his new wife into the small hut. Two days after they had moved there, a leopard came and killed both of them. The next morning an alarm was raised, and the people followed the tracks. They found that the girl had been completely eaten and that only her skull was left and that the husband had been eaten except for one arm.

Six months after those people had been killed, my mother became pregnant with me. When I had been in her womb seven months she went into the maize garden. There she met a god called Mpuga. She went there at midday and fell down unconscious. Mosumba went to

---

[1] All of these children died before Mpuga was born.

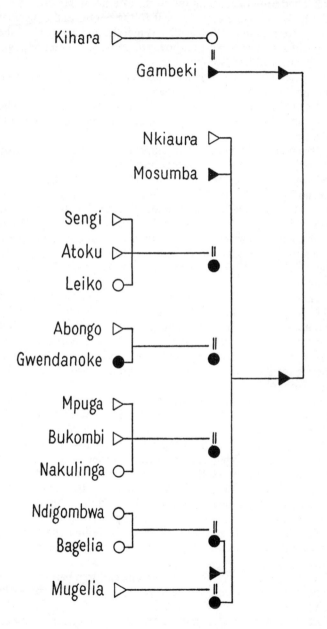

look for her and found her about five in the afternoon. He carried her home. Then, on the same day, he went to the doctor and consulted him. The doctor told him, 'Your wife has met the god Mpuga. As she is pregnant, if she gives birth to a boy, you must name him Mpuga. If she has a girl, call her Nambijo.'

That very day they started dancing and the ceremony lasted seven days. During those seven days they made a special small spear which they kept at the head of the bed until the baby boy was born. The child was named Mpuga and they gave him that small spear, and it is mine even now.

One of the first things I remember happened when I was a very tiny boy. One night my mother, my father and I were all sleeping in the same bed when a man came and opened the door. He came to the fireplace and lighted the fire while we were all still asleep. He called Mosumba. That man was so importunate that they had to cook food for him at night. They killed a chicken for him. My mother and I did not see him. Only Mosumba saw him in another room where there was no fire. When he was eating he asked for water to drink. My father gave him salt, and that was the most amazing thing I have ever heard of in my life.

After the man had left, my father told us the things that he had been told. The stranger had said, 'Mbongwe is trying to kill you by sending out a leopard, and you might have died in a day or two, but since you are my friend, I am trying my best to save your life. Now, as you have given me good things and good food, you won't die, but tomorrow or the day after one of your neighbours near here will be killed by a leopard.'

Two days after that a neighbour, Babusumbe, and his son, Kabinga, were sitting around their fire at night. There were some goats tied in the same room. They heard a goat crying and went with a lighted bunch of reeds to look at the goat. They discovered that a leopard was killing it. When it saw them, it started to growl. They ran. They jumped on the platform where food is hung to dry and shouted to people outside to tell them what was happening. The people came and cut a hole in the roof and pulled them out one at a time. They covered the hole and shot the leopard. I wondered very much about this and realized that the man was telling the truth to my father about what was going to take place. That is the first thing I remember,

The next thing I saw was this: there were six children bathing in the river. When we were bathing, we used to dip our heads completely under the water. While we were doing that Mugelia's son put his head down and swallowed some water. He went under and was drowned. When we saw him struggling, we thought that he was playing. As the river flowed on, the boy was carried on the surface of it. We went along, one boy on each side of him, splashing the water, thinking that he was playing. The wife of his brother came along and found us doing this. She asked, 'What are you doing in the water?'

'We are playing with our neighbour who is a good swimmer.'

She said, 'Why is he facing down into the water? You boys are going to kill your friend.'

She came running to us and when she touched the boy, discovered that he was already dead. She said, 'You have been playing with a corpse.'

So we had to pull him out of the water. At that time we did not know what death was. Then we saw that the woman was starting to cry. She left her pot and carried the dead boy home. We followed her. That is the second thing I remember.

When I was about nine years old my mother went over to the Congo to have iron necklaces made for her. While she was away, a niece of the Bandinyama from Bohanda visited our home. She was smoking hashish about eight in the evening when she was overcome by it and let the pipe fall from her hand. The coal dropped on my left leg, and I tried to brush it off my leg. I tried several times, but it would not come away until that woman who had been smoking the hashish got some water and poured it on my leg. She paid a fine of one chicken for the accident, and I was very sick.

Two months after my leg had been burned my father married another wife, Nyagimanywa of the Babandi, who already had two children and brought them with her. A month after the marriage my mother returned from the Congo. When she returned, she was pregnant with Bukombi. I still had the sore from the burn when she gave birth to him. Two days after his birth, I had a fight with one of the children who had come with my father's new wife. I started fighting with him at my mother's house and chased him away. When we reached his mother's house, he fell at her feet, and I boxed him on both ears. The wife said, 'This boy is always beating my children. I hope that the sore on his leg will be serious and make him lose it.'

My father had been thinking of leaving the Bandinyama and going to settle in the Congo, and he had been away for three weeks at this time. I returned from the fight and told my mother the whole story. I said, 'That wife has said bad things to me.'

The fight took place about four o'clock. At five on the same day the sore started to bleed and would not stop. Mother and I stayed by the fire all night and did not go to sleep at all. I felt much pain. On the following morning the sore was about two inches in diameter. In the afternoon Gambeki came to see us after he had heard all the quarrelling and my mother's weeping. We explained the whole affair to him. He was amazed that the thing had started so quickly. He went to this woman and told her, 'It is you who have said a bad thing to Mosumba's son. You had better stop this sore from getting any larger. If you haven't stopped it by tomorrow morning, I am going to tie you up.'

By night-time I had no strength and was in a coma. People ran to Gambeki and called him. When he arrived, he found me almost dying. He was very angry to see that Mosumba's son was going to die, so he asked Kihara to tie the woman up. When she began to feel very great pain, she said, 'Although you are killing me, I am not the only person who is injuring this boy. The god Mpuga is also responsible, because the mother of the child Mpuga went to the Congo for a long time, and it is possible that the god was annoyed with her for staying there such a long time.'

So they released the woman. They had to cut plantains and put them in the ground in preparation for a ceremony. Before it started, some people asked Gambeki, 'Why don't you get the true house-holder from the Congo?'

But Gambeki said, 'No. That man seems to be foolish. I have sent him many messages for him to come back, but he hasn't arrived. I can't lose the son of the lineage so I will carry out the ceremony my-self.'

Gambeki did all this because I was the son of his brother. He used three goats, fourteen fowls, five hundred baskets of food and a big bundle of salt, which was very expensive at that time. The dried meat cost him five big baskets of plantain flour. There were many other things which I do not remember. So you see how much my illness cost him. When I was healed, he did not ask my father to refund these things.

I did not listen to any of the ceremonies and most of it has been told to me since then. I was in great pain, and most of the people thought that I was going to die. They were doing all these things to try to save my life. The god Mpuga said that he would not come on that night, but he came at nine the next morning. He came to my mother's head, and they fed him. My mother had acted for that god be-fore. He said, 'Even though you have called me, I haven't caused any trouble in your home, and I am sure that the child must be bewitched by someone. It is not trouble from me.'

The god spoke through my mother, and the person who asked the questions was Gambeki who was the householder. I was lying on the floor nearby.

The night the ceremony ended they put one big pot of beer on the fireplace and Gambeki's son, Erungu, was serving it. He was passing beer to all the people. That woman who had bewitched me came

34

and gave a small calabash to the boy and said, 'Give me some beer.'

But the boy said, 'No. You belong to this home and are near the pot, so get some yourself.'

When the woman took the calabash to the pot, she did not intend to get beer. She had some human flesh (which is considered poisonous) in the vessel. She poured the flesh into the beer and turned up the empty calabash. She pretended that it was full of beer and put it to her mouth and pretended that she was drinking. When the son, Erungu, went to get some more beer, he felt something against his hand. He said, 'What is the thing which has touched me?'

Gambeki told him, 'Pour your beer out of the calabash.'

He filtered it through his hands into the pot and emptied the calabash. There was something left behind. They brought a plantain leaf and poured it on to that and discovered that it was flesh. Gambeki asked, 'Who has put his arm into this pot besides you?'

Erungu said, 'This woman just asked me for some beer, but she was near the pot and I told her to get it.'

Gambeki said to the woman, 'You are a true witch now.'

He kept quiet until the ceremony was over at noon on the next day. The beer which was left in the pot after the flesh had been found was thrown away. They kept the flesh. About four on the same day, I became seriously ill. Gambeki had discovered that it was true that this woman was the one who was killing his 'son', so he told all his sons, including Kihara, to tie up the woman very tightly. They put a rope around her neck and when they saw me getting worse, they would tighten the rope. One of the sons of this woman was very angry to see his mother tied like a thief and the people nearly killing her, so he untied the rope. Gambeki asked, 'Who is undoing the woman who is a witch?'

'Her son.'

Gambeki ordered the son to be beaten and while he was being punished, he ordered the mother to be beaten also. They both started bleeding from the mouth, nose and anus. After they had been beaten badly and Gambeki saw that there was much blood, he told his sons to stop. He said, 'You wait and watch them. If they die, it is all right, and if they don't die, it is all right.'

The mother was still tied, but the son had enough strength to reach the sub-county headquarters and accuse the people. The sub-county chief sent down a policeman, who arrested seven sons of Gambeki but left Gambeki himself behind. They also carried the woman who had been beaten to the headquarters. On the following morning they sent for me. They tried the case and had an exhibit of the human flesh, and the case was decided against the woman and her son.

Gambeki was told to keep the suspected woman until his child Mpuga had healed. Two days later the son of that woman became ill and he died two days after that. Then the suspected woman went back to the chief to accuse them and said, 'You see. These people have killed my son because they beat him badly.'

Kihara was arrested again. Then the case was tried and it went against the woman again, the reason being that it had been six days since the boy had been beaten. 'If it were just a question of the beating, he would have died on the same day.'

The man was buried. Gambeki decided to take me from Bundinyama to the home of Rukungu in Busaru. At that time Gambeki was very annoyed with Mosumba because he had neglected me badly during my illness. Mosumba was afraid to come while I was still at Bundinyama, but when he heard that I was at Busaru, he came by night and carried me off to the Congo, carefully and secretly, going by the long route. My mother did not want to go with me because she was afraid of Gambeki. She thought that it would look very odd if she ran away with Mosumba, since Gambeki was performing all the duties of a father and taking care of all her needs and mine. If she ran away, it would show that she did not agree with Gambeki, because she and he had been saying that Mosumba was a bad man for not coming to see me when I was sick. She told her husband to take his son and that she would stay behind. Then my father found a doctor who treated my sore and cured it within two months. After I was healed I stayed in the Congo for another three months, and then Mosumba brought me secretly at night to his home here. When he handed me to my mother, Gambeki heard him say, 'Here is your son.'

Gambeki said, 'Who is that speaking in my house?'

When Mosumba heard that, he ran back to the Congo. He stayed for six months, but he did not get along well there, so he moved back. He came and settled across the road. One day Gambeki heard the news that he was back and said, 'I won't go to Mosumba's house for three months and that will show him that I was very angry with him.'

Gambeki told Mosumba that he would not get his wife, that is, my mother, and his two sons until the punishment was over. Then, when the three months had passed, Mosumba came and reported to Gambeki, and Gambeki told him, 'You go and prepare beer and find one big male goat.'

Gambeki came in the morning to Mosumba's house with four of his sons, Kamohanda, Atube, Kyabongo and Erungu. Then he gathered together all the Bandinyama and stood up and made a speech to the people. 'Mosumba acted very badly because he refused to come home when I called him. His people were sick. I tried my best to heal his son. Now his son is all right. He left his wife while she was pregnant. The child was born here while he was away, and he hasn't seen him. Now, Mosumba, I am handing your whole family over to you, but I do not want you to do this any more. If you go away again, you will stay away for life and never come back to me.'

They ate and drank the whole night. On the following morning Mosumba gave one goat to Gambeki as a present for the things he had done for him, and he gave him three chickens as a relish for vegetables. Gambeki took the goat alive back to his home. I, Bukombi and my mother stayed with Mosumba.

A year later the wife who had gone with Mosumba to the Congo divorced him. The brideprice was refunded, and two months later the wife remarried. She stayed with her new husband seven months and then got dysentery and died at Bundikahuku. When she divorced Mosumba, she had two of his children who were also sick with dysentery. When Mosumba heard that his children were sick, he went to Gambeki and asked him for medicine for that disease. He took the medicine to the children, and they recovered. When they were well, they returned to their father's home.

Once, when I was a small child, Gambeki sent for me to go to look after his rice. One day, when some boys and myself were in the garden watching his rice, he called me and one of his sons to go and look after his goats. When we went off, we started to play football and forgot about the goats. They ran off and ruined someone's garden. Gambeki caught them and took them back home. When he saw the owner of the garden, he said, 'Don't worry about this, but go home. I will pay you for the damage.'

Then he sent someone to call us to come home. We sent back the message, 'We are still grazing the goats.' But when we looked for them, we could not find them. When we reached home, Gambeki gave me six blows with a stick. After that I ran back to my home and did not go to his home again until he died. He sent Atube to ask me to come back, but I said, 'I have had enough.'

Even though Gambeki hit me six times that day, he was a more useful man to me than my father, who neglected me very often. Gambeki spent a lot of money curing my sore, and when it was finally gone, he gave me a very good feast.

The child next to me in age was the daughter of another wife of Mosumba. She died when she was grown, but before she was married. I do not remember her birth because I was only a year old then, but I remember one thing which happened to her when I had the sore on my leg. Mosomba was drunk one day and when he came home at night the mother of the girl was sitting just beyond the light of the fire. She had the child on her thigh with her legs on the floor. Mosumba stuck his spear into the ground thinking that there was no one there and, unluckily, the iron of the spear went through the child's leg. She had that wound for a very long time. My father consulted with doctors for something like two years. He found that it was the goddess Nyakala, who had never been brought into the house, who was causing the sore. Then he brought in a priestess of Nyakala who came and spoke in the room of the gods and said, 'If it is you, Nyakala, who is making my "daughter" sick, I wish that she may be healed within two weeks. After that, I will call you into the house.'

The result was that in two weeks the sore was getting better, so Mosumba had to bring in the goddess Nyakala and have a ceremony. Within the seven days that the ceremony lasted the child's sore healed. That was the story of her illness.

I remember two things about Bukombi's birth. First, my mother was very angry because she had lost the three children she had brought with her from her first marriage. Secondly, I was her first child by this husband, and I was very ill with the sore on my leg. When she gave birth to Bukombi, she rejected him. She put him aside and said, 'I am not going to give him the breast.'

Other people had to feed him on sugar-cane and goat's milk for two months. By that time my leg had healed and my mother was feeling happy, so she gave Bukombi the breast. While he was still sucking, Gambeki came and saw the child. He said, 'This child does not resemble any of the Bandinyama people, so it is possible that the wife conceived him elsewhere.'

My mother denied this. 'This is a Bandinyama child.'

Gambeki said, 'I will give him the test.'

Gambeki's test was to bring the teeth of a leopard and tie them around the child's neck.[1] He put on the necklace about two o'clock in the afternoon, and the next morning the whole of Bukombi's body had swollen. That day Mosumba happened to have beer. Gambeki brought the child out into the courtyard where the people were sitting drinking, and explained to them what his idea had been. He said, 'You see, this is what our totem has done. Now the child's body has swollen. It will be bad if the child dies, but as there are many old people here, we will be advised what to do to save him.'

He was given medicine with which to wash the child. It was used to wash him in the morning. Then the child's body was healed, but he had sores on the swelling. That lasted a long time and, when they saw it was not going to heal, they took the child to a doctor called

---

[1] Each lineage in Bwamba has something, usually a species of animal or bird, which the lineage members must avoid. Contact with it causes illness. In the case of the Bandinyama it is the leopard.

Kaswera, who gave Bukombi some medicine which healed him. He asked one goat for a fee, and they gave it to him.

The accusation against my mother caused much trouble between the Bandinyama and the Bamati, my mother's lineage. When Mother told her father about this, he asked the Bandinyama to come and meet him at Mosumba's home. From Bumati came Nyamimbo, her father, Jagalijagali, his brother, Bakamaki, Nyamimbo's son, and a nephew of that lineage, Mangahulu. They called Gambeki and Mosumba, Kihara, Erungu and other Bandinyama. My mother's father stood up and accused the Bandinyama, and they were found guilty. After the case had been judged, Gambeki denied the judgment saying that the case had not been fair, but they asked him one question, 'Who tried the test on the child?'

Gambeki said, 'It was I.'

They said, 'What was the result?'

Gambeki just laughed. He said, 'Oh, yes, we are guilty, but we will pay you only one goat.'

My mother's father refused it completely and said, 'If you don't pay three goats now, I will take back our daughter and pay back your brideprice.'

The Bandinyama wanted to reduce the number to two goats, but her father would not have that and said, 'Don't you know that my child is married here for nothing now? The one with whom I exchanged her died together with my son, so if you don't pay me three goats now, I will take back my daughter.'

The Bandinyama refused to pay three goats, so her father was very angry, and he did not even eat the food which was prepared for him. He went home and the following morning my mother left Bandinyama and went to her home at Bumati. She took Bukombi with her, but I stayed here. Four days later Gambeki and Mosumba selected three goats and sent them to Bumati with Erungu and Kamohanda. Then those two boys asked the wife of Mosumba to come back, as they had paid the three goats. But the father refused to give them the wife, 'As a punishment to you Bandinyama who have annoyed me, I will keep this daughter of mine here for a month.'

She stayed there for a month. When that time was over, her father gave her one goat and two pots of banana beer and sent her back. The nephew of the Bamati who accompanied my mother explained to the Bandinyama how they had annoyed her father and why he had punished them. Then he said, 'From now on you must treat her better, in a good way, or he will come and take her back again.'

The Bandinyama agreed and kept my mother. Six months later her father died. Bukamaki, who was the successor of her father, sent down to Bundinyama and asked for the brideprice of my mother.

They gave him seven goats. Gambeki said, 'As you want the goats for your daughter, we ought to give you six, but we are giving you seven so now you should give us five for our daughter who died, as this is the rule in the country.'

That uncle of mine agreed, but when he returned to Bumati other people gave him advice. 'As we have a new government now, you must not pay him his five goats at all. If he asks you for five goats, you tell him to go and accuse you to the sub-county chief.'

So Mosumba took Bukamaki to court for the five goats, and the case was judged against Mosumba. He and Gambeki were very annoyed. At that time there was one Mumati staying with the Bandinyama. When they returned home, they told him to leave on that very day or he would be badly treated, so he had to go.

After a time the Bandinyama started a ceremony to put the goddess Nyakala on my mother's head, and they did not tell the Bamati. The Bamati came down here and asked them for one goat for making that mistake. Gambeki and the rest of the Bandinyama refused to give the goat. The Bamati accused them at the sub-county headquarters. The chief (a Toro) had to find out from the local people what the custom was, and the people said, 'When you are doing such a thing, you should tell the father of the girl or his lineage.'

So Mosumba was wrong again. Gambeki was very annoyed; 'These Bamati are going to get all our goats for this one wife.'

Before the Bandinyama returned home, they told the Bamati, 'You are lucky that there is the new government. Otherwise you would have been killed.'

Mosumba gave them the goat with a disdainful gesture. Before the man who had come for the goat left, Gambeki said, 'The Bamati must not come to this ceremony for Nyakala. If there is one here, he must leave.'

So they drove all the Bamati away. After that ceremony for Nyakala, Gambeki and Mosumba sent a message to them, 'You have our eight goats and our daughter. From now on we do not want to see any Bamati coming down here looking for beer. If one comes here, we will beat him to death, and we will all go to jail.'

Three years after that warning Gambeki died, and from that time my father used to allow the Bamati to come here, letting them in slowly by degrees. In 1940 my uncle Bukamaki died. Then, after a while, Mosumba died also, so that now all the Bamati come here as they want, since the people who used to prohibit them are dead.

At this time in my life I had a very good friend, Mulako, who called me his brother. He used to visit me, and we would sleep in the same bed, and I would kill a fowl for him. Mulako would stay for two or three days, since our houses were quite close. When I visited him, I

40

would stay there for three days and would have a big feast. Later when I went to Butogu, he used to leave his home and come and stay with me for a couple of months. At that time I was married, but I would not dare to let him sleep alone, so he, my wife and I would all sleep together in the same bed. When I was young, he was my very best friend, and he is about the same age as I am. He had a nurse then. Mulako's father had asked the father of this girl if he could take her to help look after the child. We are not looked after like Europeans, but, as soon as we can walk, the nurse leaves. When my mother used to go out to the garden, they would carry me to Mulako's house and leave me there with the nurse. That went on until I reached the age of understanding. Then, as my mother left me at home alone, I would go to Mulako's house and stay there playing with him. As we grew up, we became very close friends. As a proof that our friendship was a very strong one, when he married his first wife, he brought her to my house. Then, when the father-in-law came to ask for the brideprice, Kihara said, 'I will pay your brideprice.'

But he waited until Mulako had two children from the wife and, since nothing had been paid, Mulako decided to ask the whole family for some goats. Batigwa gave him one goat, and the man who had married his mother gave him three. I also gave him one goat. It was a mistake for Mulako not to tell me at first, in which case I would have given him more than that, but I had used most of my goats by the time he asked. Then Mulako paid the five goats to his father-in-law. In 1949 his father-in-law wanted to complete the payment, so he asked for fifty shillings from Mulako. He came to me, and I offered him twenty shillings. He made up the rest and paid the debt. That is my friend.

It was about this time that I made my first blood-brother. This man was called Byaigoro. The people called Banyambinde who live on the other side of the mountain used to bring salt to the house of my nephew Ngilime. I used to visit my nephew and I often saw these people there. One day I asked him, 'Who is the best man among these?'

He told me that it was Byaigoro. At that time in Bwamba getting salt was a problem, so I thought of making friends with one of the salt carriers so I would not have to worry about getting it. I began to act as his friend, and when he came to my house, my mother welcomed him with a meal. He returned to his home and, when he came to Bwamba again, he brought me a big bundle of salt. That time he slept at our house for two days and after that we cut ourselves and became blood-friends. I took three shillings in ten-cent pieces, strung them on a piece of palm and tied them around his waist. He took the mat that he had sat on. As he did not eat chicken, I gave him a he-goat for his food. I also gave him a she-goat in thanks for the bundle of salt he had brought. He tied two shillings around my waist. Then he went home, and we continued to help each other.

I went to see him in 1943 and found that his children were very ill. I offered him ten shillings to help them, but, unfortunately, they died and I had to be of help in burying them. I learned from that that it is a very useful thing to have a blood-brother. In 1946, when Byaigoro heard that my father had died, he brought me fifteen shillings to show how sorry he was for me. When he returned home, I gave him one of the goats that I had received from Mosumba. He became sick in 1947, and after he was well I asked him to come here and gave him a he-goat. In 1948 when I went to visit him, he had a big feast for me. He gathered most of his relatives and friends and told them how helpful we were to each other. He came down here in 1949 and again in 1950 when my mother died. Each time he brought me something, salt or beans or meat.

In 1929 the rulers passed this order: 'You must select some young boys to go and attend school and become candidates for baptism.' I was chosen by the teacher to go to Fort Portal and study to become a Christian. Two of my brothers, Sengi and Atoku, and myself had been attending the Sunday service. We used to go even though we were pagans. The teacher used to come and visit all the villages asking people to come to the services. The teacher wanted to take all three of us, but Mosumba refused to let my brothers go, saying, 'I must keep two here to serve me.'

The teacher was not satisfied with this answer, so he took two. Atoku and myself, and at last Mosumba agreed to that. Sengi did not have to go. First of all we attended classes here in Bwamba for a year. We studied for a year, learning prayers and the catechism and how to read. I liked it very much. At the end of that year the White Father called Peri Deri came down to Bwamba and we were tested. Only five of us out of sixty passed the test and we were baptized. I was named Tomasi. Then the priest wanted to take us to Fort Portal with the others who had passed. In the past they had taken married people, but now he said, 'We should take the younger people so that they can be trained in schools after they have been baptized.'

The local teacher said, 'The parents of these children are refusing to send them to Fort Portal for study because they think they will die there. I want all the teachers to meet tomorrow at Bundihugyo to decide about this thing. If it is true, the parents will be forced to send their children away to Fort Portal.'

At the meeting they decided to write a letter to the county chief to ask him to force the parents to let their children go. Then the county chief wrote letters to all his sub-county chiefs. The chiefs gathered together the parents of all the children who had passed the examination and told them, 'We are going to use force if you don't give us your sons.'

Many people were called. They were asked why they refused to send their children to Fort Portal. This was the answer: 'We know that Fort Portal is far away from Bwamba and we thought that the children would be unhappy if they went there.'

In the end our parents agreed that we should be taken. They were afraid that otherwise they would be put in prison. We were taken up to Toro to the place where candidates for confirmation lived. We started learning Lutoro. When I first arrived, I thought, 'I am lost, because I don't see any of my relatives or tribe members.'

The first thing which made me feel better was that the bark cloth in which we had arrived was thrown away, and we were given two sets of uniforms. We were very happy to see ourselves in clothes. We were very well looked after. We used to eat a lot of food, plenty of meat on Sunday and fish on Friday. We received free salt and everything we needed. Then we began to feel at home.

About six months later one of the members who had come with us died. After he died, the priest told us that the results of the post mortem showed that the child had eaten too much food and it had got mixed up inside him. He said, 'This was the only reason for his death. You Amba must cut down on your eating or you will all die. This child was eating the heads of goats. Possibly he ate some of the small bones in the head, with the result that they went into his intestines and caused his death.'

Then we were very angry with the priest because he was going to cut down on our food. We were used to having four meals a day and whenever we had less than that we would rebel. We would not go to class or to handicraft, but would just stay in our beds. The priest tried to cut down on our food, but we all refused to allow that. We said, 'If you reduce our food, we will all run away.'

So we continued to have our meals. Then, in December of the same year, the king of Toro died. They had planned to confirm us then, but it was postponed until the next month which was January.

That year there were a lot of earthquakes, and we were very afraid of Toro because we had never known earthquakes before. They used to come in the day and at night. So we were very unhappy during that time and decided to run away. The leader of the rebellion was a man named Kakumba, who had been in Fort Portal before we arrived. He gave us a lot of reasons for going and these are the main ones: 'First, I have heard a rumour that the Mukama, the king of Toro, has died. They are going to bury him with one Amba, and perhaps they will choose one of us. Second, we have been in this place for a long

43

time, and I have been here longer than you, but I have never heard of these earthquakes before, so this may be the way that we will all die. Third, the priest said that our neighbour died because he ate too much food. This is all wrong. We used to eat ten times this much at our home continuously and without a rest. We never died from eating too much. Now if you won't take my advice, you may stay here. I am going.'

As we were leaving, the houseboy of the monk saw us, so he went and reported it to the priests. A messenger was sent on a bicycle to bring us back and found us at Kusinga, ten miles from Fort Portal at the foot of the mountain. He called the teacher who was nearest there, and they both said, 'If you don't go back, we will call the police and they will arrest you.' After we had been taken back, we were locked in the house for two days. We were given four strokes each by the head priest. He planned to take away our clothes, but finally forgave us and did not. When it was time for our confirmation, we were punished. Our friends who had not run away were confirmed a week before we were.

Three weeks after our first communion we were confirmed. We went into the church, up to the altar, and the priest opened his Bible and set it up on end. They chose two children, a girl and a boy, who had never touched the tree of Adam. The boy went up on the right hand side and the girl on the left. The whole group of people raised their right hands. The priest started to read, and all said after him, 'I am making an agreement. I am repeating my agreement made at baptism. I have left Satan; I have left all his traps and all his ways. I do agree to follow Jesus Christ and to stay in his religion all my life. Amen.'

Then the priest took some holy water in his right hand and sprinkled it on us as the water of grace. After that he gave us scapularies which he put over our heads individually. It was about eight-thirty in the morning when the mass ended. We went out of the church and back to our houses and waited for the priest to come and say good-bye. When he came, we all knelt down. We put our hands together and then the priest said, 'Since you have decided to make the agreement with Jesus, you must copy the ways of true Christians and stay with your religion until your last day. Keep the religion all the time; don't give up. I am sending off other candidates, but I am keeping the twenty Amba who ran away, because if I let them go, they won't come back to school again.'

So the ones who ran away, all unmarried children, stayed in the school. When school started again, we forgot all our complaints and felt as though we were at home, because of all the good things they were doing for us. The priest promised us that we should have a holi-

day. The next term went from February until May and in May we
had our holiday. We had one month in Bwamba. In the beginning
there had been thirty people from Bwamba, but only twenty were
taken into the school. Ten of these were being trained as teachers.
When the holiday began, the twenty people came down to Bwamba,
but at the end only fifteen went back to Toro. We were asked, 'Where
are the five who are missing?'

We said, 'We don't know about them because they have stayed
down in Bwamba.'

My father had not wanted me to return to Toro. When the holiday
ended, all the boys were told to gather one evening at Bundibugyo.
That evening Mosumba came to Bundibugyo and told me that my
mother was very ill. He asked me to return home in order to see her.
His tale was not true. A friend of my father's had given him the leg of
a pig, and he wanted me to join the feast.

I refused his request and went to Fort Portal. I told him, 'If she is
dying, let her die. God will help her, but I am going.'

A week after I arrived at the mission, my mother and father came
to see me. I wondered how she had managed to get well so quickly.
They brought me some of the meat which had been given to them
and which they had dried. At last they told me, 'This is why we asked
you to come home. We wanted you to have the meat with us.'

I asked them, 'If you had prevented me from leaving then, with
whom could I have come to Toro?'

They said, 'We would have brought you.'

I said, 'That is a lie. You wouldn't have done it.'

They stayed for four days. Before they began their return journey
to Bwamba, the priest gave them a bundle of salt as a present.

At the end of the term we were tested, and the people who could
write went to class two. I was one of the five Amba who were accepted. In December of that year I went back home for the holidays.

It was during this holiday that my father did for me the one good
thing he ever did. We were sitting around one evening when he called
his wife Nabaswaga. He said, 'I want to divide my girls among my
boys, because I have grown old, and I want each son to look after
his girl. Nkiaura, my brother, is older and is married, but I will give
him a young girl now.'

My mother asked, 'Who is given to Nkiaura?'

'Bagelia. Mpuga's girl is Ndigombwa; Sengi will take Aleko; Abongo will take his sister Gwendanoke. Bukombi will take Nakulinga.'

He said to the girls, 'Now you have seen your "fathers". You must
obey them, and whenever they want to exchange you for a wife, you
must go along with it, because it is I who have told you to do so, and
I am the one who is your father.'

45

My brothers and I were very happy about this. I was especially glad, because my girl was old enough to be married. I did not have to give her anything because I was young, and I did not have to put her in a separate hut, because we boys were living in my father's house and the girls were all living in my mother's house. I kept Ndigombwa for about a month, and then I saw a beautiful girl and fell in love with her. That was Paulina.[1] I came and told my father, and he allowed me to have her and exchanged Ndigombwa for her. Nidgombwa was not told about this; father and I talked about it ourselves. Mosumba told her on the day that she was to leave home. She had come from the garden about midday, after lunch, and Father said, 'Ndigombwa, you are going today. You have been exchanged for a wife for Mpuga.'

She was silent until she left. Mosumba said, 'Even if you say nothing, you are going to be taken today.'

Ndigombwa did not cry, but she was very angry with Mosumba and me because we had forced her to go. The intermediary came on that very day, and she went with him. Later on she was happy, because she found that her new husband was all right. To prove that she was happy, she is still living in that home, and she has had six children. Three children died and three are alive. I was the one who lost out, because my wife died later. Ndigombwa loves us for all the things we do for her. Whenever we kill a goat at our home, she gets a leg. Whenever we sell our crops she gets two or three shillings from the proceeds. She always comes and collects some of any crop we harvest. We always tell her to come and get some of the harvest, and she does not help us with the harvest because she is the eldest daughter.

Although I had been given Paulina, I did not want to marry a pagan, so I sent her to the teacher to have her baptized. When I returned to Toro to school in January, there were only ten of us, because five had stayed behind. The five members who had been in class two were all promoted to class three. We were not paying anything, but getting free uniforms, free books, free accommodation and free education. In March my wife was included in the group which came up to Fort Portal to be candidates for confirmation. She kept on with her religious training. I continued my schooling. The missionary said that the engaged girls would be confirmed soon, so that they could be married. In November my wife was confirmed and in December, on the eighteenth, we were married.

My wife and I were both very young. To prove to you that we were very young, for four months we slept in the same bed using different

[1] *Mpuga's Wives in Order of Marriage:*
Paulina, Angweka, Mambaiye, Nyakajuli, Beliki, Nyakala, Lubangi, Bakweziba, Beabusa, Budedyo, Nyabasulu, Mambiabo, Likerenge, Koke, Kijungu.

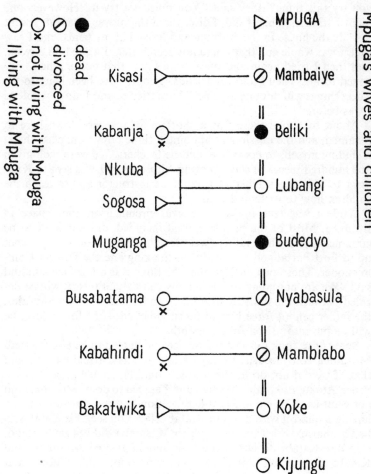

Mpuga's wives and children

blankets. Kihara had told me that if I put my penis in a woman's vagina, the vagina would bite me. However, I used to see husbands and wives sleeping together at night and no one cried out. My friends and I used to meet and discuss these things. When I asked, 'Could you try this thing?' they said, 'You must not try it.' However, one night I tried it. When I did, I discovered that it was pleasant. I went outside the house in the morning and looked at my penis, and I saw that it was whole and that it had not been bitten. I waited for a week, and then I tried again and once more I saw that nothing had happened to me. Then I told my friends, 'People have been lying to us. These things will not bite anyone. I have tried it, and I am as whole as I was before.'

About that time there was a shortage of teachers down here in Bwamba, and the missionary appointed three boys from class three, including myself, to come here and be teachers. We were each given one hundred pieces of slate to bring with us, and I was sent to Kitengya to help the teacher as a religious instructor and to teach the children how to write and read.

While I was teaching at Kitengya, circumcision took place in Bwamba. Most of the people, myself included, did not want to be circumcised, but their fathers were forcing them to do so. We went up to Fort Portal and reported it to the king and the District Commissioner. Those two decided that the thing was a local custom and said, 'We are not going to put out any rules about this. It will be decided between the individuals, fathers and sons. If the son refuses, the father cannot force him to be circumcised. If he forces him, he will be put into prison for six months.'

Some of us took our fathers' advice and agreed to be circumcised. Mosumba convinced us by saying that it was a tribal custom and that, if we did not do it, the people would laugh at him and at us. Sengi, Atoku, Bukombi, Abongo and I agreed to do it. Mosumba did not want us to be circumcised here at Bundinyama, because he was having a quarrel with a certain Katabwita.[1] You see, this Katabwita had a quarrel with Mosumba which Mosumba did not understand. One day Katabwita had made beer and he invited Mosumba and Kinaba to come to his place early in the morning. They killed a goat and, while they were sitting down in chairs drinking their beer, Katabwita went into the house, got a stick, and hit Mosumba on the head with it. He got up and when he asked, 'Why are you killing me?' Katabwita said, 'You haven't even seen me yet. I'm going to kill you now.' And he gave Mosumba a blow on the back which broke his backbone. Then Kinaba ran away, and Katabwita said, 'Oh, yes. I will do what I said.'

[1] Katabwita is also a Mundinyama.

By that time Mosumba had fallen down. Then another man called Nkonisiani came along and said, 'Don't kill the man.'

He caught Katabwita and then carried Mosumba to his home and bound up the wound on his head. When we saw our father, we were very angry, so Sengi, Atoku, Kihara and I took our bows and arrows and went to kill this man. We went and stayed at Katabwita's house for two nights and two days, but he had run off and we could not find him. He had hidden in the bush. The sub-county chief sent some people to get him, and they caught him. Kihara gave him a blow which made him vomit blood. Atoku was there also and gave him a blow on the head which brought blood. That blow was so heavy that it blacked his eyes, so they did not put him in prison but took him to the hospital. He eventually lost the use of one of his eyes. The blow on Mosumba's back made him impotent, and he used to go about bent over, holding his back. That is the reason that my father did not want to have the circumcision at his home. This fight took place in 1932 on May 15th. The circumcision was on July 13th. Gambeki was staying at upper Bundinyama at that time and he said, 'The people at lower Bundinyama will stay there, and I will come and circumcise their children. The Bandinyama who are up here with me will have their circumcision here.'

But my father did not want to join this group, even though Gambeki was going to do the work. So he had to take us up to Busaru to the house of Mugelia who was his true nephew. Gambeki was very angry with Mosumba for this. He said, 'If you are angry with those Bandinyama down there, you could bring your children up to my place.'

So the matter ended by Mosumba paying a fine of one goat to Gambeki. We all went to Mugelia's on Thursday. In the afternoon they took off all our clothes, and we were dressed in green plantain leaves. We were locked in the house about seven-thirty in the evening. In that house were most of the Basaru who were going to be circumcised. All the parents of the boys came into that village. They did not speak at all, and they did not go into the house, but stayed in the courtyard and passed the night singing. We were like prisoners. When we wanted to go to the latrine, we were taken by five guards. At the first crowing of the cock, we were given a meal which contained some medicine which gave us diarrhea. We had to follow a lot of rules in that house. We slept on the floor and had only two plantain leaves as a mat. We were told to sleep on our stomachs and not to turn on our sides or to lie on our backs. We started having bowel movements as soon as we had eaten that meal. By the time it was daylight, each person had had four movements.

The Basaru have a god called Kilagozi who lives in a big tree and in that tree are lianas. Whenever there is a circumcision, they get the lianas and tie them around the waists of the boys. So we were kept waiting that morning till they fetched them. When they put them around our waists, some of the boys started crying, even before the circumcision, because the sap of the lianas was stinging them. At about ten in the morning the first boy was circumcised. He was a nephew of that clan, and, after he had been circumcised, they started on the son of the householder. After those two, five boys were brought at the same time, and they stood in a line. There were five men performing the circumcision and each took one boy. After twelve had been done, the teacher Kirima came to the place and wanted to see the ceremony since I was in it. He asked, 'Where is Mpuga?'

They told him, 'Mpuga is still locked in the house.'

He said, 'Let him out to watch what is being done to his friends.'

So they brought out a group, and I was in it. If you are very strong and brave, you can break down the door of the house and come and watch what is going on. The boys who do that are called up first. Kirima was right to bring us out. Otherwise we would have thought that we had been treated differently from the other boys. You do not know who your enemy is among the people who are circumcising you. We watched our friends for about ten minutes, and then we were called to take our places. My father did not want to have the five circumcisers do his children, but wanted one of them to cut all of them. He knew which man was best. Some circumcisers have ways of bewitching boys that they cannot capture wives. When they have circumcised the boy, they take the blade of the knife, put it in ashes, and call the name of the boy they want to bewitch. For instance, they would say, 'Mpuga, you must not capture a woman. You will marry wives only for the brideprice.'

That is a bad thing in our country. If you do not capture a woman, people will say that you are not a real man. Then there are some circumcisers who bewitch in this way: when they pull the foreskin and see that the penis is erect, good specialists will stop and take another boy and wait until the first boy's penis is limp, but a bad man would turn the blade of the knife and touch the penis while it is erect. That would make you impotent, and you would not have an erection until the day you die.

My father also said, 'Mpuga must be the first.'

But the old people said 'No. We must start with one of your twins. Then we can have Mpuga, and after him the other twin.' So Atoku was the first. When they cut his foreskin, the knife became blunt before they had finished, so they had to stop and go away and sharpen it. When they came back, they started to cut him again. When they were ready for me, another man who had a very small child said, 'Go

50

first, my young child,' so they took that boy first. His father wanted
to bring him early, because he knew that his child would be afraid
if he had to wait and saw many people being circumcised.

They had dressed me in a red hat (fez) like the policemen wear and
a white hen was tied around my neck. Then they started cutting. The
way they do it is to push the penis in and pull out the foreskin. Then
they cut quickly. When it is done like this, you do not feel anything;
it is as though you were being cut by a reed.

They said, 'Mpuga has always been a troublesome boy, so go and
get him a piece of sugar-cane, and he can eat it while he is being
circumcised.'

Eating the sugar-cane is one of the tests given to a man to prove
that he is brave. The people said, 'You are always troublesome, fighting with your neighbours, bothering us, and pretending to be brave.
So let us see how brave you are during the circumcision.'

Mosumba made me eat the sugar-cane. I was the bravest boy in
our village and that is why he gave it to me. I had been proved the
bravest when I was grazing goats one day with the other Bandinyama
boys. A leopard came and caught some goats. When the other boys
saw that it was a leopard, they ran home. I did not like to do that, so
I went after the leopard, chased it away and got the goats back. So
my father and my lineage knew that I was the bravest boy.

It was very painful during the second part of the cutting when they
were tearing the skin. While they were doing that, I was chewing on
the sugar-cane, and I wanted to spit it out from pain. They said,
'Don't spit,' and I said, 'No. I am feeling quite well.'

That was a lie. I was really feeling great pain. They took roughly
ten minutes with me. Then my father wanted to bring Sengi, but the
people said, 'No. You must bring a boy who is not a twin,' so they
brought Abongo. When they were tearing his skin, he was leaning
against a tree, and he started wiggling. Mosumba came and boxed
him on the ear. Then he stood still, and they took a medicine which
they give to anyone who is showing fear and slapped it on his chest.
After they had finished with him, they took Sengi. He did not have
any trouble; he was the bravest of all. Then they started on Bukombi,
but since he was very young, he did not stand up. They put him on his
father's thigh. After they had cut his skin, he said 'Oh! Can't you give
me a rest? You are doing this like people who are hurrying to finish
a contract.'

Their answer was, 'No, we are trying to do it quickly so you won't
feel it. If we do it slowly, it will be more painful.'

The circumcision went on like that until one in the afternoon. Then
the circumcisers went up the road and started on another group of
boys. There were not many people in that group, only about eighteen,

so they did not stay there long. On their way back, they called at our place to see if anyone had done anything wrong. If a person had, he would have been reported and if anyone was bleeding, they would see the penis and cut it again. I was lucky; when they came to me, they found that it was not bleeding and they did not even put water on the wound. Four boys were cut again, and then late in the afternoon we were put in one house. For a bed each boy had two chairs arranged with the seats facing each other and a space between them so that the penis was hanging down. We slept on them all the time. When you got tired of leaning on the back of one chair, you would lean forward on to the other one. We stayed in the hut for two days, but had to stay in the village six days altogether before we could leave home to go into the bush.

In that house I had the worst experience I have ever had in my life. I was sitting on two logs in such a way that my penis hung down between my legs. While I was sitting there, a snake came and settled under the logs. He was twisted around a stick near my left thigh. It saw my penis and was about to bite me. When I saw it, I was very frightened and I had no strength to stand up, so I shouted to the people. At the time that I saw it, the fellow who had sent it had something like a shock, which caused him to jump from his seat and fall into the fire. After they had taken him out, they lit a torch to find the snake, but they did not see it. It had disappeared.

There was a boy called Mpweria who had hired the snake which was bewitched to come and kill me. The reason he wanted to kill me was that my mother had been married to a member of his lineage, and when he saw us, he felt jealous and said, 'Oh, if that woman had stayed at our place, all of these boys would be my brothers now.'

After all this had happened, my father told the householder, 'You see, Mugelia, I consulted many doctors before I came here, and I knew that there would be some kind of incident such as this. So this boy is the one who was going to kill my son?'

The boy replied, 'Oh, now you have taught me a good lesson. I am not going to persecute your son any more.'

Mosumba said, 'If you go on and try this again, they will carry your dead body back from this ceremony. But nothing will happen to my son.'

This was the second time in my life that I had been bewitched.

Four days later we were taken into the bush. We stayed there for one month, and at the end of that time the young boys, like Bukombi, had healed. But there was some trouble between my brothers, Atoku and Sengi, and myself. I quarrelled with these brothers about water; they were not washing themselves. I told them, 'You must not be afraid of this hot water. It is the only thing which helps.'

They told me, 'Oh, you, who don't fear hot water! We will be healed first!'

The same night that we had started this, while I was sitting I felt something drop on my leg, and I asked the people who were taking care of us to come and see me. They found blood dripping from my penis. One man warmed some water and put it on my penis. In the morning it was inflamed, so I sent someone to tell my father to come and see me. When he came, I explained the whole thing to him, and he judged that the case was against my brothers. A week after that they both had the same trouble. After a few days they were worse. Then, seeing that three of his sons had infections and that only two of them were well, my father decided to take us away from that place. He said that we should be brought to the house of Beyali, who was his nearest friend and clan member. As we were coming back, we met a messenger sent by Katabwita who is my father's 'brother'. This man said to us, 'Since Mosumba took his children to Busaru, thus making himself a Musaru, and left the other Bandinyama to have their circumcision ceremony by themselves here, he will not know the thing which will make him bring those sons back.'

When Mosumba heard this, he was worried. He had thought at first that he would take us straight back to Bundinyama, but then he said, 'Since they are saying that they have bewitched my children, I will take them to Gambeki's home, and I will see if the other Bandinyama are stronger than I am.'

We had our first bath when we reached Beyali's house, and had a good sleep, which we had not had at Busaru. Two days later my sore was better, but those of my brothers became very serious, and they had to call the doctor to take them to his house. On the first of October we went out of our seclusion period, and we were well. They burnt the hut that we had stayed in. At that time Atoku and Sengi were still at the doctor's house. During the three months that we were in seclusion we did not see a woman. No one is allowed to see one, even his own mother. When we came out, some of the boys had feasts given by their fathers, but our father did not give one for us because, as he said, 'My other sons are still in danger, so I am not happy yet.' A month and a half after this my brothers had also healed, and they came home.

The other trouble with circumcision is that they keep you apart from your wife for two months. I had my wife Paulina at that time, and I was away from her for five months altogether. After being home for two months we were allowed to have our women. I discovered that circumcision has no effect upon intercourse. We entered our home, and we have stayed there ever since.

I started as a teacher here at Kitengya, near Bundinyama, and

E   53

stayed there for two years. The reason I had to leave was that, whenever I used to beat someone for a mistake, he would come and beat me, because all the people knew me and we had grown up together. I had much trouble with Erikanjero, because he was not attending classes regularly. When I used to give my class figures to write, he would not do anything, but would start annoying his neighbours. So once I had to beat him with a cane on the top of his head to rid him of that habit. Then he was very angry and said, 'You will buy the road you will use today.'

Then he stood outside the door with his stick. Yohanna, the senior teacher, went outside and told him, 'I don't like such disobedience. You go to your home.'

So he went away. He went home crying and told his parents that I had beaten him on the head. He said, 'I wanted to beat him, but Yohanna stopped me.'

His parents told him, 'Get your stick. You will go and beat him while we are present.'

By that time school was over, and I had gone home to get my lunch. The parents and their child arrived at the chapel and found that I had gone. They saw Yohanna and asked, 'Where is Mpuga?'

'He has gone to get his lunch.'

They said, 'We have brought this boy to fight with him, because Mpuga has beaten him severely.'

Yohanna said, 'You must not do this; it is no good. Your child had been disobedient. Whenever the teacher gives him some work, he won't do it. He starts to whisper to his neighbours and troubles them. Mpuga reported this to me several times. At last he beat him with a stick, and it was not a heavy beating at all. So don't fight.'

But they said, 'No, no. We must go to Mpuga's house and fight with him.'

So they came to my place and found me resting in bed. They started talking to my father and mother, who were sitting in the dining hall. After he had heard the whole story of both sides, Mosumba said, 'Mpuga is here in the house, but what do you want to do to him?'

They said, 'We want him to explain the whole thing to us. After we have heard him, if we find that he is in the wrong, we will tell our boy to fight with him.'

So Mosumba called me to come out. My mother said, 'You all seem to have come prepared to fight, because you have sticks. If you had gone to his house and found him, would you have fought with him?'

They said, 'No, we just want to hear about the affair and judge it.'

Then Yohanna Kirima explained the matter to them as he had done before, and I did the same. Mosumba and Kirima judged that case was against the child, but the parents were not satisfied. They said to me and my family, 'If Mpuga tries to beat this child again, we will all fight with him.'

A week later, Kabanga, the father of that child, brewed some beer. While he was talking at the beer party he said, 'Mosumba's son has been sent down here just to beat our children, not to teach them. If one of the children he beats dies, we will carry the body to the house of Mosumba.'

He brought some beer to Yohanna Kirima and said, 'Don't give any of my beer to Mpuga.'

So I did not get any of that beer. At the same time, Mosumba came to us and told us all that had been said at the beer party. So, when I realized that a feud was starting, I asked for a transfer. I was sent to Butogu.

I got along well there, and the children obeyed me. My work was to teach the students how to write and read and teach them the first book, called the catechism.

A teacher's pay was three shillings a month; there were free dresses for our wives, no taxes, two uniforms a year, free text-books, free chalk and a free house. We used to have two free servants picked from our students. When we went up to Fort Portal, we had free porters. We used to get an allowance when we were in Fort Portal, and free food and servants while we were there. We had a free garden from which we made a lot of money. You were allowed to use the students to work in the garden and, when it was harvest-time, you could eat the crop or sell it, and no one asked you about it. One could make about thirty shillings a month from the garden, from the plantains, sweet potatoes and maize. Any teacher who was lazy used to be transferred to a place where there was food, so that he would not bother the priests asking for money for it. I used to make a lot of money from beer made from the plantains in these gardens. When our supervisor was going around, I used to make beer and have it ready for him. He would hold a beer party on the day that the local men reported to him.

I was the leader of the choir and used to read the Gospels. When the chief catechist was away, I used to do it all. And I used to preach. I taught the ten laws of God from the first to the tenth, and that involved all the ways of people and their behaviour towards their God. I used to preach, 'People, you must marry only one wife, as is the order of the Roman Catholic religion, and you must not fornicate with the wives of your friends. You must not kill your friends for nothing. That is forbidden by God. You must not covet other people's goods.'

There were a lot of other things, but these are the ones I most remember. Every Sunday I told them these things. They liked it very much, and every teacher used to have to pass the test at the main church in Bugombwa, and I passed that satisfactorily.

The bad thing about teaching is that it locks you in your hut as though you were in a prison. You cannot love women. You are watched carefully, and you have no leave. That is why I used to call it a lock. Another bad thing about the job is that you have to train people who have no idea about education.

I stayed one year there doing that work. After that year we received a qualified teacher who came to Bugombwa, the main Catholic school down here, so they took all the children from the bush schools and sent them to Bugombwa. That qualified teacher was Erinesti Kakumba, the man who had influenced us to run away when we were at school at Fort Portal. Until that time there had been two teachers at Butogu, Alosio Tibinyata and myself. When Kakumba came to Bugombwa, they discharged Alosio, and I was the only one left there. They discharged him because of his sins. He used to bring women and have intercourse with them in the chapel. He was reported by the wife of Manweri, the Amba who was our leader at the church at Bugombwa. He came down here to check on the story and found out that it was true. He called Alosio and discharged him. After he had been discharged, he captured one of the school-girls whom he was teaching and took her away.

An instance of my father's neglect of me is shown while I was a teacher at Butogu. I accidentally hit one child with an arrow on his wrist which made me liable to a fine of one hen and one goat. I had to pay that fine by myself, even though I had a father. And he never came to see me.

During that time at Butogu Gambeki died suddenly, and I went back for his burial. Kihara was the speaker at the first death ceremony, but I did not understand what they were talking about. The only thing I heard was at the first death ceremony, after the trial, when Kihara said, 'Now that Batigwa has been appointed as the head of this home, everything is all right. The only thing I ask is that each son have his share of his mother's property.'

He said this because his mother was the favourite wife of Gambeki. At that time, Batigwa's mother had only come to Bundinyama because of the illness of her husband; she had divorced him earlier, so she had no property at that time. Therefore we knew that Kihara intended to keep all the property for himself. Batigwa only took one spear from his father's home and two daughters. Kihara got the rest. He used to go where each daughter had been married and demand the brideprice, and whenever Batigwa went to the same places, the people would say, 'We have already paid Kihara,' and there was nothing Batigwa could say. He might have had some goats which were owed by people outside the home, but all the goats left in the home were taken by Kihara.

About this time Paulina had her first miscarriage. 'It was a ghost,' people said, 'from her family which caused this.' My father started to carry out a ceremony, as is done down here, but I refused to have it because I was a Christian. He said, 'Since you refuse to do this, I won't give you any more advice. It is you who are causing the death of my grandson.' Paulina agreed with me and did not want the ceremony.

After the miscarriage, the White Father visited my place, and he was very sad that my wife had miscarriage. He asked me how I got my water. I said that there was a swamp near my house where we used to go and bathe. He said that this might have been the cause of my wife's miscarriage, and he advised me to boil the water before using it for a bath. But by that time it was too late, because my wife was pregnant again.

While I was teaching at Butogu, I once attended a meeting at the church at Bugombwa. I had thought that it would last only one day, but the White Father said that it would take four days, so I came and stayed here at Bundinyama. At that time, I had left my wife behind. I met a Bunyangule girl, Alumbya, who was staying next door to my father's house. The first night that I stayed at Bundinyama, after I had had my meal, I went down to see Batigwa, who was also a teacher at that time. On my way back, I passed the house I mentioned and stayed there for a while talking to the household and that girl, Alumbya. Then I went on to my house where I stayed until dinner-time. After I had finished dinner, I went to bed. But Alumbya sent down my younger sister, Nakulinga, to tell me to come up to her home. The message was this, 'Just come up. I want to tell you something.'

So I went to that house and found her sitting on a chair, and she gave me half of the chair. I asked her, 'Are we going to share this chair?' and she said, 'Yes.'

We sat on the chair and talked a lot, and when the householder went to bed I said, 'I'm going back home.'

When I said good-bye to her, she replied, 'Hhmmmm.'

I asked her, 'Why are you so sad?'

She said, 'You are leaving and telling me good-bye, since you are standing up.'

I did not pay any attention to her. I went home and slept. Late in the night I woke when someone was beating on my shoulders and saying, 'Are you asleep?'

'Yes.'

57

The girl said, 'It is I.'

'What do you want?'

She said, 'I have come to sleep here.'

I wanted to call someone to come and make a bed for her, but she said, 'I have a bed at my house; I want to sleep with you. But if you don't want to sleep with me, I will go back home.'

So I got up and went to my elder brother and asked him what to do about this, and he advised me to sleep with her, so I came and enjoyed her. That was the first woman I had ever slept with outside of marriage. I continued to be her lover for some time. Whenever I saw her, I had intercourse with her until 1945, when she was married. I never thought of marrying her myself because I was told that she would not have any children and she never did. She became a prostitute later on and went as far away as Buganda. Then she was married to Paolo, and after that she was married by a Munyanguli. She is a very nice-looking girl.

During the time that I was teaching at Butogu I also met another girl at the house of Ereneko who was my friend. I asked him to approach her for me and he did. She said, 'Yes.' So I went and slept with her one night. I did not go back to her again, because I went up to Fort Portal on a visit.

In 1935 or 1936 I was transferred to Buhundu for a change, because I had been teaching at Butogu for a long time. After I had been there for a month, I had trouble with my eyes and became sick. After I was well, I returned to my teaching.

At Buhundu I met a girl who was receiving religious training to become a candidate for baptism. Her name was Angweka. I loved her and asked her tò come and stay at night with me. I was her lover for a while, but when my wife Paulina died, she was the first wife I captured.

In July, 1936, I went to Fort Portal for a meeting. At this meeting one teacher at Busaru was discharged, because he had captured a girl and his marriage was not approved. Now the priest said, 'Busaru is a big place and an important one, so we will transfer Mpuga from Buhundu and give him Busaru.'

At that time my wife had been sick for a long while and I said, 'It is difficult for me to move so far from my home.'

The priest said, 'If you are a good teacher, you will go.'

So I agreed to go there.

After a month I had my first bad time. The people of Busaru used to come and take drums from the church at night and carry them to pagan ceremonies. I reported this to the leader, Manweri, at Bugombwa. After that I thought that all my troubles would stop, but the people refused to obey. I used to tell them in the daytime not to take the drums, but at night I was afraid to go out myself, because they might spear me. When we would go out after the noise had stopped to see what had happened, we would find that there were no drums in the chapel. Manweri gave me a letter to the sub-county chief. He gathered all the people in that village and asked them about the affair, and they said that no one had ever touched the drums. The chief said, 'I am going to put my policeman on guard, and if anyone is caught, he will get six months in prison.'

Three days after this the Busaru people were drunk, and when they passed by my house they called to me, 'You teacher! Get up and listen to what we are saying. You reported us to the chief. If you are a fool, you will stay here; if you have any sense, you will move.'

I went outside with the lamp, because I wanted to get the names of some of these men. I recognized two—Kisaka and Mugindi. In the morning I went and accused them at the sub-county headquarters. The case went against them, and they were sentenced to two months in prison. The Busaru people carried on the feud, but our leader Manweri told me to live at Bugombwa and to go to Busaru in the daytime.

At this time Paulina was very ill. She was pregnant for a second time, and she had the same trouble which she had had the first time. When I took her to the dispensary at Bundibugyo, Musa was in charge. He told me that the disease was too much for him and that I had better take my wife to Fort Portal. I took her to the mission hospital where she had six injections. She stayed there for three months, but the doctors told me that she was very ill and they could not heal her. So they advised me to take her to the large hospital. I had a letter from them and took her to the Government hospital. They told me, 'The child in her womb is not healthy. It is very weak and may die unborn or during birth.'

I stayed there for four days, and then they gave me a note to take back to the mission hospital. The lady doctor there told me to take Paulina to the Protestant hospital, but the doctor there told me the same story. He said, 'Don't bother to give her medicine, because it will be of no use.'

Then I decided to bring her back to Bwamba, so I did. Four days after we arrived home, she had a child. It lived for six days and then died. So it was proved to me that the doctors were right. The people here said the same things they have said when she miscarried before, 'Mpuga has been very disobedient, because he has not taken our advice to hold a ceremony. That is why his children are dying. It is he who is allowing them to die.'

Paulina agreed with me and trusted only in God until she died. She was sick for a long time. I took her to the hospitals in Fort Portal.

She was in the Roman Catholic hospital and in the Church Missionary hospital. They did their best, but they failed to cure her. Then I had to bring her back here. At that time I had to give up teaching. The White Father told me that I should not stop, but I said, 'No. I will go and look after my wife till she dies. After that, I will come back to the job.'

Before she died, I had gone to Bubandi to fetch my father's goats. I stayed there for three days, and during that period a sister of my wife came down to my house to visit and stayed a night with my wife. Late in the night, she ran away with Paulina to her home. When my father went to my wife's house early in the morning, he could not find her. He discovered her at her sister's and asked why she had been brought there. The sister said, 'I wanted to get this sister of mine so that I could try to save her. You people are not trying to do anything for her illness.'

When I returned to my home and discovered what had happened, I went to her sister's and asked if Paulina could come back, but my sister-in-law said she could not. When she had been there for a week she died, and one morning the Bandinyama saw the people coming to tell them the news. They were going to bring the body back to Bundinyama, but our people refused to have it saying, 'You had better bury your own body.'[1]

These people had already carried the body, and when the Bandinyama would not have it, they left it outside and went and accused us to the sub-county chief. They said that the Bandinyama wanted to fight with them, and they also accused me of refusing the body. If her relatives had buried the body, they would have lost the brideprice. After they had explained the affair, the chief asked me. 'How long have you been with your wife?'

'Seven years.'

'Was she a legal or a temporary wife?'

'Legal.'

The chief said, 'Why do you refuse to bury your body? You had better go and bury it.'

So I had to do it. Then at the first ceremony after death, I did not say anything, but Mosumba stood up and spoke to the Bobandi, 'You were very wrong to steal our patient. We know that she got the disease from this place. She could have died in our home. If you had

---

[1] Paulina's lineage by taking her away and keeping her against Mpuga's will assumed responsibility for her. By so doing they became responsible for her burial in their own land in the event of death. This in turn made them liable for the repayment of whatever they had received from the Bandinyama, in this case a girl. They took the point of view that since the illness had been contracted while Paulina was living with Mpuga, he and his lineage were ultimately responsible for her death. Thus they thought the Bandinyama should bury her.

done such a thing in the past, we could have taken our daughter back, but now that there is this new government we are going to let this pass.'

At the same time Kihara stood up and said, 'No. We'll pay for this body. The price is five goats. We must get our daughter, Ndigombwa, back today.'

Ndigombwa was at the ceremony then, and Kihara caught her. The Babandi were very angry, so they went home before the ceremony was over. They played a trick on us by taking the dress of our daughter and putting it in the room of the god. This made the girl sick. She had a swelling on her leg which became a very bad sore. We tried for a year to treat her, but it was in vain. Then we sent a message to her husband and he said, 'If you don't send my wife back to me, she will not get well.'

Then Mosumba decided to send her back. When they arrived there, they held a meeting in which they asked the boy what kind of god he had used to bewitch the girl. He said, 'Kihara.'

The old man said, 'That is very bad. It is most doubtful whether the girl will get well. That god is always a very difficult one.'

So the wife still has a sore. It is thirteen years since it started. We held a second death ceremony for Paulina, but there was no inquest. After her death her ghost bothered me, and I dreamed of her three times, so I told my father about it. He told me that I should go and call her while I was defecating in the latrine. After I had done that, I was not bothered again, and I have never dreamed of her since.

My marriage to Angweka, whose lover I had been, came about this way. I met her at the market and walked away with her and asked her, 'Are you still at home?'

'Yes.'

I said, 'Would you like to marry me?'

First she asked me, 'You are a teacher and teachers can only marry one wife, so how can you marry me?'

I said, 'No, I am not teaching.'

So the girl agreed, and I told her to come to my home. She asked me to visit at her home on the following Wednesday, and I went and we arranged the business of coming to my home.

She said, 'You will find me in the market next Monday.'

I captured her at the market and took her to Busaru to the house of Mugelia. We stayed there for three days and then I brought her back to my house. That day, about six in the evening, her brother arrived. Mosumba asked him, 'Have you come for your goats?'

'No. I have come for my sister.'

Mosumba said, 'Do you want to take her at night?'

'Yes. Even if I have to walk all night, I will take her.'

Mosumba refused to give him the girl. That brother replied, 'As you refuse to give me my sister, I will stay here overnight without eating. I will not go into the house, but will stay outside.'

He stayed there the whole night. Then at seven in the morning he said to Mosumba, 'Since you have refused to give me my sister, I'll go. I will return shortly.'

He returned about seven that same evening. Mosumba said,'What is wrong with you?'

Her brother said, 'I want to stay here for another night.'

Mosumba said, 'All right, go ahead.'

Mosumba went outside about midnight to see what the man was doing. He found him lying near the wall outside of the house near where my bed was, and he was trying to hear what I was doing with the girl.   Mosumba said, 'This is a very bad thing, which is not done in the whole of Bwamba, so wait until the morning and I will give you back your sister.'

My father called Kihara in the morning and explained the whole thing to him; how I captured the wife, how the brother-in-law came down, how he tried to give him fowls and how her brother had refused them, how he spent two nights here, and the worst thing how he was found trying to hear what my wife and I were doing in the bed. Kihara told Mosumba to do as he liked. So my father gave the woman back. He told the girl before she went, 'We loved you and would have married you, but the habits of your brother are not good; you will go and go forever. Never return to this home.' The girl was very angry and went away crying, but I was on my father's side because her brother had acted very badly.

Then I married Mambaiye. Two months after I had married her, I decided to get another wife, because when you have only one wife, she makes trouble and does not behave well. Two weeks after I had married Mambaiye she became disobedient. If I had discovered this before, I would not have married her. One day I went to visit at Bubomboli, and when I came back, she would not let me have any food and said that I had been with other women. I asked her politely to give me food, but she refused completely so I had to go and get some from my mother's house. That instance showed me that she was a bad woman.

We often quarrelled about food. One day I said to her, 'Why don't you get my food ready on time? Whenever I come here for food, you tell me it isn't ready.'

She was very angry. She did not say anything to me, but she seized a spear from the wall and said, 'Can't I kill you now?' and thrust the spear at me. It went through my shorts and cut my back. I was very angry and wanted to spear her, but my father stopped me. He called Kihara to attend to the wound. Kihara found that it was not very serious, so they treated me by themselves. Mambaiye's punishment was to stay in the house all of the time that I was in bed, carrying water, washing my wound and preparing my food.

After that, whenever I wanted to beat her, I used to hide all of the spears and knives. When I did beat her, I used to stay away from her for four days afterwards. I would not go near her or eat her food or go to her house, because I was afraid that she might have something with which she might kill me.

I became the lover of a girl who was visiting at Kihara's homestead. Mambaiye discovered that I had gone to the house where the girl was, so she came there at night time and found me and the girl taking a bath together. Both of us were completely naked. Mambaiye began to beat the girl. I stood up and tried to put my shorts on, but Mambaiye grabbed them, struck me twice and then began to beat both of us with the shorts. I finally managed to get them away from Mambaiye. I put them on and then I began to fight with her. I gave her some very good blows, so she ran home.

Early the next morning the girl ran away and went back to her home in Bunyanguli. Mambaiye asked, 'Where is the girl who is trying to take Mpuga away from me? Is she still here?'

The people said, 'No, she left very early in the morning.'

Mambaiye was a very fierce woman. Once there were some men who were dancing the death dance and they went around Bundinyama begging for food. They came to my father's house, and he offered them one hen. They said that that was not enough for the six houses in his group, so they said that they would take some sorghum. They were about to take it from the dining hall when my father said, 'I am very weak and can't prevent you from taking it, but you are only taking it because Mpuga isn't here.'

At this, the wife, Mambaiye said, 'What do you mean? Am I not here?'

She rushed out and caught the man who was taking the sorghum and pushed him. He fell down and dropped the grain on the ground. There were about twenty men there, and they slapped her, but she knocked almost all of them down. They did not get the sorghum.

She also used to abuse me. Whenever I asked for water to wash my feet, she would say, 'You go and get it yourself. You are just an ugly fellow. All the women have refused you; I am the only one who would marry you.'

I said, 'Oh huh. We'll see. We'll see. I'll get another wife.'

She also had many other bad habits which I cannot remember or explain. Most of these things were slight mistakes, but she took correction badly, and I knew that she was a hopeless woman. I did not take any interest in what she did. I used to beat her, but that was not enough. The only way to teach her was to get more wives. I did not tell her when I was going to bring another woman home, because when we are trying to marry new wives down here in Bwamba, we do not tell our present wife about it. If you do that, the wife will do her best to stop you. She will either hide the keys to the box where your clothes are kept or make herself ill so that you cannot leave. When I brought my new wife, Nyakajuli, to Bundinyama, I had to take her to my brother Sengi's house, because I had only one small house. Down here when you get a new wife and do not have a house for her, you take her to your brother. As for sleeping with the wives, it is done alternatively. When your brother goes out, you come in.

When I appeared with Nyakajuli, Mambaiye did a very bad thing to me. I did not blame her for this because, if I had, she could say that I was trying to get rid of her because I had married a second wife. Four days after I had married Nyakajuli, Mambaiye bewitched my penis so that it was very lazy and I could not raise it at all. I had to go and ask the older people what was happening to me, and they told me, 'You have been bewitched by your first wife. The only way to save yourself, is to get up about midnight, leave Nyakajuli's bed, and go to Mambaiye's bed. When you get to her house, you must not call her, but call the child to come and open the door. If she has bewitched you with medicine, this child will find an odd thing on the door.'

About three in the morning I got up and went to her house. I went to the window near the child's bed and called to him to come and open the door. When he came to open it, he found a very odd thing on it which he told me about. I told him to take it, and he did and handed it to me. I went and hid it.

This thing was the bark cloth which is used as a loincloth. When your wife wants you to stop sleeping with other women, she takes off her loincloth at night and puts it on the main door of the house, and she says, 'My husband must not do anything where he has gone. He will not get anything, even if he sends a telegram to the Pope.'

After I had hidden the cloth, I went into her house and awakened her. When she got up she said, 'Who opened the door for you?'

'I opened it myself.'

She jumped up and went to the fire to get a light so that she could get the thing from the door. She did not find it there, so she came back and sat down at the fireplace where she stayed all night while I slept in the bed. I tried to get her to come to bed, but she would not. I said, 'What did you have on the door?'

She would not say. In the morning I had to report all this to Mosumba. Then he called that wife and asked her about all of these matters which I had told him. He said, 'Do you have anything to say to defend yourself?'

'No, I am guilty.'

Mosumba told her, 'As you are a girl for whom we paid no bride-price, it is all right, and we are going to let you stay in the house, but if we had paid anything for you, you would have been sent away today. From now on, you must not do anything like this.'

Mosumba sent both me and my wife home. That night I was strong and enjoyed my new wife.

Nyakajuli knew that Mambaiye was trying to cause trouble for her. Two weeks later they had a quarrel, and when Nyakajuli said, 'I know that you are trying to harm me, and I can prove it by the case you had recently,' that witch kicked her, and they started fighting. I was not present, as I had gone away for a visit, so Mosumba stopped them by himself. When I returned, my father explained the whole thing to me, but I did not do anything about it that night. In the morning the witch went to her family's home. She stayed there for four days, and I had to go there in order to see her. When she saw me, she said, 'Oh! Now you have come to tell me about my spells.' She asked me politely, 'Don't say anything about them.'

I was very kind and did not say anything about them. I did not stay there for the night but came back home the same day. She had told me, 'My father is trying to stop me from leaving home, and we cannot both go together. You go ahead, and I will come sometime at night.'

She came the same night. She and I lived together happily, but she used to quarrel a lot with the other wife.

During this period I stayed at home. Then the Government wanted young men who knew how to read and write to be trained to become agricultural instructors. I wanted to become one for the sake of the money.

We went to be trained at the foot of the mountain here in Bwamba by Erika Mukasa, a Ganda. We were in training for a month and a half and then we were sent to our posts. I was sent to Bubandi with two other men. We earned fifteen shillings a month. I stayed there for six months, and then I was transferred to another part of Bwamba. I worked very well and made no mistakes. After I had been in my new post for five months the European agricultural officer said, 'I want all the instructors in Bwamba to come to Kyenjojo (in Toro) for training.'

At that point I became ill with fever. I went to the dispensary for treatment. I stayed there and was given many injections. To prove to you that I was very sick, they called the priest to come and give me the last rites. I did not see him until he slapped my leg and said, 'Do you know that I am a priest?'

'Hmmmm.'

65

He said, 'Do you know what a Christian does when he is going to die?'

Nyakajuli and Mambaiye were there. He saw them and said, 'Who are these women?'

They told him that they were my wives. Then he said, 'Why have I been called here to such a sinner?' He raised his right arm and said, 'I am leaving you, Mpuga. I am speaking in the name of Jesus Christ. It is not I who am being cruel to you, but you yourself, because you have forgotten your religion. Either repent in your heart or die with your sins. As I am only a man, I can't know whether you have repented or not, but Jesus will know where to put you if you die, either in hell or in one of the chairs.' He went out of the room.

After I was discharged, I had a relapse on the way home. While my people were crying, the dispenser came and drove them away and felt my heart. He found that I was still alive, and he immediately sent a message to the doctor at the Yellow Fever Camp. He asked him to come and see me. When the doctor came, he gave me two injections which I did not feel. Then he gave me some medicine from a spoon. After that they gave me an enema. A little later I began to feel better. Later in the evening the doctor came again and bled me. Then he ordered the dispenser to give me an injection every day. I began to recover. I stayed in the dispensary for two weeks. At the end of that time they told my father to take me away.

My father took me to the house of one of my mother's brothers in Bumati, where I stayed for two months. While I was there, my father did not allow any of the Bandinyama with the exception of Kihara and Batigwa to visit me. My father was afraid that some of the other Bandinyama might bewitch me. Also he was afraid of one of Kihara's wives, Kageye. Kageye had fallen in love with me and wanted me to have intercourse with her. My father had told Kihara, 'You should tell your wives not to trouble my sons in the future.'

Kihara had asked him, 'Which wife is it. If you tell me which one it is, I will cut off her ears.' My father had refused to tell him, because he knew that Kihara would do as he had threatened.

At the end of the two months my father made beer. When the beer was ready, he sent a messenger to me and I returned to my father's house at night with the messenger. We arrived there at the first cockcrow. My father hid me in the house. Early in the morning a fat goat was killed and food was prepared. Most of the Bandinyama were there. First, they ate their food. Then the beer was brought out, but before they began to drink, my father took me out of the house and showed me to the people. He said, 'I prepared this feast for my son who was going to die, but who is now alive. I am very happy and I am thankful that I have my son again. Since he has recovered from this illness, may he grow old and get grey hairs on his head such as I now have. Don't think that I am giving this feast for the sake of the witches, as is the custom here in Bwamba. I have made a feast because I am happy to have son well again.'

They all looked at me, and they saw that I had not lost any of my limbs and that I was as strong as I had been before. Then they began to drink beer.

While I had been ill, the other men had gone to Toro for their agricultural training and had returned. When I had recovered, I went to see Erika, but he said that I could not begin my work again until I had seen the Agricultural Officer. He gave me a letter to take to the officer in Fort Portal which explained my illness. The Agricultural Officer said, 'I am sorry, but your place has been given to another man because you were ill. There isn't a place for you now.'

I returned home and stayed there. A month after that some of the other men were sent away because they were cutting down the staff. Some of them were discharged, and some of them were sent to the Forestry Department. They called me back and sent me to the Forestry Department, since I had been discharged without a bad mark. I worked in Fort Portal for two months. Then they told me that they were going to send me to Busongora (southern Toro near Lake Edward), but I refused to go, because Busongora is a bad place and there is much fever there. Then they said they would send me up into the mountains, but I told them that that was also a bad place. The Forestry Officer said, 'I have no post for you. If you like, you can give up this work.'

I said, 'All right.' I returned home.

At this time I started staying seven days in the house of each woman. This is a good system, but if you make a mistake and stay, for example, eight days in one house, the other wife makes a lot of trouble. I still use this method. My wives, Mambaiye and Nyakajuli, continued to quarrel. They would not eat together, and neither wife would go to her neighbour's house. I could not send them to do one job at the same time. They kept entirely apart.

One day I visited my father's sister, Mabulumba, who lived at Busaru, and I met a girl named Beliki there. I visited for five days and during that time I became her lover and slept with her.

Later at the Bundibugyo market I met Beliki and told her, 'I want to marry you.'

She said, 'Yes. I also want to marry you.'

I said, 'I will come to your house on Wednesday.'

I went there on Wednesday evening and found her sitting in the dining hall. The householder was a member of a lineage which has a feud with the Bandinyama. The girl and I went into the house and

67

while we were there talking the father, who was outside, asked, 'Who has entered the house?'

The people told him, 'It is a son of the Bandinyama.'

He began to talk about the feud. He asked, 'Whose son is it?'

The people told him, 'It is the son of Mosumba.'

He said, 'Oh! Mosumba and Gambeki who killed my brother! He must go out of this house. If it were the old days, I would kill him.'

I ran out of the house. The girl started to follow me, but her father stopped her and said, 'Go back.'

She went back into the house, but came out by the back door and met me. I brought her home.

Nyakajuli and Mambaiye did not like the fact that I had brought a new wife. They were rather angry, and it is well known down here that the more wives you marry, the more jealousy you get among them.

In the morning her father was afraid to come to our village, so he sent one of his sons. Mosumba drove him away. He said, 'Go away. Don't you remember what your father said to my son last night? You are safe because of this new government. Otherwise I would kill you.' The son asked for the fowls, but Mosumba refused to give them to him, so he returned home. Then Beliki's father sent a member of his lineage who is a sister's son of the Bandinyama to say, 'Since you have said what you have said, I don't want your fowls. Take the girl and marry her for nothing. No one of our lineage will ever come to see her. Until my daughter visits me here at my home, I will do what I can.'

After a year her father said, 'I want one of your daughters for my girl. If I come for fowls, I want both the fowls and the girl.'

Mosumba refused this and said, 'I have no adult daughters.'

Then her father said, 'Even though the girls are young, I will come and choose one for myself.'

He came and chose a girl. He was given the choice of Nakulinga and Leiko. He chose Leiko. He was offered five fowls, but he refused them because he said he wanted seven, and in the end he was given seven.

Later Beliki became pregnant. When she was pregnant, she left my home and after two months, I brought back my sister. Beliki's child was born at Busaru. A few days after his birth she died. The child had no milk so they asked for a goat to pay for the medicine which was necessary in order to bring milk into the breast of Beliki's mother. The milk came, and the child began to drink it.

Two years later I went there to ask my mother-in-law to give me the child. She said, 'I will keep the child. Don't worry. Let him stay at the breast.'

Then a sister of Beliki, who was married to a man in the Congo, came and took the child away. That was three years ago and I have never seen the child since. They did not tell me that they were going to take him to the Congo. I had tried to get the child, but everything has been in vain. Last year my mother-in-law died, and I went to her death ceremony. I spoke to the people about the child. Mugelia, who is the child's mother's brother, said, 'Don't worry about him. I will do my best in this affair.'

Mugelia sent a messenger to find out about the matter. The answer from the Congo was this 'They want three goats.'

I said, 'Three goats is too much. I shall give them one goat.'

That was the last message I have had. I have planned with Mugelia that whenever the child comes to visit him, he should call me so that I may go and catch the child. It is very difficult. The cost of taking care of the child in the Congo is too much. They want three goats. Here in Bwamba it is only one goat, and in the government court it is only fifty shillings.

Because of the trouble between Mambaiye and Nyakajuli I decided to marry the third wife, Nyakala of the Babomboli. I thought that she might be better than the others. I used to visit her at her house, and I started having intercourse with her.

It is the custom here in Bwamba to sleep with a girl several times to try her out. One cannot capture a wife unless one knows she is all right. Sometimes a woman is married before she is tried, but in that case the husband worries very much about the wife, and the wife worries about whether the husband is virile. The wife wants to know if the man's penis is strong, and the husband wants to know that the woman does not have a bone which would make it impossible for him to enter. That does not happen often, but sometimes it does. Another reason for sleeping with a woman is to find out whether she knows about sleeping with men. If she does not, she may lie on her left side, which is a bad thing. The side she lies on is a matter of individual preference. I always lie on my left side and whenever I change and lie on the right, I beget daughters. If the woman does not lie on the side which is correct for the man, it can cause a change in him.

There is another reason for trying a woman. Once I went to a girl who had a vagina large enough to hold me, but when I had an orgasm, I could not manage another erection and had intercourse only once the whole night. That was bad, and I had to give up the girl. The reason for it was that the girl's vagina was too cold. I sent that woman away on the second day, having had intercourse with her only once.

When one tries out a girl, she should not be taken in her mother's or father's home. The girls down here have their own house when

F   69

they grow up. If she is the only girl in the home, she can be taken either to her brother's house or to the house of a friend or to one of her relatives. She is forbidden to have intercourse in her mother's or father's house because it would give the parents worms.

When I had been Nyakala's lover for some time, she became pregnant. Her parents asked her who was responsible for it, and she said, 'Mpuga.'

Her father sent a message to my father, 'Your son has impregnated my daughter, so you must come and heal my home.'

Mosumba selected Mulako, Sengi, Mambaiye and Nyakajuli to go with me with the following things: one goat, one white hen, dried meat, mushrooms and millet flour. The woman went to carry the things and see what was going to be done. When we arrived, we found the people ready. They killed one goat for us. They took the small intestine out, cut a piece of it, and tied one end to my arm and the other to Nyakala's arm. Then the millet flour was prepared. In preparing it, we each took hold of the stirrer and stirred. They brought the skin of the goat, and my wife put it on my back first and then I did the same to her. Then we got a plantain stem shredded so that it formed a brush. I went with the wife, who was holding a pot of the goat's blood, and dipped the brush in the blood and painted it on each house in the group. After we had done all this, we had a meal. Then they gave me the girl to take home.

Mosumba and I were very glad that the girl had become pregnant. Her parents were not so happy, because in this instance it seemed that their daughter was being taken free. They should have had chickens and many other things, may be even a large brideprice, which they might not actually get in a case of this kind. My other two wives were not happy. 'Oh, this is another wife coming now.'

They did not make any trouble until four months had passed, and that trouble was caused by my mother. It happened one day when my new wife was away at her home. My mother had beans in her garden ready to be picked. She took Nyakajuli and Mambaiye into the garden and gave them each an equal amount of beans. When the new wife, Nyakala, returned from her home my mother took her also into the garden and gave her a large amount of beans. The other wives were very annoyed and said, 'Why did she get so many beans, when we did not get that many?'

Then they quarrelled and that was the start of a feud. When the new wife saw that there was a lot of trouble, and she was due to give birth, she had to go back to her home to have the baby. She was there for one month and then had her child. I was very much annoyed at this, but I did not try to do anything, because I knew that the wife was right to go home.

About this time I had a bit of trouble. One Monday I left my wife, Nyakajuli, in labour and as I was returning, I met Mambaiye in the courtyard. She shouted to me rudely, 'You big-headed man! You left your wife in the middle of labour, and you went after other women in the market. Now you will see what your punishment is.'

I started wondering what it was all about and asked her. She replied, 'You won't have any food this day. You will see what the matter is. You are always a lot of trouble around here.'

I asked her again to tell me, but she just went on abusing me. She was a very fierce wife. So finally I tried to get into the house, but the women hit me on the head and said, 'Go back.'

I cried, 'What is it? Has my wife died?'

They said, 'No, go and find some one to come and wash the babies and cut the cords.'

My senses faded; I lost all my strength and began to think about the expenses. At last I said to myself, 'Oh, my father is alive; I won't worry.'

Twins are a very bad thing and a lot of trouble. There are many things that you must do in Bwamba when you have twins. The midwife brought to help your wife takes some chickens, dried meat, white mushrooms and ten shillings, which are tied on her arm. You have to make a feast before she leaves the home, and at that feast you have to kill a goat, get mushrooms, millet flour and one white hen. When you have all this settled, you get a sister's son, who is given one goat, one white fowl, mushrooms and dried meat, and he is sent as a messenger to tell the wife's parents the news. When he arrives at her home, he does not go into the house but stays about a hundred feet away, and he ties the goat to the elephant grass. Then he shouts, 'You people have twins.'

When those people hear the news, they come armed with sticks and run after the sister's son until they catch him. Then they beat him. If he is strong enough, he will run away and leave the people behind. They go back and get the things he has left and take them into their houses.

In your house, when twins are born, you make a lean-to thatched with dry plantain leaves against the side of the house, and you get a drum. When either of the twins cries, the drum has to be beaten until the child stops. The mother and father of twins are in trouble for a whole month. The parents of the woman cannot come to the house until the children start walking, unlike in a usual birth. The day my twins were born I did not have anything to eat until late at night, when they finally gave me some food. I could not eat it. All the people who had been having beer at Kabonga's came to my home and started insulting me and my wife. You know how drunkards are when they insult you. It is so bad that you could weep. First the men would insult the mother, 'Oh mother of twins! Mother of twins has a huge belly!' Then the women would turn to me and say, 'The father of twins has a long penis, long penis.' Then the men would turn to the mother and say, 'Mother of twins, you have a wide vagina.' This is done alternately, the men abusing the mother and the women abusing the father. So you do not enjoy yourselves all during this time and you begin to regret it. 'Why did I have these children who are so much trouble?'

We always feel sorry for Batigwa who has had twins twice. Mosumba was happy to have the twins, because he had had them before. He wanted me to have more children. I was annoyed, because the people were insulting me and I would have to spend a lot of money. Nyakajuli was much more annoyed than I, because she had the trouble of the birth in addition to the abuse of the people.'

One of the twins lived for four days, and the other died after a fortnight. I did not know what killed them. Twins do not get sick; they just die suddenly. We thought that it was the will of God. The burial of the twins was a lot of trouble. When they died, they were taken out of the home and into the bush where a special tree called the Kiroko is found and were buried there.

All these troubles with wives annoyed me very much and because of them I was converted back to my religion in which I could marry only one wife. So I had to look for someone to marry me legally. That is when I met Lubangi. I went to her father and spoke to him about marrying his daughter. He asked me for fifteen goats. I told my father, and he gave me the goats, which I paid to my father-in-law. All these things were done secretly so as not to let the other wives know, but when they saw the goats going away, they knew that I was marrying another wife, and, as a matter of fact, they did not cook any food for me that day. I went for two whole days without food. At this time, the teacher came to see me and said, 'Since you are engaged to a Christian girl, you must send away all these wives.'

The next morning I told them, 'You all go home, because I have repented and I want to marry one single wife and return to my religion.'

Mambaiye said, 'I will go and become a Christian, and I will have a ring marriage as you are having.'

Nyakajuli said, 'I was a Christian, and I thought you would marry me in a ring ceremony, but as you have chosen another wife I will go away and get married again.'

The third wife, Nyakala, was away at her home after the baby boy had been born. I did not tell her about it, but she heard that I was

getting a ring marriage, so she never bothered to come and say anything.

I had to give the wives all their dresses and all their other things.
Then I sent them away. At that time I had three children. Nyakajuli
had one boy, Kalisa. Mambaiye had a boy, Kisasi, and there was the
new baby, the child of Nyakala. They all went with their mothers, because I knew that they would be back when they were grown.[1]

Mosumba was very annoyed, and if he had known that I was going
to send away the three wives, he would not have given me the goats
for the new one He said, 'You have ruined your home. I have been
very happy having three individuals here with our blood, and our
blood has been making me happy all the time, but now you have sent
them away and you have sent off your own blood to stay outside.'

My mother was of the same opinion as Mosumba. The Christians
all thought that it was a good idea, and the families of the wives I had
sent home were glad because I had not paid anything for the girls.

During our engagement, which lasted four months, I heard a
rumour that people had bewitched my future wife with a medicine
which is put in a cut and keeps a man from having an erection. There
is a special charm down here which is made when a girl refuses to
sleep with you. You get a razor blade and put some medicine on it
and go to her. When you are trying to persuade her, you cut her back
slightly. When she feels it, you say, 'No, I just touched you; I have
not cut you.' It is impossible for her to see her back. That charm will
keep the girl from having intercourse with another man. That is the
way a man named Sesinga had been bewitched.

I came and told my father and he sent me to my grandfather, my
mother's father. On the way there, I was informed that he did not
have any medicine, so I came back home and told my father. The
same day my father sent me to my future father-in-law to find out
about the rumour. The only way to find out was to sleep with the
woman. I slept with her and came and told my father that the
rumours were not true. When it was time to be married, we went up
to Fort Portal to be married in the church. After the ceremony we
returned the same day by the mountain path. We had a feast here and
settled down. Lubangi had her first child which was a daughter. The
child lived one year and then died. Three months after the child died,
she went home and asked her father, 'Why has my child died?'

I did not know what her father answered. Lubangi stayed there for
a month. During that time I would go up and ask her to come home,
but she would refuse.

Then I married another wife, Bakweziba, of the Babomboli. She

[1] Of these children only Kisasi is now alive. Mambaiye later returned to Mpuga
after he had married Lubangi.

was at her father's home, and I used to visit there now and then. Sometimes I would stay at night. I started by staying two nights, then four nights, and then five nights. On the last night I captured that girl. Four days after that, her father said, 'I want the brideprice; I don't want chickens.'

My father, Mosumba, refused his demand and said, 'That has never been done in the whole history of the world. It is better that I should watch your daughter's habits, and then I will pay you for her.'

Her father gave him three months and said that in that time Mosumba would be able to judge the ways of his daughter. When that time had passed, he came and was given five goats. After I had paid the brideprice, my wife became pregnant. She hated me while she was pregnant. I asked my father, 'What is wrong with my wife? Why does she hate me so?'

Mosumba said, 'This is just because she is pregnant.'

About this time I had my fight with Balikengo, the sub-parish chief. He came and sat in my doorway early one morning. He had come to get my wife to carry food to a European at Kirumia. My wife got up in the morning without any clothes and, when she opened the door, she saw Balikengo sitting there. She ran back into the house crying, 'Oh! You have seen me naked!'

I was very angry. I said, 'Who is that?'

She said, 'It was Balikengo.'

I said, 'What is wrong? Why have you come to my house so early in the morning?'

He replied, 'I have come to get your wife to carry some food.'

I got up, put on my shorts, and picked up my stick. I kicked him first. He fell down, and I hit him with my stick. I hit him twice, and then he cried, so my father got up. He said, 'Don't do that. If he becomes angry enough, he will accuse you in court.'

Balikengo ran to the sub-county headquarters, and they sent a policeman to arrest me. He found me in my garden. The trial went against me, and they wanted to put me in prison, but they decided to send me up on the road gang at the Public Works Department station, and they said, 'This will teach him.'

So I was taken to Sempaya to work on the road. We used to start working at four in the morning. The roll-call took four hours because there were many people. There were nine hundred and fifty porters. The job was very bad. We did not make out well because we started very early and worked until late in the day. We could not run away, because we knew that we would be brought back or punished. Since I had been a lot of trouble, I was put on hard work for two weeks, but then I was promoted to be a sub-headman. Most of the headmen were not able to read and write, so the clerk had much difficulty giving out tickets and marking absences. The headmen used to come and bring the tickets to me so that I could give them to their owners, but when they discovered that I knew how to read and write, they promoted me. There I was happier because I was not doing manual work, but only talking to the people. I worked for two months in that position, and then I went back home. When I arrived, they sent a policeman to arrest me. I was brought into the court, and they asked me whether I had been sent by the county chief for poll-tax exemption. I gave my note to the sub-county chief which showed that I was exempt, but the parish chief said, 'This fellow is disobedient and a trouble-maker.'

The note, which I had, said that I had still five months before I had to pay the poll tax, but the chief and his court decided to make me pay it then. So the sub-county chief tore up my note and gave it to a policeman and said that, if I did not pay my tax, I would be put in prison. I saw that they were all ready to put me into prison if I did not pay the tax, which was six shillings, so I had to pay it. But when I asked the chief to give me permission to go and get the money from my home, he refused, saying, 'You are a prisoner now.'

So I had to send my brother, Bukombi, home to get the money. He returned with thirteen shillings. After I had paid the six shillings for the tax, they told the clerk to write down my name for the work one has to do if one does not have cash for the tax. It was to work for one month at the king's palace. That will make you obedient.

So I put my hand in my pocket and paid seven more shillings. They told me, 'Good-bye.' That is how I came to pay the tax.

I stayed at home four months after the court case, and then I went back to work on the road, because I had a friend there who was working as the headman. I stayed there quite happily for six months. Then I asked my friend if I could come home, and he agreed to let me, so I came here and had a rest. When they began to build the road the rules were good. A man could go there and work for a month and then return home, but later they made a rule that each porter had to work at least three months. When he signed the agreement to work for three months, he was given a blanket, a sack to use as a sleeping mat, and free food, beans and corn meal.

When I returned to work the second time, I made a blood-brother of a man called Zedoro, who was the inspector's cook. At that time his wife was having trouble; she had pain at the time of her monthly period and this prevented her from having children. Zedoro knew that my mother had medicine to take care of this trouble, so he asked if I could get some for him. I came down here and asked my mother, and she showed me a tree whose bark should be prepared by the husband as an enema for his wife. He did all the things as instructed by my mother. A month later, he told me that his wife was pregnant, and he wanted to give me some money for the medicine, but I refused him and said, 'You are my friend. If you have a child, it will be due to our friendship, so why should I take money from you?'

At that time, he had left his job. He came down to see me and brought me a half a sack of beans and a basket of onions. He brought my mother a big basket of millet, because she is very fond of it. Mother was surprised to see that this man had come back, and she said, 'You are the best Toro I have ever known. We did those things for you, and we thought that you had forgotten, but since you have brought us these nice gifts, Mpuga had better make you his blood-friend.'

Zedoro said, 'No. We can't have the ceremony now, because I am not ready, but wait until the end of the month, and I will return with my brothers.'

Mother, Mosumba and myself decided to give him a goat to take back with him. Mother gave him a basket of rice in return for the millet. He returned with his brothers when he had promised. He stayed for two nights, and on the third day we had our ceremony of cutting our brotherhood. I tied five shillings on him, and he tied four on me. I gave him a he-goat for food, and he gave me forty-five shillings. My mother was very surprised by this, so she and my father decided to give him a she-goat with her twins. The people thanked us very much and went away on that day.

A month after they had gone, I received a letter from his brother which said, 'Your friend is being taken away to fight in the war.'

When he returned from service, he heard that my father had died, and he only stayed four days in Fort Portal. He was down here on the fifth day. He was unable to bring down the goat he had promised, so he brought twenty shillings instead. He also brought me a new shirt and a pair of shorts. He brought my mother a big bundle of beans and a basket of them for Lubangi. He also brought three shillings worth of salt. He stayed here for three days and when he left on the fourth day I gave him a she-goat from the goats left me by Mosumba.

Later when he heard that my mother had died, he brought me ten shillings and stayed here for six days. When he was ready to go, I gave him twenty shillings. That is what I have done for him and what he has done for me. He is a very good friend.

When I returned from working on the road, I spent four nights with my wife, Bakweziba, and then she went back to her home. I did not know why she left, so I had to go there and find out. She said, 'I have come to give birth at my home, so that my mother can take care of me.'

Mosumba asked why she had gone, and I told him. He said, 'Oh, it is all right. You had better wait for her.'

A month later she had a son who was named Kamotia. When the child was born, I took her some salt, some butter, some bark cloth and a chicken. After six days, the people took the child out of the house. Six months after the baby was born, I went back to work on the road at Sempaya. Then she came down here to Bundinyama while I was away. I spent seven months at Sempaya, and during that period I heard that the wife had gone back to her own home. When I asked why, Bukombi told me that she was not getting along well with Lubangi. A month after she left she came to visit me at Sempaya. She told me the same story that Bukombi had told me. She stayed at Sempaya for four days and then went back to her mother's. Three weeks after she had returned there, Bukombi wrote me saying that the child had died. Then I asked permission from the inspector to leave, and he allowed me to come down here for seven days. I passed through my home, but I did not eat. I went to see that wife. When I got there, I simply complained to the people and told her father, 'You see. Your daughter has brought my child here. I asked her to go back and she refused. Is this what she wanted?'

I did not stay there overnight but returned here. It is the custom of the Amba that when such a thing happens, on the day before the first burial ceremony takes place, the husband and wife have to stay in the same house together. When I asked my father, Mosumba, if I should go to her father's home for a night, he refused. 'It is not good for you to go, and there is no sense in taking back this woman again. So you go to the ceremony in the morning and, when it is over, ask for your brideprice and return here with five goats.' I went in the morning with my mother, Lubangi, and my sisters, Leiko and Nakulinga. I said to her lineage, 'No. I am not interested in this woman, so you must pay back the brideprice.'

They gave me five goats. Bakweziba married again later on.

I found Beabusa, whom I captured from her home, at the River Humia. The first time I went there I stayed for two days, and the second time, I stayed for five days. During those five days her father did not know about me, but one week later, I went there again. That night the old man heard me speaking, and he asked his daughter, 'Who is speaking in your house?'

'Nobody—just us girls!'

He came in and found me sitting there. He said, 'Why have you come here?'

'I love your daughter.'

'Which daughter?'

I pointed out the girl, and the father was very angry. He said, 'You

proud boys just come here to capture my daughters for nothing.
That way I lose a girl in exchange, or goats. Get out of here.'

As I was leaving, the girl said, 'Come and get me tomorrow.'

So I went back the following night, got the girl and brought her to
my home. Three days after that, her lineage came and demanded
chickens. We spent three good months together, because Lubangi
got along well with this woman and they were fond of each other.
Beabusa had been a priestess, and when she was asleep, she would
dream and talk a lot. I asked her, 'What is wrong with you?'

She said, 'Oh, I am a priestess. If you don't get something to feed
my god, I won't stay well.'

I said, 'Oh, I didn't know that you were a priestess. If I had, I
wouldn't have married you.'

She kept on acting that way so I divorced her. I hate priestesses,
and I do not have any of them in my house. It is very bad to see a
Christian home carrying on ceremonies and beating drums now and
then and to have it known that you have a priestess in your house.
That annoys the Christian people as well as God. But Beabusa was
very angry and did not believe that that was the reason I divorced
her. She thought that I had other reasons which were bad ones.
Mosumba and my mother were very angry also. They said, 'If you
had no property to pay for the ceremony, we would have paid for it,'
but I said, 'No. It is unlawful in my religion.'

Lubangi laughed at me and said, 'Even though these words come
out of your mouth, "I don't like priestesses," you are ready to get
them because you are marrying so many wives. That is not the behaviour of a Christian.'

I replied, 'Even though I am a sinner, I will still have one point in
my favour in God's presence—though I have married many wives,
none of them was a priestess.'

After I had sent away Beabusa, I stayed alone with Lubangi for
six months. After that I married another wife, Budedyo, a daughter
of the Babomboli. I became her lover while she was still at her own
home. She became pregnant by me. Before the pregnancy was
noticeable, I attended a spirit ceremony at the home of Erungu, the
spear-maker. My mother was a priestess in that ceremony and this
girl was there too, but not as a priestess. While the ceremony was
going on, Budedyo told my mother that she had become pregnant
by her son. When Mother returned home, I was at Bugombwa. She
told Mosumba, 'One of the girls in the ceremony has told me that she
is pregnant by Mpuga.'

When I returned home, my father asked me, 'Your mother has told
me that you seduced a girl at Bubomboli and now she is pregnant. Is
that true?'

'Yes.'

Then Mosumba sent a message to the girl, 'My son has admitted that he has seduced you. So what do you say?'

Budedyo replied, 'After the ceremony, Mpuga will come and see me.'

I went to Bubomboli, met the girl and discussed it with her. I said, 'If you stay here till your parents find out that you are pregnant, we will have to do many things, and I will have to bring a goat.' The girl said, 'No, I wouldn't like that. I want you to come and get me two days from now.'

So I went home and returned two days later. When I brought her home, Lubangi did not make any trouble with her. The Babomboli sent a messenger to us two days later. They sent Erungu, who is their sister's son. He was told to say to the Bandinyama, 'You had better bring back the girl, so that Mpuga can come and have the ceremony for her pregnancy.'

Mosumba refused to do that and said, 'It is impossible to return the wife and then have the ceremony. It is too late.'

Erungu returned and told the Babomboli this. He was then sent back to the Bandinyama by the father-in-law to say, 'As you have refused to hold the ceremony, I won't come for the chickens.'

So we lived together until she gave birth. Erungu was sent back again to ask for one goat as a fine, and my father paid it. I stayed a year with Budedyo. Then I caught her making some mistakes. The wife of Erikangero was pregnant and she had been having trouble with him. So she thought of causing a miscarriage. This wife of mine was one who was known to be able to cause it, so she was hired. Budedyo gave her some medicine to cause the miscarriage. We discovered the plan one day when the pregnant wife had gone to the stream for water. She came back with a parcel tied up in banana leaves which she hid from her husband. When her husband went out, she put some water in a small pot and started to make the medicine. When her husband came in, she tried to hide it, but he saw it and said 'What are you hiding?'

'I am just making medicine for an enema.'

'So little?'

'Yes.'

'What is wrong with you?'

'I have a stomach ache.'

He said, 'We slept together last night and I didn't hear you complain of any trouble with your stomach. This is not an enema at all. I will take it.'

Her husband took the pot and the medicine and started to beat his wife. She said, 'Do not kill me. This is medicine I got from Mpuga's wife to make me miscarry.'

So he brought his wife and the medicine to my home. We held a trial, and it was decided against my wife. She was very angry and the next morning she went away to her home and stayed six months. I tried to get her to come back but she said, 'No, I'm having a rest.'

She was not a good wife. She also used to make medicine to give to me to make me love her. She put the medicine on my pillow. I found it and took it to my father. He judged the case, and it went against her. He advised her not to do it any more. The medicine had not affected me, because it had not been there long when I discovered it. She never tried it again.

Also, whenever my mother wanted to send her on an errand, she often refused to go. When you called her, even if she were near by, she would not answer.

After six months she returned and spent one night in Budinyama. In the morning she was sitting in the sun, and my mother saw some marks on her. She called me to look at them. When we told Budedyo that the marks were leprosy, she denied it saying that it was just scabies. We got some medicine for scabies and put it on the marks, but they did not go away, so I had to send her away. She was very angry and wept a lot and said, 'They must have bewitched me at my father's home.'

Her baby is the child Muganga, and he is still living. When his mother took him, I waited only a few days and then went down and fetched him. I brought him back because I was afraid that he also would get leprosy. When I brought Muganga home, Lubangi said that she would not take care of him, because she was afraid that her children would become infected. Lubangi refused completely to take care of him, but my mother said, 'I am very old. If the child gives me the disease, it will not be very bad. Don't worry; I will look after the child.' My mother took care of him. He stayed with her for three years and then she died. I asked Koke to take care of him, but I found that she did not look after him properly, so finally I had to take him to my sister Nakulinga. He stayed there for six months. My sister looked after him very well, but when she was away her husband did not give him any food. When my sister told me about this, I went there and saw her husband and talked to him about the matter, but he paid no attention to what I said to him, so I have brought the child back to my home.

The next wife I captured was Nyabasulu, the wife of Nterabuki, the policeman at Hakitengya. He used to sleep with most of the wives of the Bandinyama. One day when he was drinking beer with Kihara, he said, 'I have slept with all the wives of the Bandinyama except Mpuga's and yours.'

80

Kihara was very annoyed. When he returned home, he explained the matter to the Bandinyama boys and they said, 'We will try our hardest to capture his wives.'

So I went around and approached one of his wives. She was agreeable. I also asked another wife if I could bring another boy to capture her. She also agreed. So one day Kabiyondo and I went down and captured these two wives. We took them to Fort Portal to the house of a man called Kandoli. He is the blood-brother whom I had met while I was training at Fort Portal. The policeman was very annoyed, as he had only two wives and they had both been captured, and by the same people. He went to Kihara and said, 'Your brothers have captured my wives. You had better tell them please to return one of them to me so that she may serve me.'

Kihara said, 'Have you forgotten what you said?'

He said, 'Oh, I have forgotten all those things, because I said them when I was drunk.' Then he said, 'What shall I do? I guess I will stay single as I am.'

Kihara said, 'If you have any witchcraft, go and cast spells.'

When Lubangi heard that I had married and had gone to Fort Portal with the wife, she thought that I would go all the way to Kampala, so she came back to my home on that day. She wrote a letter: 'If you are annoyed about my leaving you, I am back now. Don't go to Kampala.'[1]

The result was that we returned with our wives. On that very day that I returned, Lubangi fought with the new wife. When he saw them fighting, my father went and stopped them. The new wife ran away. She went to Bundibugyo and slept there for a night. In the morning I went to see her. The first question I asked her was, 'Why did you run away?'

'Oh, your wife is very tiring. I couldn't stand her.'

When I came back, I told Lubangi, 'You have done a very bad thing, fighting with my new wife, and now she has run away.'

Lubangi said, 'Why did you take her to Fort Portal? Why didn't you keep her in the house? Is the wife with whom you ran to Fort Portal the most beautiful girl in the world?'

That wife, Nyabasulu, stayed with the Bandibugyo for three months, and I used to go up here and stay for a night or two at a time. When I went to see her, I would always ask her to come back, but she completely refused, saying, 'If you want to marry me, you had better give me a house here in Bundibugyo.'

My father refused to allow me to build a house there, because he did not want to be separated from me. Then I stayed home for a

---

[1] Lubangi and Mpuga had quarrelled and Lubangi had gone to her father's house.

month and did not go to see her. By that time the wife had become pregnant, so she came down here and told Mosumba, 'Your son has refused to give me a house at Bundibugyo. Now he has made me pregnant, so call him and hear what he says.'

Then Mosumba asked me, 'Do you want this wife?' and I said, 'Yes.'

Mosumba said, 'What do you think about her now?'

I said, 'It is you who prevented me from building a house at Bundibugyo.'

Mosumba said to the woman, 'Don't you want to come down here and live?'

She said, 'No, I can't come here, because Lubangi is very fierce.'

Then I said, 'As you have refused to come down here, I am no longer your husband. Even though you are carrying my child in your womb, you can go wherever you like.'

That was the end; she went back to Bundibugyo and later gave birth to a girl who is still living.

Lubangi is a lion. Whenever I want to fight with her, I first remove all my clothes and get ready. When we begin to fight, she scratches me like a leopard and tears my clothes like a leopard. If I want to beat her only a little with a stick, not wanting to kill her, she can beat me to death. She is merciless. If I kick her, her kicks will be ten times as hard as mine. Some of the reasons why I fight with her are shameful ones and I cannot tell anybody about them, but I will tell you about some of them. For example, I once gave her some very good kicks which sent her to the sub-county chief and to the dispensary. She had left me for a month and when she returned, she found me carrying my son while I was grazing my goats. She came to me, but did not greet me; she merely said, 'Give me my child.'

I said, 'What do you mean? You left the child here for a month while you were away and you have just returned. When you return, you rush up and try to take the child away without asking my permission.' By that time I had half the child and she had the other half. I said, 'Leave my child alone. If you don't, I will beat you.'

Lubangi said, 'Am I a stone? Can't I beat you?'

Then I said, 'If you aren't a stone, I will beat you.'

She did not say anything. She struck me on the ear. I took the child and put it down, and came back. I said, 'You are the one who started this fight. I am going to give you a very good fight.'

I hit her on the ear. That was nothing to Lubangi; she hit me twice on my ear. I changed my mind and decided to punch her. I gave her a blow which caused her to fall down and then I kicked her twice while she was on the ground. She got up and caught me and started to put her fingers in my mouth to tear my lips. When I held my lips closed, she held my nose and scratched it, but I did the same to her nose. We were near the road and many people were watching us. Then I left her and stood about five yards away. I saw her coming towards me so I told her, 'I did not intend to fight with you, so I want to stop fighting.'

She said, 'No, I must fight with you. I want to catch you by the chest and throw you on the ground.'

I wanted to stop the fight, but, seeing that she was eager to continue, I caught her. She was thrown on the ground. She tried to choke me. I said, 'All right, I will choke you.' Each of us squeezed the neck of the other and, as you know, men's fingers are stronger than women's so I bested her. Lubangi became very weak and her hands fell from my throat. I stood up. I kicked her three times. After that I gave her a number of blows. Then I got a stick and hit her with that four times. By that time she was unconscious. A woman, a Toro, came and said, 'Don't kill her.' I stopped beating her. She lay there for a few minutes, and they poured water on her in order to revive her. After she had regained enough strength, she went to the headquarters of the sub-county chief. She said that she had been badly beaten, and the chief gave her a letter to take to the dispensary so that she could be examined.

When she arrived at the dispensary, it was late in the evening, so the dispenser told her that it was too late and that she should come back in the morning. She returned to Bundinyama, but she did not return to my home.

When I heard what had happened, I went to see the dispenser's assistant during the night time. I explained the whole thing to him, the connection I had with the woman and what the trouble was about. In the morning Lubangi went to the dispensary again and was examined. The man to whom I had spoken examined her and he wrote a letter to the chief telling him that he had found that the woman had been beaten, but not badly. Lubangi took the letter to the chief and when he read that she had not been beaten severely and understood that Lubangi was my legal wife, he told her, 'You are the one who has done wrong in this affair. You left your husband and you stayed away and did not come to see him or your children. When you came back and found him with the child looking after the goats, you forced him to give you the child whom you had forgotten about completely until that time. You are the one who began the fight so, if Mpuga had killed you, you are the one who would have been wrong. Never do such a thing again.'

Lubangi left the court crying. When she met me she said, 'Oh, those people are your friends.'

A bit later I married another woman, Mambiabo. One Saturday I met her at the Bundibugyo market and spoke to her. She promised to go to my home on Tuesday, but instead I went to her home that day and talked to her some more. I had a good meal with her, and then it rained hard. I asked her if I could stay for a night and she said, 'No. I'm afraid of my father, because he lives in the same house. But he has two houses and perhaps he will stay in the other one. So you had better go to Mwange's house where you can stay till late in the evening. I will make sure about what my father is going to do, and I will either come and stay with you or bring you down here.'

I saw her late that evening. We enjoyed the night together, and she went back to her home very early in the morning. When she arrived, she found her father beating her mother. He had seen the girl when she was going off to me the night before, and he knew that she was going after men. So he had gone to her house late at night to see if she was there where she should have been. He had asked his wife first, 'Where is your daughter?'

'She is inside.'

The father had gone in with a light and found nobody. He came out and beat his wife and said, 'It is you who are allowing our daughter to go out.'

When the girl returned that morning, her father caught her and started to beat her. He asked her, 'Where did you sleep?'

'I slept at Mwange's place.'

The father asked, 'Why did you stay there?'

'I visited those people and while I was there it rained hard, so I didn't come back.'

Her father did not believe that. He said, 'If you deny that you went to visit men, why is that boy staying at Mwange's too?'

She replied, 'Of course, that boy slept at Mwange's, but I didn't sleep there. I stayed in another house.'

So the father shouted for Mwange, 'You, Mwange, it is you who are leading my daughter to your mother's brother (Mpuga) and if they capture her, it is you who are going to pay me the goats.'

I told my 'sister's son', Mwange, 'I am leaving, because this old man is very fierce! My idea was that I could always have this girl through you, but if her father is angry with you in this way, we may all get into trouble.'

Mwange accompanied me on my way home, and, when we reached the river, we met the girl's mother carrying water to her home. She said, 'Who is that?'

Mwange said, 'The one who stayed the night in my house.'

She said, 'Oh, my son, I have been beaten badly for you, and I don't know how we will be able to live with my husband.'

I said, 'Don't mind, my mother-in-law.' I had two shillings and fifty cents in my pocket which I gave her.

She said, 'Thank you very much, my boy. If you are going now, wait here a few minutes. I will go and call the girl to come and tell you good-bye.'

After a short time the girl came back with some food, rice and a hen. We ate there by the river. After that I dropped one shilling which I had left in my pocket into her basket. I said, 'Now I am going. What is your decision about the whole thing?'

She said, 'Oh, I will be coming to meet you next Saturday. Don't go into the market, but go to a certain place and hide, because if you stay by the roadside, my father will see you as he is also going to the market. When I come by, whistle to me, and I will know that you are there.'

So I went away. The next Saturday I went to the market. I did not stay there long, but passed by and went to the place she had told me and waited for her there. When I saw her coming, I whistled to her, and she came to me. We started talking and I asked her, 'What do you think now? Are you ready to come?'

She said, 'Of course. But I have left my bark cloth behind. I'll go and get it.'

So she went back and got the bark cloth and we came down here. I put her in Bukombi's house where she stayed for a short time until I built her a house. Early the next morning Mwange came, sent by her father. He said, 'I want seven chickens and one girl in exchange for this girl.'

Mosumba refused. 'I can't give you a girl unless this one has stayed here for a month or two, but I will give you six chickens.'

They were given to him, and he went back. He handed the chickens to the father and explained to him what had been said. The father said, 'All right. I'll wait.'

Two weeks later the girl said, 'I'm going to visit my mother.'

While she was visiting there, she was caught by her father. I went to see what had happened to my wife and saw my father-in-law and asked him what was wrong with her. He said, 'Oh, your father said that I must wait too long. Why did you take my daughter if you did not know all ready that she was satisfactory? I won't give her back to you unless you pay me.'

I went home and explained it all to Mosumba. He said, 'You write a letter to Mwange and ask him to come and get a girl in exchange for your wife.'

Mwange came and took Leiko. When my father-in-law saw her, he said, 'All right. This is what I wanted. You take his wife back to him tomorrow.'

G   85

Mwange brought my wife in the morning, and we lived together happily. Leiko's husband used to treat her badly, so she left him. Her husband came after her four days later. Then they heard the case, and the husband was found guilty. Mosumba told him, 'You must not treat my daughter badly like that. If she comes home again, I will give back your daughter.'

So the husband took Leiko with him. She stayed with him four months longer and then he started to beat her again, so she came home. My father told her to stay at home until she had given birth. The next day her husband came. My father said, 'You might as well go back. I'm going to keep your wife until she has the baby.'

One month later Leiko was captured by a Muhuku boy. I was very annoyed that she had been captured while she was pregnant, so I refused to go there for the chickens but told my father to go. He sent my mother. This was the message sent with my mother, 'You should bring that girl back with you, because she is pregnant.'

But when my mother arrived there and asked the man to give Leiko to her, he refused to do so and said, 'There is no law about exchanging girls. If you want to accuse us, go on to the sub-county headquarters.'

My mother returned and explained all this to us. I wrote a letter to Mwange telling him that Leiko had run away and married. In the morning he came with the husband of Leiko. The latter said, 'We don't want anything except our sister.'

By that time my wife had had a daughter. Mosumba said, 'How can you take the woman who has our baby? Let me give you some goats instead.'

The husband said, 'No, we don't want goats,' so they took their sister away. My wife stayed with them for six months, and I used to go there often, asking them to give her back to me, but they refused. They exchanged her with another man for another girl. That is all. She is still with the same man.

In 1943 I fought with the sub-parish chief, Balikengo, again and with Babito, who was also a sub-parish chief. During the war we used to pay money to the Red Cross. Those two chiefs came to my house one day and found Kalisa giving me an enema. They did not see me, but my father was there, so they said to him, 'Every poll-tax payer has to give us fifty cents for the Red Cross, so if Mpuga is not here, we will have to take one of his chickens instead. When he comes to us with the fifty cents, we will give him his hen.'

So they chased a hen. Mosumba tried to stop them, but they pretended not to hear him. I was very annoyed. I stopped the enema and rushed out to find that the hen had been caught. I said, 'Leave that hen alone.'

They said, 'No. Give us fifty cents. We won't let go of your hen, so do what you like.'

I was very angry then and ran and took hold of the hen's legs. Arungu, who had come with the two chiefs, had hold of its head. Balikengo and Babito told the man, 'Don't let go of the hen.'

Arungu twisted the hen's head and it parted from the rest of the body. He was left holding only the head. Then I did not bother to go and get a stick. I took the hen's body and started to beat Balikengo and Babito with it. The man Arungu, said, 'Oh, he is fighting with my elders! Leave him for me. I will fight him.'

So I started fighting with Arungu. I found that the fellow was very strong and I could not get rid of him, so I left him and went and kicked Balikengo so hard that he fell down. Babito hit me hard on the ear. I deliberately bumped into Balikengo with my head, and he fell down. Kalisa ran to Kihara to tell him of the fight going on at my house. When I saw that he had done that, I said to myself, 'I'll go and get my stick, and it will be a very nice fight indeed.'

When I went into the house, my mother, who was outside, locked me in. I tried to get out but could not because there were no windows and no other doors. So I started weeping in the house and saying, 'My mother has done a great wrong.'

The chiefs said, 'Aha! We will go and accuse him at the sub-county court, because he has beaten us.'

When Kihara came, he was very angry with my mother and said, 'Why did you lock him in? We could have beaten all of them. Even if we had been put in prison for a few months, it would have been all right.'

I was accused, and the chief knew that the people had been beaten because of the blood and mud on them. The sub-county chief was not at his headquarters, but Kabaleta, my parish chief, was. When these people came complaining of so many things, and he saw that they had been beaten, he sent for me. They sent a policeman for me who came and arrested me. When I arrived at the headquarters, I was not even given a chance to plead, but I was sent off to prison. I refused to go and said, 'You can't take me to prison without even hearing my case.'

The chief, 'No, you Bandinyama are disobedient.'

So I was taken to prison. The man who is county chief now was a sub-county chief then and was inspecting the prison when I arrived there. He asked, 'What is wrong with you, Mpuga?'

I said, 'I have fought with the sub-parish chiefs.'

The sub-county chief said, 'They should hear your plea before they put you in prison.'

He sent me back to plead my case. I asked him for a note confirming what he had said and he gave it to me. When I returned with the note, I was sent home and told to return the next court day, which was Friday. When I came into court on that day, the case went against the chiefs, because they had come and eaten my pineapple and sugar-cane and after that had caught my hen. They had not asked anyone if they could eat that food. Their fine was to pay for my hen, which was two shillings. But I have never fought with the chiefs again.

In 1944 I married another wife called Likerenge. I married her from the Busaru market. Babute and I were selling the goods of Juma, the Nubian, at Bundibugyo. A girl friend of Babute came along accompanied by this girl, Likerenge, and Babute told me to talk with her. I did not have a chance to speak with her because I was busy, so we promised the girls that we would call at their home on our way back from the market. When the market was over, we went there. An old woman asked the girl, 'Why are these two boys coming here?'

The reason she asked was that the girl I was interested in had been married. She had been with her husband for three years and had a child by him. Then she had fallen sick and so had to come to her home to be treated. The girl who was free was Babute's friend. My girl replied to the old woman, 'He has come with Babute, the friend of my neighbour, but he has no girl friend here.'

The old woman said, 'No. You want to leave my brother and be married to someone else.'

The girl denied it, 'He is not my lover.'

Then the woman rushed into the house where I was and said, 'Is this man more handsome than my brother?'

Likerenge did not answer. While these two girls were preparing a meal for Babute and me, the woman put out the fire and said, 'It is I who grew this food. You're not going to give it to your friends.'

The girls were angry at that, so they told us, 'You had better go home.'

Only the friend of Babute was allowed to accompany us. The girl in whom I was interested said, 'Since they have been rude to me when I haven't even taken you as my lover, come to the Bundibugyo market on Monday, and I will meet you there.'

We met there and talked a long time, and I bought her a packet of cigarettes for fifty cents. I also bought her some fish. Then she said, 'Are you interested in me?'

'Of course. I want to marry you.'

She said, 'Oh. I have already been exchanged for another girl. What are you going to do?'

'The government has stopped exchange marriage,' I said. 'I will marry you and pay the goats for you.'

So she replied, 'You meet me at the Busaru market on Wednesday.'

On Wednesday the old woman knew that the girls were going to run away, because they had prepared some food during the night which they intended to bring for us, so they were kept from the market. They had to wait until the woman went out to the market herself. They then ran away with the food and met us on our way from the market. They gave us the food and explained what had been happening. They said, 'You be ready on Monday. We will come and you can take us on that day.'

So we had to go home empty-handed. By that time, the father had discovered that the girls were going to run away, so he appointed a brother to watch them. He gave them some ground nuts to sell in the market and told their brother, 'As soon as you have finished selling, come back with these girls, because the Bandinyama are very bad for them.'

They were kept under guard all the time. It was very difficult for us. We knew that they were being watched. I, myself, was afraid to go near them, but Babute tried to go. The brother spoke rudely to him, 'What do you want with my girls?'

So Babute had no luck. We failed completely that day. Then we decided that we could go up and steal the girls from their home during the night, since we had no other way to get them. But, unluckily, that day Babute hurt his leg with a stick, so he was unable to go.

On Wednesday Babute and I went back to the market. As soon as we reached it, we met the girl friend of Babute who told us that their father had given them a very severe punishment. 'He beat us, and then in the morning, he decided to take Mpuga's friend back to her old home. This made her run away to Bundibugyo, where she is now.'

I was very surprised. 'Oh, I didn't know that I had passed my girl on the way here.'

So I sold all my goods in a hurry. About two in the afternoon I left the market, came home, handed the cash and the goods which remained to their owner, and then I immediately went to see Likerenge. I left her, and she told me to come and wait for her at another place. We met and I brought her down here. I put her in Bukombi's house.

Early in the morning the father of the girl and Benya, the man at Bundibugyo from whose house I had taken the girl, came to my house. They did not greet us. They did not sit on chairs, but they only said, 'We have come to tell you that the woman you have captured is a married woman.'

Mosumba was unable to try the case or hear the affair by himself, so he called Batigwa and Kihara. Batigwa thought that we should keep the woman and let the father-in-law go and accuse us in court, but Kihara said, 'No. Whenever you take a thing by force, you don't get any good in return.'

So we gave Likerenge to them. This was the agreement made with her father: 'If the girl comes back here, you won't complain about these matters again. In that case, you will come and collect the bride-price, either goats or shillings.'

So the girl was taken away. But one day the father appointed a man to accompany her back to her husband and, when they were on the way, Likerenge escaped and returned to my home. When her father heard of this he was very annoyed and sent word to Benya, 'You go and tell the Bandinyama that they can have the girl for nothing. I will not go there for anything.'

Benya came and told us and Mosumba said, 'Thank you very much for the gift.'

I lived with her eight months. She and Lubangi did not get along well. Likerenge used to bring my mother's water for her. And my mother heard someone say that Lubangi wanted Likerenge to bring her water also as she was the favourite wife. My mother was annoyed that Lubangi was trying to take her position, so she called her and asked, 'Why do you say these things to this woman?'

Lubangi asked, 'What things?'

My mother told her and Lubangi said, 'Who told you this?'

'Likerenge.'

Then Lubangi asked Likerenge, 'Is it true that I wanted you to bring me water?'

'Yes, don't you remember?'

'No. If you are starting lies in this house, I will teach you.'

So they started to fight. I saw that they were fighting and came out and stopped them. Lubangi was the one who was at fault, because Likerenge was a good wife with good habits and she cultivated well. I got three goats from the food that she grew.

After eight months Likerenge became pregnant. When her father heard that he said, 'Oh God! I'm not going to let my daughter go for nothing. I'd better go and ask them for the brideprice.'

So he came down here and asked for it. Mosumba said, 'I'm going to give you goats,' but the father-in-law said, 'No, I want a girl.'

Mosumba said, 'I have a girl I could give you now, but your daughter is pregnant, and it is unlawful to pay for a pregnant wife.'

So my father-in-law said, 'All right. I'll wait until she has given birth.'

Four days after her father had gone, Likerenge visited her parents. She stayed there for five days. On the sixth day I was to go there and stay for a night. I heard the news when I was at Bundibugyo, 'Your wife has been captured.' Then I went and told my father about it and he said, 'You must not mind about that woman, because it is not good for a wife to be captured when she is pregnant.'

So I kept quiet. Likerenge stayed at the house of Sigio, who had captured her, for a month. Then she left him and went back to her father. She stayed there for two months, and then her father said, 'Now you had better go back to the place where you became pregnant.'

So she returned to me. I did not want her to stay the night with me, so I sent her back to her father. I did this because of misbehaviour. The same day, her father took her to Benya and said, 'You had better take this woman to the Bandinyama and let her give birth there, because I cannot put up with all these difficulties. If this woman has twins, what will I do?'

When that happened, the Bandinyama had to keep Likerenge until she gave birth. She stayed here for one month and then had her baby. It died after two days. It was a boy. The woman fell sick with a special illness which comes from childbirth. She takes fire and throws it on all her things, and she loses her hair. This illness is caused by the fact that the woman has gone about having intercourse with men while she was pregnant. My mother found out that this was the sort of disease that she had and asked me if I could do anything about it. I refused to do anything and said, 'Let her be taught a lesson.'

Mosumba was very angry and sent messages to her home to inform them about what was going on. He wanted to give the girl back to her father, but her father refused to have her, saying, 'It was you who ruined my daughter. She didn't go to your house pregnant; she became pregnant by your son. So you must cure her before I will take her back.'

Then Mosumba told me to look for a doctor, so I went to Kirwana. I paid him three shillings, and he gave me some medicine which cured her. A month after she was well, I sent her away to her home. She never returned.

In 1944 Alubeni became my blood-brother. That man was staying in the Bambutuku village. Those Bambutuku had come from the Congo to work for the Public Works Department. One day I had brewed some beer and was selling it. Those people passed my house and bought one shilling and fifty cents worth of beer. Alubeni and a man called Berinarugo were with them. Lubangi brought out some food, and I asked them to have it with me because they were coming from work. They thanked both of us for our kindness. Three days later they brought Lubangi a shilling and a gift. I was not home at the time, but they said to her, 'It is bad luck not to find Mpuga here, but tell him when he comes back that we want to make him a blood-brother.'

Lubangi told me this when I arrived, and I agreed to it. They returned two days later and I killed a fowl for them and Lubangi cooked rice. They told me, 'At the end of this month, we will have a ceremony and you will come to our place.'

Then Berinarugo sent me out a letter which said that my friend Alubani wanted to come to my house to have the ceremony. They came and slept at my home and in the morning we had the cutting. I tied two shillings on him and gave him a he-goat for food. They were about to tie money on me, but Kihara stopped them from doing it and said, 'You are living far away from your home in the Congo now. You go home and when you have returned from there, you can tie the money on him.'

Kihara was being kind to them. He thought that they were buying their food and possibly renting the house where they were living and that they might not have enough money or property to give to their friends. He thought that when they went home, they would be able to get things to give me.

Then I gave them one young female goat. They said, 'We will spend two days at our village here and then we will come to say good-bye to you. After that we will go back to our home in the Congo.'

When they came to tell me good-bye, they asked, 'What would you like most from the Congo?'

'I would like some plates. You could bring me seven plates and one cup.'

Then I asked them, 'How long are you going to be there?'

'A week.'

So I gave them twenty-five shillings to buy some clothes for me. I gave them two fowls and bought one shilling's worth of salt for their wives. I went with them part of the way. Then I waited a week and a half and they did not return. It turned out later that on their way they did not go to the Congo but got on a lorry at Sempaya and went to Fort Portal. They were there for two days and their goods were stolen, so on the third day, they went to Kampala. A year and a half later, they had more trouble with people stealing their property. A brother of my friend said to him, 'This bad luck is coming from you. If we stay here in Kampala any longer we will probably die. Let's go back home.'

His brother returned home, but my friend, Alubeni, stayed in Kampala. He finally decided to come home himself, and at that time the road to Bwamba had been washed out by the rains, so he came over the mountain and stayed the night at the dispensary. Leaving there, he was afraid to pass my house, so he took another path. But he was caught by the parish chief for not paying his poll tax. The chief asked him for his receipt, because he knew that the man had been working for the Public Works Department. When Alubeni could not produce the receipt, the chief brought him to the sub-county headquarters. The people there asked him, 'Do you have any friends or relatives in this country?'

He said, 'I have a blood-brother, Mpuga, and a sister's son, Berinarugo.'

I had found all this out from the policeman, Sengi, that afternoon, so I went along to see who was saying that he was my blood-brother. I could not see him, so I went home. The next day, the prisoner asked the policeman, 'Is Mpuga living here now?'

He was told that I was in Bwamba. Then he wrote me a letter in which he said, 'Even though we treated you badly, don't remember that. Come and see me.'

When I met him and asked, 'Where have you come from?' he told me the whole story. After he had finished, he said, "Don't think about all the things we did to you. Lend me eighteen shillings and save me from prison. You will see me in the future.'

When I went home, I told the whole story to my mother and she said, 'You must do this, even though they did play a trick on you, because it is the duty of a blood-brother to be generous.'

So I took eighteen shillings and paid the tax. When I got him out of prison, he thanked me very much, and I took him to my house and fed him. He stayed there for two nights. Then he went to the Congo. Before he left, he said, 'I will be coming back shortly.'

I have never seen his face since then. I will not have any more friendships with Congo men. I have heard that he has gone further into the Congo. Whenever I think of all the things I gave this man, it gives me a shock.

The next wife I married was Koke of the Basaru. I got her from her mother's father's house. I went there one afternoon, captured her and brought her to Atube's house. At that time her brother was working near here for one of the Toro. When he went home, he was told, 'Koke has been captured by a man called Mpuga from Bundinyama.'

The brother asked, 'Then why didn't I meet them on the way to this house?'

He thought that I might have hidden the woman at Atube's. When night came, I wanted to bring my wife to Bundinyama, because I thought that at night nobody would be in the road waiting for us. But when we reached a place on the road, we met her brother. He asked, 'Where are you going, Koke?'

She said nothing to him. He hit her with a stick, and, when he was about to hit her for a second time, I said, 'No. Don't do that. You are lucky; I would have fought with you, but since you are so young,

I can't. You are of an age to fight my brother, Bukombi, so stop and go home.'

Then the boy shouted to some people, and they came. They told me, 'You are a thief stealing this girl. You had better leave her so that her brother can take her home.'

Then her brother said, 'Oh, it is night-time now. I cannot go back home with my sister all alone, so Mpuga must go with us.'

I agreed to this. When we reached Atube's place on the way back, I rebelled, and took my stick and laid it across the path saying, 'I am angry now. I want to fight you.'

The brother-in-law said, 'Oh, no! Let me pass. You can remain here with your wife.'

I replied, 'No. I must fight you, because you have caused me a lot of trouble.'

By that time the girl had rushed into Atube's house, where she had spent the day. Her brother said, 'No, you told me at first that I was too young to fight with you and that I should fight with your brother Bukombi, so what do you mean by fighting with me now? I don't want to fight. If you do, go ahead and kill me.'

I went into the house where my wife was. Then the brother said, 'Oh. Now that you have been so clever, I will stay here the night and guard my sister.'

Atube had gone to drink beer, and on his way home, he passed by the house of Koke's brother. He asked, 'Where is Makoso?'

They told him, 'He has gone to get his sister who has been captured by a man of your lineage—Mpuga.'

Atube was annoyed and said, 'Why is Makoso getting mixed up in these things? His sister is not married, and this will be the first time that she has married. He could go to Mpuga and collect his bride-price. If I meet him at my house, I will tell him to come back.'

So when he reached his home and found Makoso standing in the courtyard, he did what he told his parents he would do.

Then early in the morning I was accompanied by Abongo and Takundese to Batigwa's house. My plan was to hide Koke with Atube, because Lubangi was not at home, and I was at work at the Yellow Fever Camp, so there was the possibility that the brother might come and take his sister back. Her brother came in the morning and when he saw my mother at her house, he asked, 'Has Mpuga come?'

My mother said, 'No, he went away about ten in the morning, and I don't know what has happened to him. He hasn't come back.'

The brother played a trick on my mother. He said, 'I went with Mpuga yesterday and captured a girl, but when we were bringing her here last night, her father came and took her again.'

Mother was very surprised. 'No, this has never happened with my son. Whenever he captures a girl, he always takes her.'

So Makoso left her and went into her house, where he found Naku-linga and some other girls. He went through the house searching everywhere, but in vain. The girls asked him, 'What are you looking for? You have told our mother that you were with Mpuga yesterday and that you captured a girl and that the girl was taken back by her father, so what are you looking for now?'

He said, 'I lost my knife yesterday, and I don't know where I lost it, so I was looking for it here.'

When Abongo arrived, he found that the brother had gone to work at Jovanni's house. Abongo explained the whole affair to our mother. She was very surprised to hear all this. She prepared some food and took it to Koke at Batigwa's house. After four o'clock that afternoon, I left the Yellow Fever Camp and passed Batigwa's house. I found that Koke was still there, and I asked about Makoso. They told me that he had come back, so I took Koke with me to my home, and we stayed there for a night. In the morning Makoso came. He told me, 'You have won now. You had better give me my one hen. The rest will be taken by my father.'

So we gave him one hen. Then after four days the father came, and we gave him six hens. Four months later he came again and asked for twenty-five goats. I offered him eight goats, and he refused them. I said, 'Hmmm, I have no more.'

So he returned to his home. Everyone was quiet about the affair except Makoso. He said, 'Why do we have to let our sister be married to a Bundinyama for nothing? I will go and accuse him to the parish chief.'

He accused me at the parish headquarters, but I was busy and did not go there when they called me, so the case was sent to the sub-county court. Chief Kachope was there, and Makoso said, 'This man offered me eight goats for my sister, but I refused them because I want twenty-five.'

The chief asked him, 'What do you want if he does not have twenty-five goats?'

'I want my sister back.'

Kachope told him, 'You go and try your hardest to get your sister, but if Mpuga beats you at his home, the case won't come back to my court. You will have to appeal to the county court.'

So the brother-in-law said to me, 'You are a witch, because you have bested me. I will go and accuse you to the county court.'

He went and explained the affair to the county chief; that the sub-county chief and his court had refused to hear his case, because they were friends of mine. After the explanation the county chief told

Makoso, 'I also agree with the sub-county chief. If you don't like the brideprice that Mpuga offered you, let the girl be married there for nothing.'

After all this advice, Makoso returned to my home and asked for the brideprice, and I gave him two goats. I said, 'Hmmmm-hmmmm. It is you who brought about your own loss. I offered you more, and you refused. Now you have less.'

At that time Koke was present. When Makoso returned the second time, I told him, 'I have the goats here, but I can't pay the brideprice because your sister is pregnant.'

After Koke had given birth, her brother came again, and he was given two more goats. He was very angry, 'You are giving me two goats at a time. What do you mean by this?'

I said, 'It is your fault, because you accused me in court. Your punishment will be that I will give you the goats in instalments.'

Then I decided later in my house, 'Since he acted very badly towards me, I will give him an instalment of two goats per year.'

When he came to my house in February this year, I gave him one goat and twenty shillings. In February of next year I will finish the payment, having given him eight goats altogether. The thing which hinders me from paying all the things at once is that the wife is lazy. She quarrels a lot. That is why I do not pay him.

She acted well the first year, but the second year she changed. It is the custom down here to give your wife a rest from intercourse after she has had a child, and it happened that when she gave birth, I stayed in her house in a different bed for the first four days. Then I went back to Lubangi's house, where I stayed for a few months. When I wanted to return and sleep with Koke, she said, 'No, I don't want you to come and sleep with me. You can come back when my child starts to walk.'

It is foolish to take such a thing seriously, so I tried again to go to her. When I went there one night, she moved all the things such as mats, blankets and grass and put them on the floor. She told me to go and sleep on her bed without mattress, blanket or her. So I was discouraged with her and gave up completely and went to stay with Lubangi. When I had been in Lubangi's house for two months, Koke started quarrelling and saying, 'Mpuga hates me.'

I said, 'You are the one who drove me from your house.'

She has continued making the same statement ever since. She complains that I hate her and do not go to her house. Yet she drives me away whenever it is time to have intercourse with her. As she has such peculiar habits, I am very slow in paying for her. I have not had intercourse with her for a whole year. When she knows that it is almost time for me to come to her house, she shuts the door before seven in the evening. The child is not walking yet, but when it starts, I will go back to her. If she begins her quarrelling again, I will send her away.

She is more trouble now that I can say. She abuses me and the new wife, but she is afraid of Kijungu, because Lubangi is very fierce.[1] When I come home for lunch, I go to Lubangi and greet her, and then I go to see the new wife at Bukombi's house and greet her, and then I go to Koke. When I enter her house, she says, 'Oh, don't come in here. I am the last one you come to see. Why do you come here last?'

For another example, just yesterday we quarrelled. Paolo Ogua has fifty cents of hers, and yesterday she was talking about him and saying, 'I will go and ask him for the fifty cents, and I can buy some cigarettes.'

I said, 'Your neighbours are spending some of their money on seeds of beans, tomatoes or rice to plant now, but you don't spend a cent of yours on those things. You simply spend all your money on your mouth.'

She was very annoyed. I was kicking the mud off the house. She came and said, 'You should hit me with this mud. If you don't, I will do it for you.'

I was afraid that we would get into a fight, so I had to run away to Kihara's house. I am tired of her ways.

She did not get along well with my mother; they used to quarrel very much over the cultivating. Once my mother brought some sugar-cane seedlings and she asked both Koke and Lubangi to go with her in the morning to help her plant them. Koke did not go to help her, but Lubangi went with our mother and they planted the seedlings. When it was harvest-time, Koke was the first person to go and get some sugar-cane. She brought a big bundle home. My mother asked her, 'Where did you get that sugar-cane?'

'I got them from over there.'

My mother went to the garden. She found that all her sugar-cane had been damaged. When she returned, she said, 'You were the one who refused to plant the cane, and now you are the first person to have it. What do you mean by this?'

They had a bad quarrel. Koke said, 'Why do you want to abuse me about food?'

Mother always used to ask Lubangi to come and have the first fruits from her garden, because she was the one who had helped her in the digging. When Koke saw this, she would complain and say, 'My mother-in-law doesn't like me.'

Last year Abongo and his wife moved into her house. He used to stay in Lubangi's house, but when her house fell down, he wanted to

[1] At this time Lubangi acted as Kijungu's protectress in relation to Koke.

go and stay with Bukombi. Bukombi did not want him, because they were not friendly, so he had to ask me if he could stay with Koke. I gave him permission. Koke was not at home when he moved into her house. I had gone to Toro, and when I returned, I found that Koke had returned from visiting her home. She asked me, 'Why is Abongo in my house?'

I said, 'What to do? Can I put him in the house of a man who is not a Bundinyama? Let him stay there until he builds his own house.'

She kept quiet, but later she began to insist that either I build her a new house or that Abongo finish his. She abuses Abongo, because he has jiggers. When he is warming himself by the fire, she goes to him and says, 'This Mpuga refuses to build me another house. This is a house of jiggers.'

Abongo says, 'You are a bad woman. Why don't you think of me as your brother-in-law?'

When he comes in at night, she shouts to him, 'Don't come in my house late at night. You must not trouble me at all.'

This is a source of quarrels. Abongo is building his own house now, so that he can leave her.

In 1945 I started working for the Yellow Fever Research people. Dr. Haddow wrote to the sub-county chief at Hakitengya asking for ten porters to be here on July 22nd. It was the 21st when the letter was received. One of the clerks came around to my house in the afternoon and said that there had been a letter asking for people to work, so I came here on the 22nd. When Dr. Haddow arrived, he told the clerk to write down the names of all the ten porters selected by the chief, so I was hired. The pay was ten shillings and fifty cents a month. I worked eight days in July, and then August started. At the end of August, Dr. Haddow was going on leave, and he said that they would reduce the staff. He told the clerk, 'Keep the good porters and discharge all the bad ones.'

I was the only one left of the ten new porters. Dr. Haddow was on leave for six months, and when he returned, he found that I was still here on duty. In 1947, I was transferred and made a monkey-boy. The monkeys were supposed to catch yellow fever. They were put in cages on platforms in the trees so that mosquitoes would come and bite them and they would get sick. I used to feed them and take their temperatures. I used to wash their cages and measure food for them and carry their water to the platforms. It was a very good job, but I used to have a lot of accidents. When the supervisor found that you had made a mistake, he would report you to Rwamba: Rwamba was very fierce, but he used to call us and advise us when we had made mistakes. I made a good many. The first thing they caught me doing was not washing the monkey cages. They took me to Rwamba and he advised me not to neglect that again. He forgave me and did not report me. The second mistake was when we were caught by the supervisor eating the monkey's food when we were hungry. We were brought to Rwamba and he advised us not to do it again. The third time, Rwamba himself caught me stealing a sugar-cane and giving it to a porter. The other trouble was that I quarrelled with my supervisor, Kasami. He brought me to Rwamba who said, 'I have forgiven you for many mistakes, but I can see that you are getting worse. I will report you to Dr. Haddow when he comes back from Entebbe.'

But when Dr. Haddow came back, Rwamba was merciful to me and reported only one mistake, that of stealing the sugar-cane, and I thought that if he had reported the mistake of fighting with the superviser, it would have been much worse. Dr. Haddow called me and said, 'I could discharge you, but I have asked your supervisor and he has told me that you haven't done very many things wrong. Since you have been here for a long time, I will give you another chance.'

I was only warned, not fined. In October, 1948, I was working at the Ntotoro River, and the game scout came and shot an elephant in the sleeping-sickness reserve. After work, we all went down to the forest to cut up the meat. We left our camp about ten in the morning and got lost in the forest. We came to the place where the elephant had been shot about four in the afternoon. We finished cutting up the meat at eight in the evening. Then we lost our way coming back and slept in the forest. That very day, the man in charge of all the monkeys, Rwamba, came to visit our camp. We had left only one boy in the camp, and when Rwamba arrived, he asked the boy where we were. The boy tried to protect us, but at last Rwamba found out where we were. He pressed the boy until he told him, 'They have gone to cut up elephant meat and they haven't come back.'

Rwamba noted that in his book. While he was on his way to the next camp, we arrived from the forest. The monkeys had not been fed all day, so we had to take food and feed them. On our way back we discovered that Rwamba had passed our camp asking for us, so I followed him and found him at the camp next to ours. He told me, 'You have made a very serious mistake. You have done it without trying to hide it, so it must come out. If you aren't lucky, you will be discharged, because this is very serious.'

When he returned to the main camp, he reported it to the doctor, who wanted to discharge us. But Rwamba said, 'That would be very bad, because we would lose a lot of people,' so they decided to fine us. I was fined two shillings because I was in charge, and the boys under me were fined one shilling each. That day Dr. Haddow wrote a letter to the Sleeping Sickness Inspector, telling him to arrest any of our staff who went into the Sleeping Sickness Area. We were watched carefully during that time.

Shortly after that, one monkey caught yellow fever, so they discontinued some of the stations. We were brought back to Hakitengya with our monkeys. In January of 1949, some boys were sent away, and some of the monkeys were sent to Entebbe. Only the laboratory monkeys were left. In March of 1949, all the monkeys were sent to Entebbe, and all the boys were discharged. I was fortunate and was kept on as the laboratory orderly here. If the work is finished, I will just stop working. If they think that I am a good man, I will go to Entebbe. I would not like to go very much, but I would go. My pay is twenty-six shillings a month and one shilling of this is a bonus.

My father's final illness started with the fight he had with Katabwita. The blow on the head was not serious, but the blow on his back caused his death. In March of 1946, Mosumba said to all of his children, 'I am not feeling well at all and it is possible that I might die when one of my sons is away from home, so I want all of you to stay near the house all the time.'

The day he said that, he sent Bukombi to call Nkiaura down from Bugombwa. He called all his daughters to come and hear what he was going to say to his people before he died. He called Kihara and Batigwa.

'I dreamed last night that Gambeki was calling me into the house. He told me, "Your house is ready. Come and enter it." That means that my home down there is prepared. So you all keep quiet and I will say my last words. I have not cursed any of my children. They are all here, except Sengi and Atoku, who have gone to Kampala. If they come back, they will not have anything from my hands; anything they get will be given to them by Mpuga. I am leaving Mpuga as my successor. Nkiaura will look after him, as he is still a young man.'

Then he spoke to Nkiaura and said, 'Come and see them now and then. Try to judge all their mistakes and any troubles which may come into the home. The only troublesome son I have is Bukombi. He does not follow my advice, and I do not think he will follow Mpuga's, so you keep an eye on him.'

'You, Kihara, I am dying now. You must not tell any of my sons to start a feud with Katabwita's sons.'

After this speech, about four o'clock, my father died. In the morning we buried him. At the time of the first death ceremony, Kihara wanted to start trouble with Katabwita's sons. They started quarrelling and Kihara drove them away. Nkiaura and I stopped him and said, 'Don't break the rules laid down by the dead.'

Kihara said, 'I don't want them here, because they are the ones who killed Mosumba.'

Nkiaura told us about the fight in 1932 and the last words of Mosumba, how he had cursed no one and did not want a feud. My father's property was divided at the time of the second death ceremony by Kihara, Batigwa and Nkiaura. According to the Bwamba custom, Sengi should have been the successor, since he was the eldest son. But my father followed the Toro custom of appointing the most logical person as heir. Gambeki had appointed the youngest son. I was made successor. There were thirty-eight goats, seventy-nine shillings, four knives, eight hoes and two spears. Bukombi got nine goats, Nkiaura got seven, Abongo got four and I got twelve. I have two knives, and Bukombi and Abongo took one each. Bukombi took one spear and I took the other. My mother took forty shillings and thirty-nine shillings were divided among the daughters. My mother refused to give away the hoes, except one for Nakulinga and one for Lubangi. The rest were hers. I got all the land. My father had two gardens in which there were one hundred and fifty coffee trees. Abongo did not get any land, but he had to stay with me. I have given him land and now he is building his house. I am going to give him land for a garden. Sengi and Atoku have never come back. They have been writing to me, but I have not had a letter from them now since the beginning of the year. They did not ask for anything in the letter, but only wanted to know how I was.

Kingano said that he would take my mother, but she refused him. 'I am quite old and I have old sons who will act as my husband. I don't want to be married again.'

I did not want her to marry either. Kingano came only once to my home, and then my mother abused him, so he did not come again. She abused him, because she did not want to be married again.

Nkiaura has helped me very much. He gave me help when I had some trouble about land with Kwehemura. He was trying to cheat me out of some of my land. There was an old boundary which was about to collapse, and he removed some of the marks. When I came one morning and saw that, I replaced them and that made Kwehemura very angry. When my wife, Likerenge, came, he wanted to beat her, so after I had seen my wife, I went to the garden to fight with him. I found that he had gone home, so I had to follow him to his place. About that time Nkiaura was coming to my house. When he arrived, he was told that I had gone to fight the man, so he came and stopped me just as we were quarrelling. He took us back to the land and fixed my boundary as the right one. That settled the quarrel.

In 1948, my sister, Bagelia, was captured. She had said, 'As there were only two sisters in this home born of the same mother, and you have sold Ndigombwa, I am not going to be sold by any of you.'

She was captured and told her husband to go with her to Kampala, which he did. They stayed there for two years, and on her return, she had a child. When we found out that she had returned, we went there to ask for the brideprice, but she refused to let her husband pay it. Nkiaura said, 'We will never get the payment for you.'

The girl said, 'A huh. Leave.'

A short while later, she divorced the man and left that home. She came and stayed with us for three months and then married again. Nkiaura thought of sending Bukombi to this new husband to ask for the brideprice, but she told him, 'Don't you remember that promise I made before, that you will never be paid for me?'

We always tried to watch her, but it is impossible to keep a person as a prisoner. Neither time did we have any warning that she was leaving, and we did not find out about it until she had gone.

A while ago I made love to the wife of another man. One day the woman came to me and told me, 'My husband is going on a journey, so come and spend the night with me.'

The husband was suspicious of her. Instead of going far away, he only went a short distance and then returned and hid in the village. After dark he returned secretly and hid in the house. I went to the house and knocked on the window. No one replied. I waited for a few minutes. Then I knocked on the window again, and it slowly opened. It was dark and I could not see anyone. I thought it was the woman who was opening the window for me to enter. I had a spear in one hand and I thought, 'Well, I should go in.'

The husband, who was the person who had actually opened the window, was trying to see who it was. Our heads came together with a bump. When he felt my head strike his, he said, 'Oh! This man must be strong; I must spear him.' He jabbed with his spear. Luckily, the spear went into my shirt. I fell down backwards, and the man also fell back inside the house. When I got up, I saw nothing except the spear and I began to run. When I had gone about twenty yards, I looked back and saw the man coming very fast with his spear. I went faster. Then, I did not have much strength left. The other man was running very fast. He threw the second spear at me. Fortunately, we were running through a coffee grove and when he threw the spear, it passed through a coffee tree. The spear head did not touch me, but the shaft struck me and made me fall. While I was on the ground the man caught my shirt as I tried to get up. I struck him with my spear and the man fell down. The man said, 'You have saved yourself.'

He would have slaughtered me as he would a goat. He picked up his spear, but by that time I had put a good distance between us. He threw the spear again, but it did not reach me. While he was trying to find his spear, he ran into a coffee tree and fell down. He shouted to me, 'Go! You have saved yourself. Kill your goat or your hen and eat it. You have saved yourself.'

I was fortunate because the man had not recognized me. When I had run a good way, I looked back and saw that nobody was following me. I stepped out of the path and sat down. I felt like a man who has had a shock.

When the man threw the spear at me the first time, I began to urinate and I did not stop urinating until I had lost him. I did not notice it when I was running, but when I rested I found that my shorts were wet. When I noticed it, I urinated again.

When I arrived home, I said nothing; I simply went to bed. Lubangi asked, 'What is wrong with you?'

I said, 'Shut up.'

When she continued to ask me, I said, 'I'll tell you tomorrow. Don't bother me.'

When the next day came, I did not get up. When my wife said, 'Get up,' I said 'No. I was in trouble last night. Leave me alone and let me sleep.'

Later in the morning my wife told me that food was ready. I said, 'No. I don't want to eat, but take my pair of shorts and wash them for me.'

She said, 'Shall I also wash the shirt?'

I said, 'No, only the shorts.'

The reason I did not want her to wash my shirt was that I did not want her to see it. It was torn in pieces and she would have asked me about it. While she was washing the shorts, she asked, 'Why are the shorts so wet? It didn't rain last night.'

I said, 'I fell in the river last night. That is why they are so wet.'

I told her, 'Ask Abongo to kill and cook my largest chicken so that I can eat it.'

When the chicken was ready, they called me to come and eat it, but I said, 'I have no strength. Give this part to so-and-so and that part to so-and-so and bring the rest to me here in bed.'

Late in the afternoon my wife said, 'Because you are sick, I have prepared a hot bath for you. Go slowly and bathe.'

While I was bathing, my wife noticed that I had some scratches on my back and she asked, 'What happened to you?'

I replied to her in a very rough manner: 'I told you that I fell in the river last night and these scratches must have come from the sticks on the bridge. I think the sticks also tore my shirt.'

She said, 'Why didn't you tell me this last night?'

I said, 'Well, I promised to tell you this morning, because I did not feel well last night. Now I am feeling all right and I explained it all to you.'

I stayed home for four days doing nothing but sleeping. I felt very weak and lost a lot of weight. That was a very bad incident in my life, but it was not the worst, because I saved my life.

My most recent wife is Kijungu. I knew I loved her, because she lived at Kihara's house for a long time, and I watched her then. Kihara married her mother in 1930. She had left Kijungu in the Congo. Then she came here in 1938, when she was a young girl. After a year her father came and took her back, and she was exchanged for a wife for her brother. A year later she became pregnant. Six months after the birth of the child, she came down to see her mother at Kihara's house. That was in 1942. I wondered how such a young girl had had a child. She said, 'I was married to an old man. That is why I conceived the child so easily. I was exchanged and I don't like the home, but I can't divorce him until the child is old enough to leave the breast.'

When she went back, it was time for the maize harvest, so she brought maize to her mother. While she was with her for a day, her child became sick and died that day. When she returned to her husband, he beat her, saying, 'My child has died outside this home, and it has been killed by the men who are your lovers.' Kihara had gone back with the girl, because he thought that they would blame her for losing the child. After she was beaten the first night, they accused Kihara. They said that he might have been the one who killed the child. But he was innocent, because Kijungu had arrived late Tuesday night, and Wednesday morning Kihara had gone to Butuku. In the evening he returned to find the child dead. So the people were satisfied that she could not have slept with him that day. They suspected the disease which is caused by a woman's sleeping with men while her child is still at the breast. It breaks out a week or more after the time of intercourse, so Kihara was free of blame. Kijungu said that the child had got the illness from its father, because the night before she left her home the child had cried very much. She had told her husband, 'The child is crying a great deal. I had better stay here today; I will go later.'

Her husband had said, 'No, it is all right. The child looks healthy.'

So this was another proof that it was illness and that no one had killed the child. But the husband told his wife, 'You will not go back to your mother's house from now on.'

So she stayed there for four years without returning home. Her husband used to treat her badly. She was living at Bubandi, but in those four years she never once went to the Bundibugyo market. She was watched like a prisoner, and there was no chance for anyone to capture her. After four years, she decided that she would not stay there any longer, so she divorced the man, and went back to her father's home. She was exchanged again for another wife. She stayed at the new place for three days and then she ran away to her mother here. She had not liked her new husband. This often happens with wives by exchange. It is rare to find a woman staying in a home where she has been married by exchange. When she came here I met her, and she told me all about her life during that period. She promised me, 'If you will wait here for three or four months, I will marry you.'

She said that she wanted to have a rest and did not want the people in the Congo to think that she was planning to be married by someone down here. They would think, 'Oh! She left here because her mother has seen a man to marry her.'

If she waited, people would think that she had found the man by herself. If a girl's mother finds a man for her, it spoils the relations between the mother and father of the girl. The father would be very angry: 'It is you who told my child to be married in Bundinyama.'

The four months passed, but then she was rather afraid to marry me because I lived near Kihara and her mother, and she thought that they would fight me. Actually Kihara was all right and he was on my side, but other people sometimes take up the quarrel of their wives. In this case her mother was angry. She said, 'Mpuga was very wrong to marry this child because I call him brother-in-law.'

Kijungu finally said, 'Come to the market at Bundibugyo, and I will find you there.'

Kitoke came to me that evening and asked to go to Butama and get his goats, so I told Bukombi to go and wait for the girl the next day, a Monday, and get her and take her to Nakulinga. When I returned, I went to Nakulinga's house and found her there. When I came down, her brother, Kimbugwe, said, 'You have captured my sister, and she has been taken by Bukombi. You must pay me ten goats today.'

But I refused and said, 'I must watch her habits first, and if she is all right, I will pay you the goats.'

That boy came to my house three times during the night, so I said to myself, 'I had better go to Fort Portal and stay there. I will come back after a while.'

That is what one always does in the custom of this country. If you marry a girl from your neighbour's home, you have to take her far away for the first week, because the family could come and take her back. Say, for example, that when her brother came for the first time to my house, he had found her there. He could have taken her. A week cools everyone's temper. No one can stay angry for a whole week. The first day I returned from Toro where I had taken her, I found that many people were very angry with me. The only thing to do in this case is to sit and put your legs across the front door. Then even if the people want to fight with you, they cannot jump over your legs. My wife was hidden in the house. I gave her brother one hen and told him to come and get the rest of the hens in the morning. Bukombi took the hen to Kimbugwe at Kihara's house. He refused the hen saying, 'I can't take one hen; I want them all.'

Kihara said, 'Since you have refused it, I will eat it. If Mpuga refuses to give you six chickens tomorrow, I will give them to you.'

Then he ate the hen. In the morning, Kihara came to my house as the intermediary. I gave him two chickens and six shillings and Bukombi gave me one hen. All this was equal to six chickens, and there was the one I had already given the day before, which made seven. Six days after that her brother asked me for ten goats. I said, 'I do not have ten goats now. I will give you five goats now and I will give you fifty shillings after two months.'

He refused this and when he returned, he told Kihara, who in turn told him, 'You shouldn't refuse that, because one by one it makes a whole. This man will pay you soon, if you take these first five goats.'

Her brother completely refused to do this. He has not taken anything so far and he has never returned to my house. He said that he wanted to have everything at one time, so he gave me until the end of this year to get them. I will have the ten goats by that time and he will take them on that day. The five goats he refused to take now have four kids, so I can pay him at the end of the year. Bukombi gave me one goat and I have to pay him back. If I find that I have no more goats for Koke, I will pay eight for my new wife.

Kijungu is a very nice wife and better than Lubangi, in that she is very calm. All the Bandinyama were glad to see that they had a mother and child in the lineage. That is how it is down here when a wife comes into the home with a child. You are glad when she marries into your lineage. The only person who was unhappy about the marriage was Koke. Lubangi was all right. I was afraid to bring the wife to Bundinyama the first day, because I knew that Koke would have told the people who were looking for her where she was. I kept her from visiting her mother for three months, because I was afraid that she would be caught and taken back to the Congo. Now she goes to see her mother all the time.

I had some trouble in May this year. Musoke, who is staying with Batigwa, went up to the Bakonjo to see a doctor. He was told, 'There is a man at Bundinyama who has lost his mother, and he wants to bewitch you. He has already brought me thirty shillings to kill Kihara and Batigwa.'

Musoke asked the name of the person who had been there, but the doctor refused to tell him. When he returned, he told this story to

Kihara and Batigwa. At that time Batigwa had lost one of his children and at the first death ceremony Kihara stood up and said, 'We have heard from a doctor that you, Mpuga, have paid thirty shillings to kill Batigwa and me. Why have you done this?'

I replied, 'There is no way now to prove that I didn't do that, but this is what we can do; all of us can go to see the doctor. Then we will find out which one went to him about this matter.'

Kihara said, 'It is not I, but Musoke, who found out all this.'

So five of us went there—Kihara, Musoke, Bukombi, Kabiyondo and myself. Batigwa was sick. Kihara said, when we arrived, 'I have come to check on the things you told Musoke the other day.'

The doctor was afraid and said, 'I told Musoke only a few words. Has this brought five men to me? Musoke, did I tell you that someone was going to kill another man?'

Musoke said, 'Don't deny it.'

Then Kihara said, 'All five of us have lost our mothers at Bundinyama. Now you pick out the person who brought you the thirty shillings.'

Siongo, the doctor, said, 'I don't know any of these people and have never seen them before.'

Now Kihara said to me, 'You see, this man is the one who said that you were a witch, so you'd better go and accuse him now.'

The doctor said, 'Oh, Kihara! Don't say that. I said that I had never seen any of these people before, and now you tell Mpuga to accuse me. Why should he do that?'

Kihara replied, 'He brought you thirty shillings, so you had better go on about your business.'

So I went and accused Siongo at the parish headquarters. I was told to come back on another day. When I returned on that day, the chief told me that Siongo had run away and gone to Toro. I went back four times, but they could never get Siongo. So the parish chief told me to appeal to the sub-county chief. I went to that court three times but still could not get Siongo to appear. He finally came one night to Atube's and asked him to go and apologize to me for him. He said, 'On this stomach I have your cut of blood-brotherhood, so you ought to go and ask Mpuga to drop the case. If he is still very angry, I will pay him a fine.'

Atube came to my home in the morning and told me all of this. I did not want to follow the advice he gave me, and I said, 'I will continue to accuse the man in court.'

Atube gathered us together—Kihara, Batigwa and myself—and he judged the case. I was found innocent of hiring the man, but I still did not want to drop my accusation against him. Kihara and Batigwa said, 'Leave this man alone. He is our blood-brother. If you accuse him, he will be arrested and put into prison for six months. That is not the way to treat a blood-brother.'

I would not agree so they told Nkiaura about it. He came and told me, 'You had better let this affair die.'

So I stopped the accusation after all this advice from my elders, but I refused to take the fine which was beer. I knew that if I drank it, my temper would be aroused and I would fight with the man. That is the first time that I have been suspected of being a witch.

LUBANGI

My mother was a daughter of the Babandi clan. My father first met her when she was a very young girl. She had very large breasts. My father became her lover at that time. While he was still courting her, he killed a large animal and gave her a big piece of it, which she took, for her mother. My grandmother could not carry that meat from the place where it had been left, so she asked her son to go and get it. He brought the meat to the house. Everyone was very happy and said, 'This is the best friend we have ever known.'

As you know, Amba women are very fond of meat, and if you take some meat to your girl friend's mother, she might offer you her daughter without even thinking about the brideprice. The family ate that meat, and my father brought another small animal, which they also ate.

My grandmother said to my father, 'Since you are feeding me like a baby, I will give you this daughter of mine. But first I want you to rebuild my house.'

My father told his brothers that she wanted him to rebuild the house and asked them to help. They agreed and all went with him. The first day they cut trees and carried them to the site. The second day they destroyed the old house, and on the third day they put up the new one. When they had finished the house, my grandmother and grandfather were very grateful. However, my mother refused to marry my father, as he was old, and she said, 'If you want me to marry him, cut off my head.'

Her father said, 'I am ready to spear you if you don't marry him.'

So my mother decided to marry the man and went off with him. They settled at Bunyamwera in the Congo and my mother became pregnant with me. She went on and on with the pregnancy. She refused to eat the meat of animals, but said, 'I want some fish to eat.'

When they were at the river, God arranged it 'That you will produce this child in the water.' While my father was fishing, my mother sat on the bank of the river. He called to her several times. She said, 'I am sitting here.'

I started biting her, and then I began to come quickly. When my father looked over, he saw that my mother was in the middle of labour. He called his father's sister, who had come with them. 'My wife is in the middle of her task. I wanted to go and see her, but she stopped me, saying that I was a man.'

I was born on the sand. Then people said, 'What is it?'

'It is a female.' Everyone said to my mother, 'Thank you very much.'

Then the second child (placenta) came, and they cut the cord. When they were coming home—my father was building a house near my mother's brother's house—they said, 'That child must be called Kagale (trouble).'

That is my name. My second name is Kahero, which means that my father impregnated my mother when she was at her father's home. Then they also said, 'This child has been born in the water. Her name will be Lubangi.'

After being named, I stayed in the house with my mother. She became stronger and started going out of the house. When she went, she would leave me with her sister and tell her, 'Look after the baby.'

One day when my mother was lighting the fire, a piece of coal flew out on to my cheek. You can see the scar now. When my father returned, he found that my cheek was swollen. He was irritated and my grandmother was very angry, so they were paid a large chicken as a fine. They ate their feast and asked my mother, 'Why did you burn the child?'

They treated the burn and healed it. After it was well, they took me outside and cooked a big feast, which was eaten by all the people. After I had gone outside, I stayed at my mother's breast for a while. Then I stopped being breast-fed, and she gave birth to another child, a son named Isoba. When he was beginning to crawl, he was killed, and the woman who was responsible for his death was killed in turn. They tied her hands and dropped her in the river. That is how they used to treat witches. After that, my mother stayed with my father. She became pregnant again and bore a girl called Monodani. Six days after she had been born, she died. With the death of that child the people of my father's lineage said, 'We were wrong to suspect that other woman. It must be a spirit who is killing these children.'

So they sent my mother to her home to get a kid. She brought it back, and they hired a doctor. They took her into the bush, made a hole and put her in it. They covered it with earth. They brought all her pots and put them on top of the hole. Then they lighted a fire and slaughtered the goat. They cooked some food and ate it while my mother was still in the hole. After they had eaten the food, they took her out and closed the spirit in it. They told my mother to run straight forward without turning back. She and the doctor went home. They wanted to give him his fee, but he said, 'No, I will get my fee when she conceives a child.'

Then my mother was killed by a man who was jealous of her. He said, 'Why did you marry that old man?'

That man followed her when she was going to fetch some water. She refused to sleep with him, so she was killed by a disease which came from the water. It stripped off her bark-cloth and she went home naked. As soon as she had come out of the water, she fell and became sick. My father was very angry and said to the man, 'Although you have bewitched my wife, you won't eat her.'

He carried her to Fort Portal to the Catholic hospital. She did not recover there, so he took her to the Anglican hospital. The doctor there told my father, 'We can't heal your wife, and we don't know what her disease is, but we suspect a witch from Bwamba.'

Then my father carried her to the foot of the mountain on the Fort Portal side. She continued to be very ill. My father came home by way of the mountain to collect people to carry her back, but could get none, so he returned. He found my mother dead outside the house. He was greatly troubled. He had to dig the grave himself. After burying her, he returned to his home. When he arrived, my mother's brothers worried him very much because he had married her without paying the brideprice, but he told them, 'You call that woman your relative now even though you refused to go and carry her home when I asked you.'

My father was still young, but he remained unmarried for a long time. People advised him to marry another wife, but he refused saying, 'If I marry a new wife, she may kill my child, Lubangi.'

He remained single for five years. When he finally decided to marry, the doctors told him, 'Kill two goats and one rooster, so that you can cook for the witches in your home. After they have eaten, they will allow you to marry a good wife.'

He performed that ceremony, and three days later he married two wives. Those women cooked food, and after a week they began driving me away from my father's bed. They bewitched me by putting something in my stomach. My father became very angry with them and sent them away.

He lived without a wife for awhile, but later he married the woman who raised me. He got a daughter from her. He cut a clearing for her, and she cultivated some food. He put a fence around the food, but his brothers set fire to the fence and started to burn the crop. When my father went out to see what was happening, his brothers beat him until he was unconscious. He was carried to the hospital, and those who had beaten him were arrested. He was in the hospital for three months. When he was released, the case began in court, and he won it. At that time there was little money in Bwamba, so the brothers were fined three goats. When he went back home, he said to them,

'You wronged me greatly by beating me, so I won't stay with you any longer.'

He returned to his lineage. His brothers were not living in the village of their lineage. The first wife he married there was called Nyampombi. When he married her, she told him, 'Since you have married me, I will cultivate the gardens, but in my lineage we don't eat without meat.'

My father said, 'I don't know how to hunt with dogs, but I do know how to make game pits.'

Then the people who had laughed at him before started to eat meat at his home.

At this time I began to be a useful person in my home, because I was following the example of a good woman, and it was then that I began to forget my mother.

At that time I was living with six older girls in a separate house from my parents. We children would watch those girls when they were having intercourse with boys in the house, and they would say, 'Oh, go away. Don't look at us.' So we would go away to our mothers.

One night I and another child were sleeping with one of those girls. She brought her boy friend to sleep with her in that bed. The other child was moved to another bed, but they left me where I was. I was asleep, but they shook the bed and I woke up. They pushed me, and I fell off the bed. My little toe was cut by a stick which was jutting out, and later I lost it. When I wanted to cry, the girl said, "Oh, keep quiet; if you cry the old people will ask you why. That will be very bad.'

I replied, 'You were very bad to push me off the bed. If you knew that you were going to bring your boy here, you should have moved me from your bed as you did the other child.'

When I got up in the morning, I was asked, 'What has injured your toe? Was it a knife?'

I said, 'No, it was a stick in our bed.'

My foot became worse and worse. It looked as though it had been burned, so I had to say how it started. I explained to them that I was sleeping with a boy and a girl and that they had pushed me. The people asked me to show them what they were doing. I said, 'I didn't see that because it was night-time.'

That girl was beaten badly because she had pushed me from the bed. She brought the boy and he paid for my treatments until I was cured.

Now my father started killing large animals, and people went out every day carrying things for feasts. They even brought money now and then. As you know, Amba women are very fond of meat and when they hear of a man who always has it, they try to approach him. As a result of killing these animals, he married a second wife, Nyabahundu. She bore one son called Ntamuhira.

One day an elephant was caught in a pit which my father had dug in the forest. Many lineages went out to cut it up before my father knew about it, as he was looking after his wife who was ill. When he heard about it, he said to the people who had cut it up, 'You simply went out and got your meat and forgot about the government's tusks.'

No one came forward and everyone was quiet. So my father went and brought the tusks from the forest to his home. Then he took me aside, showed me the two tusks, and said, 'You are the only child of mine who is sensible. You can keep this secret.'

One evening, two months after the elephant had been killed, the police came. My father was away trying to cure Nyabahundu who was ill. They arrested two boys in our home and asked them, 'Where are the elephant tusks?'

The boys replied, 'We don't know,' so I stood up and said, 'I know where they are.'

The police said, 'Come and show us.'

I took them and showed them the tusks, and I was arrested together with the two boys. They took us to Kapeka, who was a parish chief, and he sent the policeman to get whips of hippopotamus hide, so that they might beat us to make us say where my father had gone. I said, 'I don't know where he is.' They asked me several times, but I refused to answer, and at last they gave me six strokes with the whip. In the morning they took us to the sub-country headquarters. The people there said, 'Let the girl sit down and rest.'

The police put the two boys to work around the courtyard. When the court convened, we were brought in and the boys were asked about the affair. They said, 'Leave the girl alone; she doesn't know anything.'

Then I stood up and said, 'I want to argue this case with them. I don't know anything about pleading cases, but I want to question these policemen.'

I asked the police one question and the chief told the man to answer, but he refused, so I started on the second question. He refused to answer that, so I started on the third. He was defeated, and they lost the case. As a result they were given twelve strokes with the whip themselves.[1] They were also sent to jail for six months and fined fifty shillings each. I was very glad about that. The chief told me, 'Go get your father's poll tax and bring it back here yourself, so that he can stay and work with his wife,' and he sent me home.

[1] They were punished for trying to obtain information by illegal methods.

I brought back the tax and Nyabahundu got well, so he brought her back, and we stayed in our house. My father thanked me very much and killed a goat for me. He said, 'It is a pity that you are a girl. If you had been a son, I would have been very lucky.'

They prepared a big feast for me and bought three pots of beer. The people cooked all day and everyone thanked me.

My father's wife Nyampombe divorced him, and we were left with Nyabahundu. Later she became sick again. My father said, 'I'm tired of having you wives sick now and again, so I'm not going to support you, even if you have had a child by me. You had better go away. I know that the only real wife I ever had who never gave me any trouble was the mother of this child Lubangi.'

Nyabahundu went away and I stayed with another daughter of my father and my father's brother. We were the ones who used to give him his meals. Later on some of his children returned from Kampala, and they married two wives who helped me in the cooking, thereby lightening my duties.

When my breasts began to grow, my brother wanted to marry, so they exchanged me for his wife. They gave me to a much older man. That man refused me and said that I was still young, but that I should stay with his mother and work as a servant. I refused to stay there, and I returned to my home. They took back their daughter.

When I returned I began my religious training to become a Protestant. But my father prevented me from attending school. Then the teachers came and asked me, 'Who has prohibited you from coming to school?'

I replied, 'My father has stopped me.'

Then he was arrested. He said, 'No, don't take me to prison. Take the child and train her as you like.'

So I began attending the classes. Nyakobe, the present parish chief, was our teacher. When I began to learn, I kept at it. I went on learning, learning, learning. But my friends persuaded me to change after three months, and I left the Protestants when I had gone a certain way in the catechism. I changed and joined the Catholics. People said, 'Our Catholic religion is very hard because they ask much. They ask prayers; they ask the catechism. They ask about books. Are you going to be able to answer all these questions?'

One week after I started, they gave me a test and I passed four books. The second week after that I was again tested and I passed five prayers. I asked the teacher if he would give me a book to keep at my house, as I had already learned to read while I was a Protestant. I did not take a long time to learn the books and then I went on to the prayers. After the prayers I came to the catechism. Then our teacher was transferred, and they brought Mpuga to take his place. At that time I was a young girl and good-looking. I was dressed only in bark cloth. Mpuga stayed there about three months, and then he was also transferred—to Busaru. No teacher replaced him, so I started going to Hakitengya to Batigwa's church.

My father told me, 'You have troubled me a lot over your religious training. I was almost put in jail. If you don't go on with the classes, you will see me.'

So I went on learning at Batigwa's. While I was a student there, my brother became engaged to a Christian lady called Helena, and I was exchanged. People said, 'Don't mind; he is a Christian boy. You will have a ring marriage when you have finished your training.'

I stayed with that boy in the same house, but I did not sleep in the same bed with him. I slept with his sisters until they sent us to the candidate school at Fort Portal. When the girl who had been exchanged finished her training, she learned more about the boy and broke the engagement. So I was free because our marriage had ended. After three months I finished the catechism and Batigwa appointed me as one of the candidates to go up to the Virika mission at Fort Portal. There were six boys and six girls. I was the first person to be tested. Only two people failed the examination. Thus I kept on with my training.

Six months after we had arrived in Fort Portal, people started dying. Sometimes in one day there would be four deaths. All the Toro were told to go to their homes. The priest told us, 'I am afraid that this disease is going to kill all the candidates. You had better go back to your homes in Bwamba, and I will send for you later.'

When we were called back, my fellow candidates refused to go. I was the only one who was determined, and I returned. After I had been there three months, I was baptized with some old women. Two days after we were baptized, we made the agreement. After the agreement, we were confirmed by the priest. Then I returned to my home.

Later some of my girl friends who had gone to Fort Portal with me were captured in marriage. I refused to be married that way.

When I returned home, men began wanting to marry me. They came to see me, and they wrote me letters three feet long, but I refused them. Leo, the son of Batwehonga, wanted to marry me. My father agreed, but I refused him. Then Berenado, a Vonona, came, and I refused to marry him also. Eria wanted to marry me; I also refused him. Anderea of the lineage of Kapeka came, and I refused to marry him also. There were about eight men who wanted to marry me, but I refused them all. Others wanted to capture me, but I refused that. Then I met a man called Mpuga when the road was being built. He had lost his Christian wife and at that time he had two other wives. He tried to court me and said, 'I want to marry you,' but I would have none of him. I said, 'You have two wives now. You want to capture me as you captured them.'

But he replied, 'No, I am going to send them away. Then I will marry you.'

Then I went to Fort Portal where my godmother lived. I explained to her that men were writing letters and wanting to marry. She advised me, 'It is better to wait a while and look around a bit longer than to get a troublesome man.'

When I went back home, Mpuga came and said, 'I want you.'

I said, 'What is wrong with you? Do you want to kill me?'

He replied, 'No, I am going to send my wives away and I will marry you.'

I said, 'One of your wives has a child. What will you do?'

'I will get rid of them all.'

Batigwa told Mpuga, 'My brother, if you don't marry that girl, I won't come to your home. I taught her and she is a good Christian.'

Mpuga said to him, 'My brother, the woman you are eager for me to marry has refused me. I have asked her twice, but she still refuses.'

My girl friends told me, 'You had better have a talk with that boy, because he is dying for you.'

I refused him also on that occasion. 'My godmother had advised me not to marry a man with bad habits such as yours.'

Mpuga was very angry. He took two shillings to a doctor and told him, 'I want medicine for getting a wife. There is a girl whom I want to marry, but she has been refusing me.'

The doctor gave him medicine which he put in some tobacco, because he knew I smoked a pipe. Then Mpuga gave it to me, and I smoked it. After I had smoked the tobacco, he asked me, 'What do you think about this business?'

I said, 'Oh, you have worn me down. I agree with your plans now. I am ready to marry you in a Christian marriage, but not in the Amba capturing kind. However, I am not the man of the house, so you had better go and see my father.'

Later my father and brother came. Mpuga told them his plans, and they refused him. Then I told them frankly, 'If you refuse to let this man marry me, I am not going to become one of the men in the home. I will be married by capture as my friends did.'

My brother said to Mpuga, 'In this case you are lucky; you will get your wife because she loves you.'

They decided the brideprice for him. While we were discussing it, I said to Mpuga, 'Before deciding on this brideprice, I want you, Mpuga, to go home and send away all of your wives, because I told you that I couldn't marry a man with bad habits.'

116

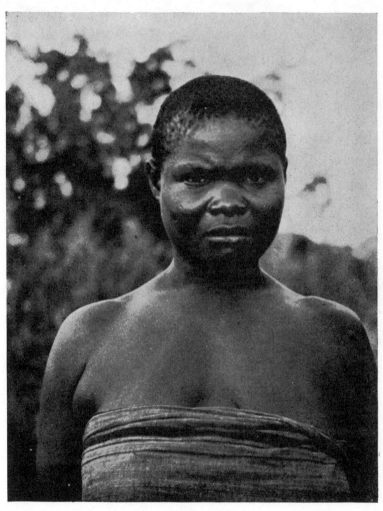

Lubangi

Interview: left to right:
F. Rwambarali, Mpuga, Dr. E. Winter

Mpuga went and dismissed all his wives. He came to our house, and they decided upon a brideprice of thirteen goats. My father was not pleased with that. He said, 'That will be the ruin of my son-in-law; we must reduce the price.'

They decided upon ten goats and that is what he paid. He came and arranged his wedding payments.

As I had refused men from time to time, people said that a certain medicine had been put in my body and that Mpuga had paid his goats for nothing because I had that medicine. Other boys who were jealous of him said, 'What do you mean by wasting your goats? That girl has medicine.'

Mpuga said, 'I will go down to her house and try to find this out for myself.'

One day he came down in the evening and saw one of his affinal relatives outside. I was also outside, so he said, 'Is there any affinal relative here?'

The affinal relative (a mother-in-law) ran into the house. Then I asked, 'Who is that? I don't want men; I have been married already.'

Mpuga said, 'It is I,' and I asked, 'What do you want?'

He said, 'I have something to ask you.'

Then I prepared water for him and he washed and went and sat on my bed. I stayed at the fireplace until about eleven. Again and again he called me to come to bed and he began to think, 'What they have told me is true.'

Then I went to bed, but I did not take off my clothes. He said, 'Take off your clothes; I am your husband. Don't fear me.'

Then I took off my dress. I embraced Mpuga, and he tried to penetrate me. I was very frightened. He tried to go slowly, but he failed that night. He said, 'I have always thought that you were an experienced woman, but you are very young.'

I gave him no answer. When he returned to his home, they asked him, 'What have you found out?'

He replied, 'The girl is still young. She has never had relations with anyone.'

He came back the next evening, and that is when he succeeded in penetrating me. That was the first intercourse I had ever had. I had recently finished a menstrual period, so he impregnated me. Seeing that I was pregnant we went to Fort Portal and had the banns put up at Virika. After the banns were announced, Mpuga came back home, but I said, 'The mountain is very steep. I will stay here until you return.'

I stayed for two weeks. Then Mpuga came and, after we had been married, we came back to Bwamba. I kept the ring at Mpuga's house for two days, and then I went back to my home. The day for the wedding ceremony arrived. I returned to Mpuga's and entered the home. For my wedding they killed three goats. The people were very happy and there were many guests, because Mpuga's father was very rich. When I married there, there were thirty goats in the home.

Then Mpuga married another wife, a daughter of the Babomboli named Bakweziba. He spat out his religion and threw it away. As you know, Amba men do not pay any attention to that, because they are accustomed to more than one wife. His parents had advised him to marry new wives because he already had a ring wife. They told him, 'If you don't marry many wives, you can't produce many children.'

I did not know that she was coming until he brought her. I thought that he had acted badly, because he brought the wife while my ring was still new. I was very annoyed and said, 'If you knew that you were going to return to your custom of marrying many women, why did you trouble to marry me in the Christian way?'

Mpuga had had intercourse with her while she was still at her home and she came here pregnant. The night she came she slept in my house. In the morning I told Mpuga, 'Remove your wife, because I carried the thatching grass for this house. I wanted to refuse to have her in my house last night, but I was rather embarrassed. Now you had better take her out.'

She never ate my food because I was annoyed with her. She ate her mother-in-law's food the entire time that she was with us. She was a very fierce woman. She used to abuse her father-in-law and mother-in-law. She predicted things which happened. She said bad things to her fellow wives. She used to abuse her husband and fight with her fellow wives. When she heard that her former husband had returned from Buganda, she went to him, and he gave her a ring. This caused a fight with Mpuga. She was very greedy for meat and was a woman of easy virtue.

After a while she gave birth to a son. She wanted to take the child to her home, but Mpuga refused to allow that. She disobeyed and took the child. It became sick and died there. When we went to the death ceremony, her lineage said, 'The child got the disease from the food which your wife carried from Sempaya.'

Mpuga said, 'No, that is wrong. My wife has been carrying food from there for a long time, and no child has died before.'

He divorced Bakweziba the same day and said to me, 'You must come back to my house.'

Mpuga's parents had been worried about the child, but when it died, they said, 'All right, let her go.'

I continued in my marriage and kept my home. A month later, Mpuga was employed by the Public Works Department at Kanyawerima as cook for the road overseer. When Bakweziba heard that he was employed on the road, she returned here. She wanted six shillings out of his pay every month to take to her mother. Mpuga said, 'I will not give you that much. If I gave it to you each month, what would happen to my proper wife, who is looking after my home, my goats and my children?'

Later Mpuga began to beat her because she was sleeping with men from other lineages. He found out because she brought back something for which Mpuga had not given her money. When he asked her where she got the thing, she said, 'From my mother.'

When Mpuga went back to the mother-in-law's home, he asked her, 'Did you give such-and-such a thing to your daughter?'

The mother denied it, 'It is you who would give things to me, not I to you.'

At this time Mpuga was not sleeping with either Bakweziba or myself, because we both had small children. He used to go and get other women. I knew about this because when a man goes out and comes in late, you ask him where he has been. He says, 'I have been there,' without specifying a particular place and you know. I did not bother about this. I used to give him food and not quarrel. I would give him water to bathe in and would go to sleep. In the morning he would go on with his usual work. He was living at my house even though I had a child and, being an Amba, would not have anything to do with him.

One day he had come from Kanyawerima to visit us. We cooked him some food, and he returned to the camp where he was working late. When he arrived there, he found that Bakweziba had locked him out. He said, 'Why have you locked me out? Is this your home?'

She asked him, 'Where have you been?'

'At my home. I want you to move out.'

He said to her, 'If you realized that you were my wife, why did you allow my child to be killed? Do you want me to divorce my wife who is looking after my wealth and family? No!'

So that wife went for ever. My mother- and father-in-law were glad, because she used to annoy them. As you know, they were old people. When they hid their vegetables, she would go and steal them. That is why they said, 'Our child, let this wife go. It is good that she leaves.'

So she ruined what she had gained. She got a house from Mpuga and went away leaving it.

One day I saw that Mambaiye, the wife who had been divorced, returning with her child. Then I said to Mpuga, 'You see what I told you? You cannot send away a wife with a child. My ring is still quite new and yet here is the wife coming back.'

Mambaiye was brought back for good, and I finally said, 'All right, let the wife stay.'

She used to get salt, vegetables and food at my house. Later I became pregnant with Nkuba. At that time Mambaiye divorced Mpuga.

When I was newly married to Mpuga, one day I went to the plantation to get some banana leaves for our bed.[1] In that garden there was a large tree which was being cut for timber. I sat down on it and went to sleep. In my sleep I heard someone calling me. The voice was coming from uphill, going downhill, saying, 'Lubangi, Lubangi.'

I got up and asked, 'Who is it? Is it Mpuga who is calling me? Or is it Eria?'

I saw no one. I wondered very much and said to myself, 'Why have I gone to sleep? I came down here feeling well. Who has called me?'

I was afraid to go home without anything, so I decided to cut some bananas. As you know, we Amba women carry large knives. I stuck my knife into a plantain stem five times, but the bunch would not fall so I left it and stood aside. Then I decided I would try again, because the plantains were almost ripe, and I was afraid to leave them behind. The sixth time I succeeded and the bunch fell. It fell into a pit, and I started to cut the plantains from the stem. It was very difficult. When I succeeded in cutting that bunch from the stem, I saw a marvellous thing. When I looked up, I saw a long snake and its lower parts looked like a man who had on a calico dress. Then I saw about a thousand people sitting on chairs. Some were dancing with bells tied on their legs. They turned to me and asked, 'Why don't you dance?'

I replied, 'No, I'm not dancing. I cannot do the dance of the Devil because I am a Christian.'

They asked me, 'Are you sure that we are people of Satan?'

I said to them, 'I have died, and I am talking to you as a dead person, because I have never met you before in my life.'

They said, 'You must dance.'

When I refused again, they asked me, 'Of which religion are you?'

I said that I was a Catholic. They said, 'No, you are deceiving us. As you have refused to dance with us because you are Christians, you must read for us; you must pray.'

I said, 'Go, I can't pray, because I don't have my teacher here.'

They said, 'No, you must pray; we are also Christians.'

There was one woman who was dressed all in white, in a white dress with a piece of white cloth on her head tied up with some pieces

---

[1] Although there are Christian elements in the account which follows, Lubangi's experience is very similar to those of pagan Amba women when they are 'caught' by gods.

of iron. When I looked at her, I saw that her eyes were set in the back of her head behind her ears. She ordered me to kneel down. I said, 'As I have died, let me kneel down.'

When I had knelt, I said three prayers. They told me to sing, so I sang one song. They told me to say the rosary, so I took my rosary and said it. After I had said the rosary, I heard a thing which looked like a snake singing the song of Christ's birth. Then I got up. When I stood up, I felt that I was in a pool of blood. Afterwards I heard something which sounded like a storm going, 'Ku, ku, ku.' And this made me fall down on the plantain stems. All these things had been seen and done in darkness. When I stood up again, I saw that it was daylight. When I got up, I used my woman's strength, took hold of the plantains, tied them in leaves and carried them home. All this time Mpuga was wondering where I was, as I had left early in the morning.

He came to look for me and met me on the path. He asked, 'Why have you been in the bush so long?'

I gave him no answer. When I reached home, I did not cook any food. At that time Bukombi was at school at Fort Portal. Mpuga went and told his mother, 'Mother, my wife has been unconscious.'

She asked, 'Where did she get this disease?'

'When she went into the garden.'

Then Bukombi arrived from Fort Portal and asked, 'What is wrong with her?'

They said, 'Your brother's wife is dying.'

He said, 'Oh God! And this is happening before I have had any food!'

They carried me to my house. As I was very ill, they said, 'Mpuga, your wife has met a god.'

They advised him to bring in priestesses, but he refused to do so. He told them, 'If you want to eat goat meat, let me know. I would rather let you have three goats than bring a god into the house.'

I was sick for a long time, and when pagans came into the house and talked about spirits, I felt worse. Whenever a teacher or Christian came in and prayed for me, I began to feel better. I finally began to recover, started to walk slowly and finally was entirely well. All this happened when I was pregnant with Yosefina. When I gave birth to the child, it was easy and I had no trouble. Mpuga was very worried about the baby and said, 'This first child of my wife is very small. I am sure that it is not going to live.'

My mother- and father-in-law denied this and said, 'It is alive and it has some hair, so it is all right.'

We stayed in the house two months, and the child began to do better. It looked like a human being, and the people who saw it were happy. By the third month we loved the child because she was very good-looking. People used to laugh at Mpuga and say, 'Why do you love the child now, when at first you said that it was not a good one?'

When the child turned out all right, we named it Kakunago. Kakunago grew up, but when she was walking by holding on to the walls, she died.

A bit later Mpuga married a woman named Beabusa. She came with two children. Mpuga put her in my house. I found her sitting by the fire. He told me, 'There is a visitor in the house.'

I asked him, 'Is the visitor from my home?'

'No.'

Then I knew when he said 'visitor' he must have brought a wife. I said to him, 'Why have you married this woman when she already has such a large family? How are you going to support her? Even if you get a house put up today, there will be four people living in it. Where are you going to get food?'

We went and greeted her and said, 'Welcome and thank you for coming to assist us in the duties of this home.' Kihara's wife came to advise me and talked to me, 'Your husband has brought a second wife. Don't drive her out. Prepare some food for her.'

So I went and prepared a good meal for my fellow wife, and I helped her cook her marriage meal. Everyone in the village ate it. After the marriage meal she moved into Bukombi's house and stayed there about two weeks. One day she asked me, 'My dear fellow wife, is this how you have been treated in this home? Why did your husband marry me if he was going to treat me like a sister?'

Then Mpuga told me, 'Since I have been married to this woman I have not been able to satisfy her. The trouble began in her bed.'

The next thing I knew was that she was carrying her children to her home and saying, 'I am leaving.'

I followed her and asked, 'Why are you leaving while you are still a bride?'

She replied, 'I can't go along with the way your husband acts towards me. He is always treating me as if he were my brother. I will not continue this way; I can't bear it. So I am going to leave.'

I was annoyed to see that she was leaving, because I liked her very much. We told Mpuga to go after her, but he refused: 'I don't want to go after that woman. I have no strength in my penis with her.'

She was a very good woman and very beautiful. She did not have any bad habits. The only reason she divorced Mpuga was because of this trouble with him. When she went, she never returned.

While Mpuga was working at the Public Works Department camp, he had another woman called Budedyo. He never brought her into the home. He met her and had intercourse with her when he was coming from the market. He took her into the bush, and they had their pleasure there. As a result of that she became pregnant with Muganga. When she was five months pregnant, she announced that Mpuga was the father, but he denied this. When the time came, she gave birth to the child Muganga. The people told Mpuga to take a chicken after she had borne the child. He refused and said, 'I had nothing at all to do with this woman.'

His father said, 'Why did you have intercourse with that woman if you knew she was a leper?'

So Mpuga admitted it and took the chicken. He said, 'I agree to accept the child, but I don't want his mother, because she has a bad case of leprosy.'

Mosumba said, 'I want to bring the woman into the home so that she can raise her child, because she is a good woman,' but Mpuga insisted, 'You don't know the disease; it is very bad. If you bring her here, she will infect you because you will use the same latrine and drink from the same gourds. If you are going to do this, I will move away from here with my wife.'

He absolutely refused to let that wife into the home. The child grew up, and Mpuga took her family the fee for raising the child and then brought it into his home. The wife was sick with leprosy until it killed her.

When I had Nkuba at the breast, Mpuga brought Nterabuki's wife called Nyabasulu. She came here and became my friend. She would bring me firewood and water. She had lived with Nterabuki eight years and did not have a child. At that time he was a policeman. Later he was discharged, and all his wives divorced him. As you know, our Amba women are forever in need of money. When the man lost his job, they thought that they were not going to get meat as before, so they divorced him. Nyabasulu went to her home, and she and Mpuga arranged a friendship between themselves. Mpuga said, 'My wife is very jealous. You can't get along with her unless you become her friend. Then at the same time, you can become my lover.'

At that time Mpuga used to have intercourse with her when she came to visit me. She would visit me and Mpuga would disappear after she had gone. I used to ask him, 'Where have you been, my dear?'

He would say, 'Oh, I have been visiting.'

This went on for about seven days. One day he said, 'You had better fix me some food. A friend has asked me to go to Toro.'

I cooked some food. He came back about four in the afternoon and had arranged the affair with Nyamanzi. Nyamanzi was also going to capture a girl. He had decided to go with her to Kampala. Luckily, Mpuga could not get the money to get him there. Then I saw a new dress, and I asked him, 'Whose dress is this?'

123

He said, 'It is someone's dress,' and he gave it to me to repair. I said to him, 'Is it possible to repair a new dress? Where is the hole you wanted fixed?'

Then Nyamanzi told Mpuga, 'Don't worry about money, because I have my bike which I left at Fort Portal. When we arrive there I will sell the bike and we will get enough money to take us to Kampala.'

They went away. A week later, I saw Kihara's wife, Kageye, and she told me, 'Oh, Lubangi! Is this the way men treat us?'

I said, 'Hmmmmm.'

She said, 'Mpuga and Nyamanzi have gone to Kampala. They aren't going to come back here.'

After three weeks, I began to think that Kageye was right, that my husband had gone to Kampala. Then I called his mother and father and told them, 'I don't know what your son intends to do. He came and asked me for some food saying that he was going up to get me some beans from Fort Portal. Now he has run to Kampala with a concubine, while I am here with a baby at the breast. I'm going back to my home.'

They told me, 'Don't you worry, our child, we will look after you. He has left some goats in the house. You can eat them and when you need clothes, we will sell some of them and get clothes for you.'

Then they said, 'If you carry our grandson away, we will follow you. God had let us be unlucky, in that we are very old people and have never had a grandson before. Now that we have one you want to take him away.'

I tied up my blanket and my baby's things. Then I started off to my home, but my father-in-law called my mother-in-law and said, 'Tie up your things so that we can go with this daughter-in-law, because I said that we must not leave this wife. We will die, but she must stay in this home.'

I saw them tying up their things and their pipes and I said, 'Oh, this is a lot of bother, so I had better give up the idea and stay here.'

Then my brother came one day to tell me that he had seen Mpuga and Nyamanzi standing on the roadside near the Fort Portal market waiting for a lorry to carry them to Kampala, because they did not have enough money to go by bus. He had asked Mpuga, 'Why have you left my sister alone with her child?'

Mpuga had replied, 'Even though I am waiting for a lorry here I am not going to Kampala, because since I have been here I have been thinking a lot about my wife and child. I left them at home and did not tell them that I was going to Kampala. I have been to Kampala before, so I have to come back. This prostitute can't take me there. I don't think that your sister is still at my home, because she is very

124

strong-minded. She may have divorced me already, so you go and see if she's there and tell her this.'

Three days later Mpuga returned. I had gone to collect firewood. When I returned, I found him at my house, and I stood in the courtyard and told him, 'Out of my house you go! This is not your house or a prostitute's house. You left it in my hands and you went after your woman, so out you go.'

His father and mother told him not to answer me, as I was very angry. Two days after that, poor tiny Mpuga, that poor little thing, began to vomit and became sick because he had eaten bad food and beans when he was wandering with his concubine. I refused to give him an enema. I told him to go and get his woman to treat his illness. I said to him, 'Where did you leave your wife? She had better come and give you an enema.'

Nyamanzi and Mpuga had left those women in Fort Portal, deceiving them by saying, 'We are going to sell some goats in Bwamba so that we can get some money to get us to Kampala, for we have not been able to sell the bicycle.'

Then one day we saw Nyamanzi's woman coming to Mpuga's homestead. She quarrelled and said, 'Oh, you acted shamefully to leave us on the road like that, saying that you were going to come back when you didn't intend to.'

She told Mpuga, 'Your girl has gone to Bundibugyo.'

Mpuga said to Nyabasulu when he arrived at Bungibugyo, 'Let us go.'

The woman refused, 'Am I your wife? What did you pay for me? You deceived me and left me at Fort Portal, saying that you were going to get money, and now, after I have struggled to get back, you want to marry me for nothing.'

Mpuga said, 'You are my wife, because I have been sleeping with you in the same bed for the last four weeks.'

After she refused to come, Mpuga said, 'Give me back those clothes, if you will not come to my house, and put your bark-cloth on again.'

Mpuga brought back his dress. When we asked him, 'Where is the wife?' he said, 'She has refused to come, saying that I have never married a woman like her.'

One day when we were going to see Nkiaura, Mpuga's adviser, we met Nyabasulu. She came and greeted her mother-in-law and greeted me too. I did not reply to the greeting, but said, 'Can I greet the person who is more beautiful than I am?'

I started abusing her. She said, 'What do you mean by saying such things to me?'

I said, 'I must abuse you. Why did you try to persuade my husband to go to Kampala with you? Was he your husband? Or did you give birth to him? Did Nterabuki take you to Kampala when he married you? You were being friendly with me, pretending to be a good woman, whereas actually you were a thief, stealing my husband.'

I wanted to fight her, but my mother-in-law told me, 'You had better leave the woman alone since she is afraid of you. You have been abusing her, and she didn't answer you.'

Then we continued our journey. Later on we heard that Nyabasulu was pregnant and that she had returned to Nterabuki. Mpuga said, 'I am the father of the child she is having.'

She stayed with Nterabuki and gave birth to a child named Busabatama, a girl. She is still there with the child. Mpuga is ready to accuse Nterabuki in court, because he wants to keep the child, and he has witnesses to prove that he is the father. He will pay one goat to the brother of Nyabasulu because he is the witness. Nterabuki could get a fee, if he were not making trouble for Mpuga, but since he is, he will lose that fee. Nterabuki will keep the wife and her other children, but Mpuga will get this child. Mpuga will not have to pay the fine for getting the wife pregnant, because she was not his wife but a concubine, a woman who was not paid for. If she had not been a concubine, Nterabuki would have gone and accused Mpuga when Mpuga had her.

Mpuga's next wife was Mambiabo. I knew that a new wife was coming because I saw her people taking Leiko (Mpuga's sister) away. When she came into the home, I gave her something to lie on and something with which to cover herself. I did not quarrel with her at all. Sometime after she had cooked the marriage meal, she became sick. She had gonorrhea and said, 'It is Mpuga who infected me.'

He denied that and said, 'I am not the one who infected you, because when you came I was alone here with my wife who is not infected with the disease. You are the one who has brought it.'

She replied, 'No, I came without disease.'

Mpuga gave her some medicine, but her illness did not lessen. Her mother-in-law started abusing her. 'Why can't you get well? That medicine heals all people who have such a disease. Why can't you be healed?'

She used to say, 'That wife is just lazy. She is well, and is only saying that she has not been cured.'

The disease continued. When the time came for the locusts to fall, she caught some. She did not offer them to her father-in-law, but cooked and ate them by herself. The people asked her, 'Where are the locusts? You're not entitled yet to eat locusts. You haven't borne any children in this home. You're still a bride. The girl who was exchanged for you had some locusts, but she gave them to her father-

126

in-law, while you have done nothing like that. The girl exchanged for you is cultivating, while you are just sitting here.'

There was much quarrelling. Then she went to the marriage intermediary and told him, 'My mother-in-law is after me. My husband loves me, but his mother is very harsh with me.'

The intermediary came and held a meeting, which set up court and judged the case. It was decided in favour of Mpuga's mother. When we used to go and cut rice, we would leave Mambiabo behind in bed, because she said she was suffering from the gonorrhea. My mother-in-law used to say to her, 'You have been saying that it is my son who infected you. You are lying. You have had that disease a long time. That is why you can't be cured.'

One day when we were cooking rice, she had her pot on the fire in her house and I had mine on the fire in my house. She left her pot there and came to my house and started talking to me. Mpuga passed her house and saw the pot on the fire. He called her and told her, 'What do you mean by leaving the food alone? Do you have a child to cook for you while you are away?'

When we went to eat her food, we found that it was burned, because there was no water in the pot. Her mother-in-law was annoyed and said, 'Why have you ruined my food, my child?'

Mambiabo refused to eat. Then she started quarrelling with her mother-in-law. After a month she became very angry and went away to her father's house. She never came back. When she first arrived here she had just finished her menstrual period, and when Mpuga slept with her, he impregnated her. She bore the child, a daughter, who is now about five years old.

After three months two new women came, one who had been taken by Babuti and one by Mpuga. Mpuga's new wife was called Likerenge, and she was a daughter of a Bandijabi. This wife ate my food and I treated her nicely. After I had taken the advice of people that it was not good to treat the other wives badly, I was good to them. Her father came to the home several times wanting to fight with spears. That is the way of old times, which we do not see now. Mpuga gave him some goats, but he refused them and said, 'I want twenty goats.'

They gave him one of their daughters in exchange, but he refused her; they gave him money and he refused that, so Mpuga said, 'What can I do?'

Her father took Likerenge away, but she would not stay and returned to our home. She had no house, so I told Mpuga to build her one, and that is when he built the small hut where Koke lives now. He cut a clearing for her which she cultivated.

Then Mpuga went and slept with a girl outside the lineage, and he caught gonorrhea. I was living in my mother-in-law's house, because mine had fallen down. One day Likerenge and I went to Bundibugyo. I saw that she was urinating painfully so I asked, 'What is wrong with you?'

We decided that it was Mpuga's disease. He denied this; 'I'm not feeling any pain. It must be your disease.'

Then I left my mother-in-law's house and started living in my own. Shortly after that, I was also infected, and that proved that Mpuga was the carrier. Likerenge had the disease for three months. At this time I was five months pregnant with Sogosa. I had the disease until I gave birth to the child. But having the child cured me. Likerenge was very angry with Mpuga. 'Why did you say that I brought that disease, when you were the one at fault?'

Likerenge and I had one fight. The reason I fought her was that she said untrue things about me. She said that I told her she ought to do no work for our mother-in-law, because no one in the home helped that woman. My parents-in-law called me and asked me, 'You are considered the first wife here. Why do you give such bad advice to the helpers?'

We had a meeting, the case was judged in my favour, and I boxed her ears. We began to fight after she had lost the case. I threw her down seven times. After I had done that, they took me to my house. When I had gone in, I heard someone saying, 'Your husband's wife is coming to beat you with a stick. Don't come out of the house.'

Then I went out and caught her, grabbed her stick away from her and pulled off her bark-cloth and rubbed her genitals with it. Mpuga came and caught Likerenge. He said, 'Your fellow wife has beaten you already. Why do you come again?'

Then Mpuga beat me with a stick, which annoyed his parents, who said, 'Why have you beaten Lubangi when it is the other woman who followed her? Let her shame that woman.'

He said, 'Lubangi was wrong to rub the bark-cloth on her genitals. It was all right to beat her, but not to rub the bark-cloth.'

My father-in-law said, 'Let her pay. Why did she go there the second time?'

Then they took Likerenge back to her house, but she returned to mine. This time Mpuga beat her, saying, 'You want to die?'

Then she stopped fighting and went and sat in her house. She told me after it was all over, 'You have shamed me. I am strong and you are weak, yet you have thrown me seven times. But you will see the consequences of that. I promise you this: if you don't feel the consequences, I am no good at all.'

Then my confinement took place. At that time the priest visited our village and wanted all the Christian wives to go and meet him.

I was in labour He called us one after the other and asked, 'Does your husband have any other wives?'

I denied this and said, 'My husband has none except me.'

That was Thursday. I went on in labour during Thursday night and the whole of Friday. On Friday night I hid myself. No one knew that I was going to have the baby. By Sunday night Mpuga was very angry, He took up his spear and started quarrelling with everyone in the home saying, 'I'm going to spear you all if my wife dies. You killed a wife some time ago, and I got another one. Now you want to kill this one.'

The people in the home said, 'It is your other wife, Likerenge, who is a witch.'

So they took her outside. On Sunday Mpuga and Bukombi went to Busaru to a woman called Nyamweuma who had medicine and brought her to our home. When she came, the house was full of Bandinyama wives and she said to them, 'Get out of this house. Have you come to dance or to cast spells? Let me do my best and if I do fail that will be bad luck which has been sent by God.'

On Monday morning I was feeling very bad and this woman gave me some medicine. She continued working the whole of Monday. The people returned from the market and found me still in the same stage, but about six o'clock Monday evening I delivered Sogosa. At that time Mpuga had gone out to consult doctors, so the people sent someone to call him. 'Your wife has been delivered.'

That child was named Sogosa, as it was a boy. If it had been a girl, we would have called her Kabomesa. The midwife who helped me wanted her fee. Mpuga offered her a young goat, but she refused. He then gave her ten shillings, but she refused these also. So finally he gave her a big she-goat, two shillings for herself and one shilling for her sister, and she went away.

A little later, Likerenge went away to see her parents. She said, 'I'll be there for a week, and after that I will come back.'

After two weeks, we heard that she had been captured by another man, named Sugyo. Then she left him and stayed with her father for a month. She was away for two months altogether and then she returned. When she came back, the householders conferred and told Mpuga, 'That woman was very wrong to leave her house when it was nearly completed. She had better pay a chicken for her action.'

So she went back and got a chicken from her home. Mpuga said, 'Even though you have brought the chicken, I am not going to build you another house. You were the one who was wrong to divorce me without any notice. You have been enjoying other men while you have been pregnant, and I don't know what the result will be.'

Three months after she returned, it was time for her confinement.

She had a lot of trouble. She nearly died with that child, because down here, when you are pregnant, you cannot have intercourse with another man. If you do, you are likely to lose the child. While she was in labour, she told the names of six men who had enjoyed her favours while she was pregnant. The baby died immediately after birth, and the woman lost all her hair. She became like a baby. Mpuga went out and looked for medicine to heal his wife. A woman gave him some medicine which had some bananas in it, and she also gave him a woman's knife. She told him, 'You should go and cook this for your wife and tell her to eat the bananas with this knife. She should cut the slices and eat them with the knife.'

Then one day Mpuga bought a lot of rice, and he told us to go and carry it. We went to fetch it. Likerenge said, 'You carry the small load and I will carry the large one.'

We did it that way. Then she lagged behind. I reached home first and took the basket in my house. When she came, she wanted to put her basket in her house, but Mpuga said, 'Take that rice into Lubangi's house.'

She brought it to my house and seemed annoyed. Then I thought, 'That is why she wanted to carry the large load and gave me the small one. She intended to take the big one to her house.'

She was actually very angry and said she would go away. Mpuga told her, 'Go ahead. It was you who angered me first by bringing some people here who caused the death of your child.'

She went off and that is the last we saw of that woman.

I heard that Mpuga had brought in another wife. When I returned, I found Koke in the home. I attended the marriage meal, and after that she stayed in her house and I stayed in mine. Then our mother-in-law lost her hen which we used to call 'mother of chickens'. She looked for it for about two days and then lost hope, thinking that it had been taken by a mongoose. When the children were in Koke's house, they heard a chicken shaking its wings in the bedroom, and they asked, 'Which chicken is that?'

Koke replied, 'I got that chicken from my fellow wife yesterday.'

But the children said, 'No, you didn't bring one chicken with you. That must be our grandmother's chicken which is missing.'

Our mother kept on looking for her chicken, but she could not find it. She said, 'I am going to take the droppings of my hen to the goddess. If any one of you has sold my chicken or eaten it, you had better say so now. If you don't, you will get in trouble.'

The children, Kisasi and Nkuba, were sleeping with Koke. She made them go to bed and, when she thought they were asleep, she went to the back of the room, got the chicken from the pot, hid it in her bark-cloth and went out. When the children asked, 'Where are you going?' she answered, 'I am going to the latrine; I will be back.'

She went out broke the legs of the chicken, broke its wings, twisted its throat and left it in the doorway of her mother-in-law's house. I heard the mother-in-law calling to me, 'I have heard something shaking its wings. Is that my chicken, returned by the mongoose?'

I said, 'I don't know.'

In the morning our mother-in-law went out and saw the chicken and accused Koke, 'It is you, my child, who have done this.'

Koke denied it. 'No, I couldn't do such a foolish thing.'

Our mother-in-law sent a message to Mpuga, saying, 'Your wife is destroying all my chickens.'

Mpuga got the message and came and set up a court. He brought the accuser and accused and witnesses for both. Koke lost the case, and the affair of the chicken ended.

They had another quarrel over sugar-cane. Koke is very fond of sugar-cane. She eats it like a civet cat. One day she went and cut ten stalks and carried them back to her house. When our mother-in-law saw that, she said, 'Come, child, even though you have your own garden, can't you get just a little bit at a time? You cut it like an elephant. What are you going to do the next time, now that you have finished the whole garden?'

'What I am going to do now is cut all my sugar-cane because I have a quarrel with you. You will go and get sick and the next thing will be for people to say that I have bewitched you.'

Then we heard her crying and we said, 'Why is she crying?'

When we asked our mother-in-law, she said, 'I have advised my child's wife not to eat food like an elephant, and now she is weeping.'

Koke replied, 'The sugar-cane you said I was cutting for myself will be cut for you, and you will have it to eat all day.'

Then we saw that the sugar-cane was being cut from the garden and being placed at the junction of the paths in the courtyard, and that the sun was beating down on it. That was Koke's way.

Shortly after that our mother-in-law became ill. When she was sick, Koke said, 'You have shamed me twice; first about the chicken and second about the sugar-cane. You will see the results.'

Koke went out again and stole some sugar-cane. When our mother-in-law went into the garden, she said, 'Who took my sugar-cane?'

Koke said, 'I got only a few.'

Our mother-in-law said, 'You acted very badly. I don't want to go on having this trouble with your stealing all my things, so I will go and destroy the whole sugar-cane garden.'

She became sick again. She continually told her relatives during her illness, 'If, by any chance I die, you must prove that I have been killed by my child's wives, Lubangi and Koke.'

The result of this was that she died. Mpuga was suspected as being the witch who killed his mother because she had died while he was in Toro. That woman was a priestess and belonged to Satan, so we we had to collect mushrooms, millet, dried meat and butter. We cooked a lot of food, which people ate on that day. They did very unusual things at her burial. They got the first pot she had used when she had the goddess, put it on her head and wrapped her in the first bark-cloth she had when she got this goddess. They filled the grave with soil and buried her. At the first ceremony they called a man named Kisangani, with whom she used to quarrel about goats. Then they began the inquest and they suspected the witches, because no one dies in Bwamba without there being a killer. Kisangani lost the case. The ceremony ended and all the people went home.

Our mother had left Bukombi a chicken. He had a guest visiting him and could not find the chicken to kill for him, so he went to Nyamanzi and borrowed a rooster, which they killed and ate at Nyamanzi's mother's house.

After they had eaten, the guest went away. Mpuga returned from work to look for some food. He went around looking into one pot after another, and he came to a small pot, where he found the back of a chicken, part of which had been eaten. So he asked Koke, 'Whose chicken is this?'

'It is Bukombi's.'

Then he said, 'Why has he killed it?'

'He killed it for his guest.'

He said, 'Why? It is the rule in Bwamba that the guest must eat the back of the chicken. Why did he leave that behind?'

She replied, 'I don't know.'

In the afternoon, Mpuga looked in the pot again and found that the meat was missing. He thought, 'I will ask Koke.'

When he asked her, she replied, 'The owner has eaten it.'

Bukombi came looking for his chicken again the next day. He asked Mpuga about it, and Mpuga said, 'I don't know about it. I haven't seen it.'

He asked all the people in the house about the chicken which his mother had left him, and no one had seen it. Later Mpuga remembered the chicken he had seen in the pot, and he said, 'What are you talking about? You have already eaten your chicken.'

Bukombi said, 'The one I ate was from Nyamanzi's. I cooked it at Nyamanzi's mother's house.'

Mpuga said, 'The reason I say this is that I found a chicken in my

132

wife's house. When I asked who had killed it, she told me that you had killed it for your guest.'

Bukombi asked Koke, 'Explain to me how I killed a chicken and ate it in your house.'

She had nothing to say. Bukombi stood up and said, 'I want your wife to repay my chicken, if she doesn't want me to accuse her to her lineage. And I think that you are eating these chickens together.'

Mpuga said, 'No. If I were eating the chickens with her, I would not have told you about it.'

They decided to let the affair drop because it would shame the wife. Then she started saying nasty things to me, and I replied to her, 'Why are you abusing me, your fellow wife? I didn't catch you with the chicken of your brother-in-law.'

Once Mpuga took some wood from my house and gave it to a carpenter, who made it into a chair. When the chair was finished, he brought it and put it in Koke's house. I asked him, 'Why have you done this? You took the wood from my house and now you have offered the chair to another wife. How is this?'

He said, 'What I have done is what I have done. If you are strong, go and get the chair from her house.'

Then I rushed out, entered the house and found Koke sitting to one side. I went and got the chair, took hold of Koke's chin and said, 'Come on, if you want to fight, come out. You have been calling yourself a strong woman here. We will see who is thrown the first time.'

Koke said, 'I am a child. You are a very old and very strong woman. I can't fight you.'

I took the chair and left her in peace.

She left recently for two weeks, because she had been told by her parents that they wanted to get the rest of the brideprice. But Mpuga said to them, 'I can't pay you any more, because your daughter is a thief and is lazy.'

They held court, and Mpuga won the case, so he got Koke back. She is not acting any better.

Kijungu is the last wife that Mpuga has brought here. She came from her home to the home of her mother's husband, who is Kihara. At that time Mpuga was building my house, and I had gone to live at my father's. Mpuga went to cut grass for the thatch, and he used to ask Koke to carry it, as I wasn't there. She refused. Mpuga said, 'You will be living in that house. You will cook in it and talk in it. Why won't you carry the grass for it?'

Koke answered, 'I won't carry your grass, because that house is not mine. It is your other wife's house.'

So Mpuga asked Kijungu to carry it for him. Koke said, 'If she carries that grass, I will beat her to death.'

Mpuga said to her, 'Are you sure? Aren't you feeling ashamed to act this way? I asked you to carry the grass and you refused. Now when I have asked my friend to carry it, you say you will beat her.'

So Kijungu carried that grass. One day they made three trips with the daughter of Kihara. Mpuga told Koke, 'If you are a strong girl, beat Kijungu. And if I don't beat you, wait until Lubangi comes to punish you.'

When they were making a second trip, I arrived from the Congo. Mpuga told me, 'Your thatching grass almost rotted in the bush because Koke refused to carry it. But my girl friend here has been carrying it for you.'

I thanked Kijungu very much and said to Koke, 'You have said that you are my enemy, since you have refused to help me by refusing to carry the grass when I was not here.'

She said, 'I want to carry grass. Let's go together, and I will help you.'

I said, 'I don't want you to come with me, because you said you would beat Kijungu. I'm going to beat you before you beat her.'

When he had finished the house, Mpuga said, 'I want to go to Toro to get some beans from my friend there, so get some food ready for my journey.'

I cooked the food. When Mpuga went up, he captured Kijungu and they stayed in Toro about three weeks. He took her to Fort Portal, because he was afraid to have her here, as her mother and her brother were on this ridge. He wanted to take her to Toro so that no one could go after them. People of Bundinyama were not pleased with the marriage then, and they still don't like it. Mpuga has paid six goats already, but they want to return them because they don't want him to marry that girl. They just seem to hate Mpuga. The Bandinyama don't like him very much, because he is the only man left in his lineage except Bukombi and Abongo.

Then people asked me, 'Haven't you had the news from your husband that he has married a wife?'

I replied, 'No.'

I was very angry that Mpuga had done this. I had no quarrel with that girl friend, but I was angry that he had left me in the house alone. When he came back, I started to abuse him. Then he said, 'Don't quarrel.'

I said, 'Do the people who marry new wives leave old wives alone?'

Then I quieted down and left him and his wife alone. That wife became my child. She used to help me with the cooking, washing and children. She used to do all these things before she went to sleep in

134

Bukombi's former house. Koke became very angry about this, and Mpuga said, 'Why are you angry? Lubangi should be the one who is angry.'

He meant that we were married publicly and all the people knew that I was his wife. It is a rule in our religion that a woman does not marry another man while her husband is living, and the man does not marry another woman while his wife is alive. Mpuga said to Koke, 'Why are you cruel to my wives when you are a thief? I married you in secret and you are illegally married, so it is not right for you to persecute Kijungu, because you two are in the same category. If you bother her, I will also bother you.'

I only watched this because I have no advice to give Mpuga and because I have failed to stop him from marrying other wives. Kijungu has no bad habits; she is a good woman.

KOKE

My father brought me to life at the foot of the mountain. Later we moved from there, because the child next to me in age became sick. We settled at Bubandi. We stayed there for a long time, and my mother gave birth to a boy. When I was young, my mother never used to go to the stream for water. I was the one who used to carry it for her. I would start early in the morning with my girl friend and work until six in the evening. Any time we took off from collecting the water we spent collecting firewood and elephant grass. When we finished, we used to go and gather pumpkin leaves to cook before our mother came from the garden.

There was a football ground near our home, and we used to play on that. Once I was playing with one of my neighbours and I pushed her so hard that she fell. She fell on a reed which injured her. They took me to the sub-county chief's headquarters to accuse me, but when the people saw that I was a young girl and that she was young also, they did not blame me for the accident, but said, 'We can't blame either of them, because they are young girls of the same age. If one were the elder, that one would have been blamed.'

One day three girls and myself went to the stream to get water. One of them struck my pot with a stone and broke it. That girl had come to our home with her mother, who married my father's brother, so she had grown up with us. I pushed her, and she fell in the water, where there was a log which she fell against. She broke her rib. There were some doctors at our home who went and treated this girl, and she was healed in two days. They said to my father, 'You must pay the fee for these doctors,' but he said, 'Why did she break Koke's pot? If Koke had started the fight, I would have paid the fee, but since this girl broke Koke's pot first, and she only pushed her in return, I won't pay the fee.'

One day we had gone to a dance, and the boy friend of the girl whom I had fought with went with me. He asked me to have intercourse with him, but I said, 'I can't do that, because you are the lover of my girl friend.'

When I was returning from the dance, she rushed up to me and hit me very hard, saying, 'You have had intercourse with my friend.'

A child of my father's sister who was with me advised me not to fight with her, because I had fought her once and had broken her rib. He said to wait and accuse her at home, where they would allow us to fight each other. When I reached home, I told my father, 'I want to fight this girl, because she hit me. I was afraid to fight her before, because they were going to fine you the last time I fought her.'

One day my father went to Toro and brought back a dress for me. He arrived home when I was out fetching some firewood, and he sent for me to come and get my dress. When I had put the dress on, that girl said, 'Oh, you lucky people whose fathers buy clothes for you!'

One day we were going to the market, and she said to me, 'Take your own path and go by yourself; I don't want to go with people who are all dressed up.'

When we were crossing the river before we reached the market, she poured water on my dress. I said, 'You have been looking for me. Now you have found me.'

I poured water on her bark-cloth in return. She turned to me, and we started to fight in the water. We both returned home, weeping. Neither of us reached the market.

One day we were all sitting at home playing, and the teacher called Batigwa came and caught us. He said, 'What do you mean by staying at home here? Why don't you go to school?'

He took us to his home, and I was given the job of being nurse-maid to his child. The other pupils used to go and collect firewood. My girl friend was very annoyed. She said, 'Did you bring Koke here to be our queen? I thought you brought her here to school.'

One day we had gone to get some beans from the garden and this girl started abusing me. 'You don't go out and gather firewood, but your work is to sit at home and gather beans. But today you will see me.'

Three days after that my father came down to the teacher's house. He said, 'What do you mean by keeping my children at your home? Our houses are not far from the church.'

The teacher gave my father that girl who used to fight with me, but he kept me there. Two days after the girl had gone, the teacher said, 'You may as well go back to your father's home, and if you want to continue with your religious training, it is all right. If not, that is your business.'

When I returned home, my father would not let me go back to school. I do not know why he would not let me go back.

My mother was the first wife of my father, and she divorced him when I was a young girl, before I had breasts. My mother's father was called Lumbala. His wife, Njabala, was a daughter of the Bandi-manda. Her first marriage was in my grandfather's home and it is there that she died. An aunt (father's sister) of my father was exchanged for my mother and has three sons and the one daughter who are alive. My mother has the same. She had six children, but two died. Whenever my father heard that they had beaten his aunt at the home where she had married, he used to beat my mother because they had been exchanged for each other. The man who married my father's aunt was a younger sibling of my mother. He used to hide when it came time to pay the poll tax.

My father and mother did not get along well, so she divorced him. My father used to say that she was sleeping with men outside the lineage and that he would beat her. He used to get out his spear and try to spear her. My father's bad habit of abusing my mother was the reason for my burning myself while I was cooking food.

When my father was divorced, my mother went back to her home. My father's lineage told him, 'Since you have let your first wife go, you won't be able to marry another. What do you mean by divorcing an old wife, one who has given you six children? Why hadn't she become a bad woman before she had all these children if she were ever going to be one?'

While my mother was still living with my father, he was a sick man. When she divorced him, all the visitors who used to come stopped coming. Now my brother is the one who is acting as house-holder. My next brother is also married. He is not yet old enough to pay the poll tax. The other brother is going to school.

When my mother left, she went to Kirumia. The people there told her to go back to my father, but she refused. Then my father's aunt, who had been exchanged for her, said, 'This man I am married to is hopeless, and I can't be married for nothing, so I'll divorce him also.'

Later my mother married at Buyali. She had two children there. The boy was very young.

Since my mother divorced him, my father has never married another wife. The wives of my brothers look after him. It is they who cook food for him. After my mother had gone, I had to look after my three brothers and my father. I used to cook for them. The most tiresome jobs were getting firewood, water, food, collecting greens and cooking. The trouble was that they gave me no help in any of these things, except cultivating. I had to do all the cooking, because all of the people at home were men. I used to quarrel with my brother Makoso. He left me at home, and he used to go and visit, and when he returned he would ask for food. I said, 'Have you cooked the food?' Because of that, he used to fight with me.

I used to cultivate, or I would have had no food to give the family. My father and Makoso did the clearing. My father used to quarrel with me when I went out to play with the other children. He would say, 'Why do you go out to play when you are the only girl in this home?'

Wasn't I a child? Didn't I want to play? I was doing a very difficult job, looking after four men and my youngest brother, who was very young. He was a lot of trouble. I had to feed him, wash him and give him enemas.

Because of all this work, another child advised me to run away to my mother, but I did not pay any attention, because my mother was the one at fault. It would have been all right for her to divorce my father if he had married another wife, or if I had been old enough to do the work. But she went away while I was a very young girl and I had to continue in my duty.

When my brother married, I remember the advice about running away which the other child had given me. Now there was another woman to take my place. I brought the food which she cooked and cooked for her the first ten days of her marriage.

The girl was quite nice. The only person who acted badly about the marriage was her brother, who came and asked to take me in exchange, but my brother refused and said, 'She is very young. You can't marry her.'

Then my brother and father started to treat me badly. They told me to help the woman in cooking and other things, while I needed a rest, because I had worked a lot in the past. My father became very mean to me. He used to shout at me when he saw me playing with the other children. He would tell me to get water and firewood for this woman who had married into the home. The wife herself used to tell me kindly, not order me. I used to help her because she did not use force. I took care of my youngest brother, but she did the rest. I showed her the gardens. My mother had left a plantation of bananas, which we used. She had also left cassava, which I used and replanted. Ndibala was too young to help. Makoso took care of the goats.

The chief reason I ran away was that my father's scolding was getting worse. I had been doing all these things myself, with no helper, and now after getting this woman, they expected me to continue, and father started abusing me from time to time.

I left about eleven in the morning. I knew that my mother was far away, so I went to my mother's father's village which was nearer. My grandfather asked me, 'Why have you come?'

I explained to him that I had run away because I had so much work to do. He told me to go to my mother, because he knew I was eager to see her. So I went to the village where she was living. She did not rebuke me, because it was she who had left me alone in that home. She greeted me. Later on, after I had explained it all to her, she laughed at my father, saying, 'Why did your father send me away, if he knew that he couldn't get another wife?'

My mother did not order me about. I used to do work there when I wanted to, and I was not forced. I lived very happily there.

The other people in my mother's home, the other three wives and her husband, also loved me.

Then one day I met Makoso's wife in the market, and she asked me to go home, so I went with her. I knew that my father's home was my true one, so I did not like to live outside it. When I arrived, Father wanted to beat me, but the other people advised him, 'If you beat her now, she will only run away again.'

After that, the other wife and I divided the work. After I had been there a while, they brought Andaiye to exchange with me. She was my age. I refused to go, her people came and took her back. When I discovered that my father was being cruel and that he wanted to exchange me while I was a young girl, I ran away again to my mother. Then my father came for me. When he realized that I was going to continue to run away, he took me to the slopes of the hills and exchanged me for a wife. They showed me the girl who was going to be exchanged with me. I learned from other people that my future husband was a leper, and I did not like that. My mother did not want to exchange me, but my father was very fond of the woman, so he did not worry about me. I was very angry, because he was simply dropping me in the fire. I said to him, 'Have you ever seen a father offer his daughter to a leper? Do you know what happens to the person who sleeps in the same bed with a leper?'

He said, 'That is not true. Leprosy never moves from the leper to another person.'

I said, 'You are lying. I know people who have moved from the house where a leper lives, because they are afraid that his breath at night will give them leprosy. So what will happen to me if I stay in the same bed with one?'

The people in my home used to quarrel with my father saying, 'What do you mean by exchanging this young girl?'

My elder brother used to quarrel with my father, 'Why do you exchange my sister with this old woman who has had seven children?'

I spent two days in the leper's village, and then I ran away to my mother. I stayed with her a month or two.

Then one day I went to a dance. While I was gone, the leper came down and told my mother, 'Get out of the way.'

Mother said, 'Where is there a son-in-law?'

The other people said, 'The one who has leprosy.'

'Leave me alone! Is that a son-in-law?' she said.

The leper said, 'I can't ignore you. It is your daughter who refused to marry me, so I will continue calling you mother-in-law.'

He brought one shilling and paid it to his mother-in-law saying, 'This is the fee for seeing you. I told you to move, but you didn't want to.'

But mother refused the money and said, 'I don't want it.'

When I returned from the dance, my mother said, 'Your so-called husband was here.'

I asked my mother, 'Why did you allow him to come here? Don't you know that he is mad? He will keep coming down here off and on now, thinking that I will eventually love him.'

She said, 'I didn't call him. He just came. Perhaps other people told him to come.'

My brother Makoso told my mother, 'My father says that whenever he sees Koke, he is going to send her back to the leper husband.'

Then I decided to go out and get married, so I told my mother and brother, 'Unless I do so, my father will send me to the leper.' So I ran and got married.

My father had not come to my mother's to get me, but he came where I was married. He arrived after about three weeks. The reason that he had not come before was that he did not know I was married. He came the day I cooked the marriage meal. He had not come to my mother's because he did not like to go there. He had only sent my brother, with instructions to catch me and bring me back, but my brother was kind enough to tell me. He told my father, 'I discovered Koke at a dance. When I tried to catch her, she ran away, and I couldn't find her.'

This marriage was not arranged. You do not have to speak or decide with anyone, because here in Bwamba when you run away to marry, you keep it secret. But when you have been paid for, people know where you have gone.

This is how I met the man. One day his sister had gods on her head, so he attended her ceremony. When the ceremony was over, he walked with me and that was when we began our courtship. One day I went to see my mother's younger sister at Ngamba. Then I left her and went to my mother's and stayed there for a few days. After that I returned to my mother's sister's home. I found that there was no one there, so I left my looking-glass on the table and went to sleep. The people came from the field and saw my looking-glass, and they knew that it was mine, so they looked for me and found me asleep on the bed.

This suitor was the brother of my mother's sister's husband. He came and asked her, 'Where is Koke?'

She said, 'I haven't seen her.'

He kept on asking her, saying, 'I know she is here.'

Then he came into the house and found me sitting there. He said to the woman, 'You have been deceiving me. Who is this?'

Then we had a talk. I said, 'Why have you come?'

'I have just come to see you.'

I said, 'I didn't come here to see you, so you had better go back home.'

He left. Then one day he sent his wife, telling her, 'Go to so-and-so's and get the girl who is there.'

That wife came, and we cooked some food for her, and she finally said, 'I have come for you.'

My mother's sister said, 'No, your husband hasn't paid for this girl. If he had paid for her, it would have been all right for you to come and get her, but as it is a capture marriage, the boy must come for the girl.'

So the woman returned. She went and told him the advice my mother's sister had given her. The boy himself came in the afternoon and found me lying on my bed. He sat on my bed and while he was sitting there, he stole my knife and my pipe and put them in his pocket. As soon as he had done that, he went out of the house. When I ran to the door, he told the people there, 'Tell that girl to come with me.'

When I went to him, I said, 'I am going back.'

He left me about ten yards behind, and then he took the knife and pipe out of his pocket and showed them to me. Then he started to walk away. I called to him, 'Give them to me.'

He would not give them back to me, so I followed him. His idea was to take me to his home. So when we reached the door, we went into his house. When I said, 'I am going back,' he told his father's wife and the other people to come and get me. So they came and asked me nicely to go into the house, and I entered.

Then my mother's sister sent word to my mother, 'Your daughter has married down here.'

My mother was angry because the husband had paid nothing to her or to my lineage. He had only brought her a shilling's worth of sugar. She said, 'I can't go there because I am very angry. I have a bad temper. I will ask her brother to go down.'

My mother thought that it was a bad thing that I had left her father to stay with her and now had run off without her permission. I had not told her that I was going, because she wanted me to go back to my father and then have my brother arrange with another man to get a wife in exchange for me. I did not like this, because I did not trust my father and thought he would take me back to the leper.

My father said to my brother, 'You, Makoso, had better follow your sister.'

Makoso said, 'No, I can't go there. It is you who are trying to make this girl marry a husband she doesn't like. You are forcing her to marry the leper.'

Three weeks after that my father asked Lorencio, another of my brothers, to take him to Ngamba where I had married. Lorencio knew the people there.

When they arrived, I was cooking my marriage meal. Until that time I had eaten my fellow wife's food. That morning I had gone and collected firewood accompanied by my fellow wife, and I got water. After that I collected the food except for the meat, which my fellow wife had got from Butuku. We started cooking the food. Three of us cooked, my husband's wife, my husband's brother's wife and myself. When we had finished cooking, the people who had come sat under a tree and ate. By that time my father had arrived, but he did not eat, because a father is not allowed to taste his daughter's marriage meal.

After the meal, when the people had begun to make mats in the courtyard, my father said to them, 'You must give me my goats if you want your wife, because she has refused to be exchanged.'

My husband said, 'I have the goats, but we will ask your daughter what she thinks about this.'

When they asked me, I said to my father, 'Can't you give me some time? I have been here for less than three weeks. You should wait until I know this home.'

He told my husband, 'You had better give me the fowls for eloping with my daughter.'

But my husband gave him a female sheep and said, 'Take this instead of fowls.'

I advised my father not to take the sheep, because I was afraid that the husband was giving my father part of the brideprice in order to avoid giving him any fowls. I said, 'You should take hens or cocks rather than sheep.'

Then they gave him seven shillings and two chickens for the elopement and my father left.

We all lived peacefully there and had no quarrels. Later I was told that my mother had a bad leg, so I went to see her. I stayed for a while and met my brother there. Then they took my mother to the doctor. After that my brother and I went to my father's home. When we arrived, Makoso went into his house, and I went into my father's house. My father asked me, 'Why have you come here.'

I said, 'Makoso came and asked me to come and see you. I will go back now.'

Then Makoso came and said to Father, 'She is not going back! I have caught her.'

143

A few days later my husband came and saw me. He asked, 'Why has my wife been captured?'

Makoso replied, 'Have you ever come to my house? I don't know you. I have caught a goat which was lost.'

My father said to my husband, 'If you want your wife, you had better give us a girl now.'

He said, 'I am willing to pay you as many goats as you want, but I don't have a girl to exchange.'

My father said, 'If you are not going to give us a girl, forget about this woman. She is no longer yours.'

The man said, 'I am going to Kampala.'

'All right.'

When he went back, he saw my mother and told her, 'I am going to Kampala, since your daughter has been captured, and I don't have a girl to give in exchange.'

He was very annoyed that he had lost me after paying his chickens, so he left his wife and went to Kampala and is still there.

My brother went to a dance and met a girl there and courted her. He asked her, 'Would you like to marry me?'

'All right, I am willing to marry you.'

Then he asked her, 'Do you have a brother?'

She said, 'Yes, I have a brother.'

Then my brother returned home. Shortly after, the brother of that woman met my brother and they talked about the matter, and the brother of the other girl said, 'I will bring my sister to your home.'

My brother agreed. The woman was brought to our home and all of the people there liked her, so she was left behind. Three days later, they sent an intermediary, who carried me back.

This man had never courted me, but I had seen him before. I was greeted nicely at his home. After one week I cooked the marriage meal, which was of beans. The people thanked me for cooking the food for them and wished me well. They said they hoped I stayed a long time in their home.

They did not examine me there because they had already done it while I was at my home. When they had brought the girl there, they had sent me outside completely naked, and they also sent the other girl outside like that. They had two men, one from this lineage and one from the other, examine us. They asked each other. 'Do you see any disease on the girls?'

Each one said, 'No,' and they left us. They examine you to see if you have leprosy. If they see that you have a scar, they tell your brother to deal with it and have you cured. This happens whether you are in your husband's house or whether you have not yet been married. Before I left, my lineage father's wives also gave me some advice. They told me to sweep my mother-in-law's house, to spend most of my time in her house and to carry her water and firewood. The mother of my husband had died, but there was another wife of his father who had brought him up. She was the only mother-in-law, so I used to treat her as the real one. We were the only women in that home, and we worked together in all things. It is I who used to carry the firewood and leave it for her, and get water for her. That woman had had many children, and none of them had lived. She became pregnant and went back to her home. On the way back she felt her labour begin. She did not eat the food which she had brought from her home, but she lay down and started labour. After every remedy had been tried, she died with the child.

After four weeks I went back to visit my father and took him a cooked chicken. I ate a lot of meat there, because I discovered that my father had killed a pig. My husband followed me, and when he found me he said, 'You must not go back to see your father again.'

That annoyed my father and was the beginning of a quarrel between him and my husband.

The next time I wanted to go and see my people my husband refused to give me permission, saying, 'I don't want you to go to your father's home, because whenever my wives return to their old homes they soon die.'

However, his sister used to come and see her parents from time to time, and I said, 'Why is your sister coming to her home, and I am not allowed to see my people?'

So I had to run away to see my father. My husband followed me there. When he arrived, I was cooking maize on the fire and people told me, 'Your husband has come.'

My father went out to see him. He took a chair for my husband, but my husband refused to sit on it. He said, 'I have come for my wife, and I want her right now.'

My father refused and said, 'No. You can't take her today. You always receive your sister from here, and no one has ever gone to your home to seize and take her away like a prisoner. You had better go away. Your wife will come back to you.'

So he left and I followed him the next morning. When I arrived, he started to abuse me and said, 'I will see how you will go back to your home.'

My father's family all wondered about this and said, 'This man must be a very bad man. This is the first time that he has come here, and yet he has shown that he is ill-tempered.'

I stayed with my husband a very long time without returning to my home. His sister used to come and see her relatives. Then one day he discovered me on the way to see my father and beat me badly. Then he wanted to take me back, but I escaped from him and went to my home. When my father saw me and asked what was wrong, I told him, 'My husband has beaten me and tried to stop me from coming here.'

My father said, 'Stay here. Let him come and take back his sister.'

One day I saw my husband on his way to our home, and he said, 'I have come for my wife.'

My father refused to give me up and said, 'Take back your sister.'

Makoso said, 'No, he must take his wife,' and Father said, 'No, he cannot go on beating my daughter like that.'

My brother was very annoyed and said, 'It is my father who is trying to stop my sister from going back to her home.'

I told him, 'You can't simply send me back like that. Haven't you considered what my husband has done? He refused to sit on the chair when he came here first, and he stopped me from coming here again. When I insisted, he beat me.'

Most of the people in my home took the side of my father, and I stayed there. My brother was very anxious to keep his wife. The people told my husband to take back his sister, but he refused and said, 'I have come for my wife, not my sister.' So he went away.

My father told him, 'As you have turned out to be a bad man, if you want another wife, you had better come and get some goats from here. Then you can marry another woman but you can't keep my daughter.'

His sister stayed at my brother's, and she is still there. She has had two children. My brother began looking for a woman to exchange for me. Two women were brought, one from the Congo and one from Butama, but my brother refused both of them. Then Nyabandu was brought, whom the people at my home accepted. I went to her home, but I was unlucky. My husband used to beat me every day, so I did not want to stay with him. I conceived my elder daughter with him.

One day I had gone to the latrine, and this man followed and beat me there. After he had beaten me, I ran and stayed in the forest, and in the morning I went back to my home. My father said, 'I am not going to give this child away again, because they are treating her badly. Their sister has never had a beating since she came into this home.'

The people at my home said, 'It is not good to keep this child here at home while she is pregnant. Let her go back to her husband and have the child there. After that, we will get her.'

When that man followed me, the people at my home wanted to beat him, and they chased him away. But they sent me back and said, 'Go and have your child there, since it is the first child. Then you will come back here.'

So I went and had the child. Then I returned to my father's when the child was very young. She became very sick when she came into our home. They sent me back saying, 'Take back your child, because it may die here.'

When I returned, the child got well. It started up. When it was starting to walk, the man began to beat me again. I divorced him. When my father saw me, he said, 'You must not go back. If they want their child, let them come for it.'

My brother said, 'Koke had better go back, because I like my wife.'

But my father said, 'You aren't Koke's father.'

When I saw that my brother was pressing me to go back to my husband, I ran away to my mother. They came for me and took me back. I stayed a short time at my father's and then I ran away again, because my brother was trying to take me back to my husband. I went to my mother's father's home.

After I left my mother's father, I came and married Mpuga. The reason I married him quickly was that my brother began looking for me with a spear and saying that, whenever he saw me, he would kill me. Mpuga gave him some chickens for the capturing fee, but he refused them and said, 'I want my sister.'

When he accused Mpuga, saying, 'He has married the wife of a man who has paid bridewealth,' he lost the case.

They asked him, 'What kind of bridewealth was this? Goat or exchange?'

I said, 'Exchange.'

They said, 'That is not bridewealth.'

They asked my brother, 'Has Mpuga refused to pay you?'

He said, 'No.'

Mpuga said, 'He has refused the money I offered, the goats I offered, and the girl I offered.'

My brother said, 'If I see Koke, I will spear her.'

They told Mpuga to get some beer and that, before he took the beer to my father's home, he should send the daughter. After giving them this beer, they would give him the woman. On the day before Mpuga squeezed the juice to make the beer, I went off to my mother's and Mpuga went to the market. He met my father there. When my father asked him where I was, he said, 'She has gone to her mother's home.'

When my brother heard that, he came at night with some relatives to catch me at my mother's house. They took me back by a roundabout way. They were afraid to take me through the country near Mpuga's home, knowing that they would be caught. I got away from them when they stopped to drink beer at a friend's house, and I came and reached the path to Atube's home. Atube was one of the Bandin-yama elders. The people there took me and hid me at the house of Mpuga's sister. When my brother arrived at Atube's, he wanted to fight him. Atube was sleeping. My brother and his relatives took off his blanket and wanted to beat him with a stick. They looked for me in all the houses, but they could not find me. So my brother came to Mpuga's house while my father stayed up at Atube's. He learned that Mpuga had gone to see the blacksmith. The people there gave him a chair, but he refused to sit down. Mpuga returned very late in the evening and found my brother on the verandah. He told him to go into the house, but my brother refused. He continued to ask him to enter and finally he did. Lubangi cooked some food, but he refused to eat it and said, 'I want my sister.'

Mpuga told him to search all the houses in the village and that, if he found his sister, he could take her. Mpuga said, 'I didn't go with you when you went to Kirumia to get her.'

My brother stayed at Mpuga's homestead overnight, and my father stayed at Atube's. My brother said to Mpuga, 'You had better take me to Atube's,' and Mpuga agreed.

He passed Batigwa's house and told him, 'I didn't intend to go up there, but these people have lost their daughter, and they think I have her at Atube's.'

Batigwa said, 'All right, go with them. If you don't know anything about their daughter, what can you say?'

While they were on their way to Atube's, they met my father coming toward them. They asked him, 'What do you mean by losing your daughter and then coming to trouble us? Did you see us at her mother's house at Kirumia?'

Then Mpuga asked his elder brother, Atube, 'Have you seen the woman these people are bothering me about?'

Atube said, 'I told them to search all the houses, but they couldn't find her.'

After my father and brother went away, we came back to Bundin-yama with Mpuga. Three days after that my brother, with three boys, came here. Mpuga gave them six goats, which my brother refused saying, 'I want fifteen goats.'

Mpuga said, 'This is all I have. I will look for some more.'

My brother took four goats. He stayed away for a week and then came back. Mpuga gave him another goat which made five alto-gether. He said, 'I am going to give you nine goats, because she has had one child.'

My brother said that he would return the goats, because they were too few, but my father said, 'No, you take ten goats for my child. Am I in trouble that I need so many?'

They quarrelled between themselves and my brother said, 'I am going to give up the daughter. You had better get the boats by yourself.'

Mpuga gave them another goat which made six. Father reduced the number he asked for and told Mpuga to pay eight instead of ten. The six goats they took were paid to my first husband for his sister. That woman has had three children at our home. Whenever I go home, my brother tries to catch me and says, 'Mpuga must pay my goats before you go back.'

My father denies that and says, 'My child cannot leave her home because of these goats.'

Then my brother says to my father, 'You were the one who was willing for Mpuga to marry your daughter. I didn't like it myself.'

So I stayed at Mpuga's only through my father's influenza. My brother told Father, 'Go and get your eight goats, which you asked for Mpuga. I had asked him for fifteen, but you reduced it to eight. I didn't want Mpuga to marry Koke.'

My father said, 'My daughter cannot go marrying from one homestead to another all over the world. Even if Mpuga doesn't want to pay the two goats that he owes, let your sister stay there. You took my child to Buhulu, and she had a child there. Now she has gone to Bandinyama, and she has had a child there. Do you want her to go someplace else? I don't want my daughter to be married elsewhere. The Bahulu took their daughter (Koke's child) back after Koke had married again, and the Bandinyama will do the same if she is married someplace else. So I want her to stay in her home and raise her child. When the child she had at Buhulu went to Mpuga's, the child ate their totem, which made her sick. So it is not good. If this Mundinyama child is moved, he will also get the totem and won't stay well. If Koke dies among the Bandinyama, it is all right, but I don't want to carry her around from place to place.'

That is how I stayed in my home because of my father. My other brothers are young boys so they have nothing to say in the matter. I said to my brother Makoso, 'I can't leave my home. The place where you had married me was a bad one. The man used to beat me. Didn't you ever see me coming home crying and saying that my husband had beaten me? Your choice was not good. When you chose a husband for me, he became cruel.'

The last time I went to my home, my brother said that he wanted to take me to the Congo. I said, 'If you want to take me to the Congo, take the six goats back to Mpuga. Then you can take and exchange me wherever you like.'

He told a Congo man to come and see me. When the man arrived, he said, 'Is that my wife?'

L   149

I said to him, 'When did you marry me? I am not your wife, but the wife of a Mundinyama. To prove it, I have their child, and I have been paid for by them, so what do you mean by coming to see me?'

My brother has married a sister of that man from the Congo, so he wishes to exchange me for that girl. My father said, 'Is that why you married a Congo girl? Did you think you would exchange Koke for your wife? Can you get two bride payments for one girl?'

The man from the Congo said, 'I want to take my sister back, because this woman he has shown me has refused me.'

So he went back to the Congo, and I returned to Mpuga's homestead. Later when my people came to Mpuga's homestead, my brother told Mpuga, 'When your wife comes down to our home, she won't come back. We will exchange her for a wife from the Congo.'

My father contradicted him and said, 'Don't mind, Mpuga. These people won't be able to send my child away to the Congo without your knowing it.'

Father said, to his son, 'Did you capture the Congo girl by saying that you would exchange Koke for her?'

My brother announced to Father, 'I am going to leave you and go to Buganda, because I exchanged your daughter for a Muhulu and you brought her back. Now she is married to Mpuga. I want to exchange her in the Congo, but you have refused me.'

Then my father said, 'Is my one daughter going to pay for all the wives you need? She has so far paid me for a pair of wives for you. Your wife Muwisa has had two children. Was she not brought in by Koke? Did you pay goats or money for her? Koke also got you the daughter of the Bahulu. Two wives have been brought into this home by my daughter, so why are you persecuting her now?'

They quarrelled a lot, the son saying, 'It is you, Father, who gave Koke to Mpuga, and it is you who are swelling her head with power. I will leave all the children of my wives and go to Buganda, and it is you who will have to look after them. Whenever I say a word of advice to my sister, you don't agree with it. Since you have said that you brought that girl into the world by yourself and she has no brother to advise her, you had better own her by yourself.'

Father said, 'All right then, I will have her.'

Whenever I have any problems and go home with them, my brother sends me to my father and says, 'Go and tell that to your father. It is he who is your father. He is father and brother to you. Even if I hear that you have died at Mpuga's, I won't call there.'

Recently he passed my house and saw that I was having trouble with my breast, which was swelling. He went home and told my father, 'I saw your child. She was joking and playing and very happy.'

Koke

When my father went to the market, he heard, 'Your child is very sick.'

After he reached home, he quarrelled with my brother, 'You were very wrong to keep Koke's illness from me.'

My brother said, 'Don't you remember what I told you? I wanted fifteen goats, and you wanted eight, so I told you to go and see her whenever she was unhappy. If I hear that Koke's child is sick, I will go there, but not if Koke herself is sick.'

Father said, 'Give me the goats which were paid for Koke and go to your Buganda, as you have been threatening.'

Makoso said, 'It is not you who will show me the road to Kampala. Let me get my cotton harvested, get some money, and I will go to Kampala and lose sight of your daughter.'

When I go home, my brother does not like for me to go into his house. Whenever he sees me, he acts as though he has seen dung. He does not like to see me eating his sugar-cane. He always says, 'Go to your father's garden or to your mother's.'

Whenever he meets my mother, he quarrels with her because 'Mpuga did not get you from your father, but from your mother.'

He says, 'My enemies are your mother and father who showed you the way to this marriage, because Mpuga had been giving a lot of presents to your mother. That is to say, it is she who told you to marry Mpuga.'

Then my mother replies, 'I was right to tell her to go, because you had already got goats with which you paid for your wife.'

He used to answer mother, 'Goats? And only these few goats! Can six goats find me a wife?'

My father's brother was irritated by this quarrel, and he said to my brother, 'Can you make this girl marry?'

So he also became the enemy of my brother. He said, 'If you want to refuse to come into my house do so, because that child is my child also.'

Makoso said, 'All right. Treat her as your daughter. You can no longer trust me.'

One day he went to Mpuga's and found that I had gone to my mother's. He followed and found me with my mother at Kirumia and beat me. He went and told Mpuga, 'I have beaten your wife.'

Mpuga said, 'If you had beaten her here, I could have accused you in court. Are you allowed to beat a woman who isn't yours? If I accused you today, wouldn't they punish you? Did we marry this girl together? I have lived with her for four years, and I have never beaten her. Why have you come to beat her? I have paid you for your property. I think you didn't intend to beat the woman, but you wanted to fight with me. If you are a man, come and fight her again when she is here. When you get home, why don't you fight with your father? You have come far from Buganda, and you have beaten my wife for nothing. Is that not enough to put you in prison?'

Then Mpuga went to my father and said, 'I nearly fought with your son. Can any man beat his sister, even an old man like you?'

Father said, 'You are very silly. Why didn't you beat him, since he attacked you in your own home?'

Mpuga said, 'If he comes again, I will fight with him. And if I fail to beat him, I will take him to court. He can come and blame me for not paying his brideprice, but he can't beat my wife like that. My brother-in-law is becoming my enemy. He came once and fought with some people while I was away. If this had happened in my presence, what would have been the end of it?'

Father said, 'He acted very badly to do that, because when any sister marries, her brother visits her. What does he mean by beating children whenever they go to see their parents?'

My brother once went to the Congo and when he returned, he found that this wife had come to my house here. He came to get her and Mpuga was very annoyed by that. He said, 'Whenever he comes to my house, I welcome him with meat and we have a talk like men. Where did he get all this ill will? Whenever I go to his place, his wives cook for me without any trouble. In that case why don't I feel the same ill will?'

Finally my brother said, 'If I meet Mpuga today, I will fight him to the death.'

Mpuga said, 'If he wants to fight, it is all right. I can't give up going to my father-in-law's home. Did I do wrong to marry his sister? Have I speared her?'

My brother said, 'I want only Koke's child in my home. I don't want her or her husband here. When I hear that Koke is sick, I won't go to see her.'

When Mpuga's mother died, Lubangi, Atoku and myself were suspected of killing her, because we used to quarrel with her. His mother became sick and died while the women were out cultivating. She was left in the house over night. And we did not eat, because she was a woman of the goddess Nyakala. Mpuga was in Toro. In the morning they had to get something to heal the house. They got a white chicken, a white sheep and millet, and they cured the house. They killed the sheep and cooked the meat. Soon after the meat was ready, they buried Mpuga's mother, and then they ate the food. After that the people went away, and we went to get our own food which we ate.

At the first ceremony Atoku accused Lubangi and me, saying, 'You have said that I am the one who killed your mother. I am not. It is the wife of her son who killed her.'

I was not angry with Atoku for saying this, because once something is said, it is said, so there is no point in being angry about it. Lubangi tried to explain what she knew about the quarrel between Mpuga's mother and Atoku. Abongo was not accused at this time. The suspicion of him has come up recently, but Mpuga's mother died a long time ago. At the second ceremony after death, Atube, Batigwa and all the Bandinyama were present, and we killed and ate a goat. There was no trial.

KIHARA

When I was a baby at my mother's breast, I had yaws. At that time there were no hospitals where we could get injections, and yaws used to stay with us for a long time. When they wanted me to stop nursing, they put chili on the breast. I continued to suck because I did not mind the chili. When my mother saw that I would not leave the breast, she put some hen's droppings on it, and then I stopped. I was annoyed, because I wanted to continue sucking my mother's breast. I did not eat any food and, when the people saw that I was not eating, they bought meat and then I drank plenty of soup, which they had made. When my mother used to go to the garden, she would leave some plantains hanging in the house to keep me from crying. I could not reach them myself, but I asked other people to get them for me. I used to eat four a day. Sometimes they left banana juice in the house. When they were outside, I would go in and drink it.

I was also troubled by jiggers. At that time jiggers sometimes killed people. They had to cut the nail of my toe.

My sister Nyabonsikali was born after me. One evening late at night, my mother started to light a fire. When she started to light it she bore a child without any trouble. Then my father shouted to his older wife to come and help my mother; I was driven away. Two days after she had borne the child my mother was troubled in her stomach. After four days they took the child outside. The child cried. She cried for two days, and then my father went to consult diviners to see what was happening. They told him, 'One of your brothers who has died is the one who has caught your child. It is he who is making the child sick.'

The doctor told my father to get a knife and a stool and to put them at the head of the bed. Nyabonsikali grew up, but she died in childbirth.

When I was a small boy my younger sister had a sore on her knee. When my mother went to work in the garden, she used to tell me to look after the infant. One day an old woman came and she removed the bandage from the child's sore. She took the bandage away with her. When my mother came back from the garden, she found that the baby was dead. My mother thought that I had fallen down with the baby and killed it. I explained to her that an old woman had taken the bandage from the sore and that as soon as the old woman had gone away the baby died. The next day my father prepared poison for the poison ordeal. All the old women were collected together. My father said, 'If one of these old women has killed my child, as soon as she takes the poison she will die.' The old woman who had killed the baby fell down as soon as she tasted the poison. My father gave instructions that she should be taken to the pond, hit on the head, speared and thrown in the water.

Once when my father was hunting, he passed under a spear trap. The spear came down, went through his shoulder and came out of his left side, breaking two of his ribs. The people who were with him sounded the alarm. They shouted that the trap had killed a man. The spear had gone through him and was sticking in the ground. My father stayed there without moving. People brought an axe and they cut out the spear shaft. Then they carried him home. Many cuts were made on his body, and medicine was put in the cuts. Then he was carried to the house of relatives at Bundimulangi. While we were carrying him, we came to a river. We found that witches had dried the river and that there was no water in the place where we were going to cross. We asked ourselves, 'Why is it that there is only sand here when the river was full before?'

When we reached the house, he was treated again. When they washed his wound, they did not use water. They got a big pot and told the women to pass urine in it and then they washed him in that urine. In the night people came to the door and passed medicine through the door. They told the people inside, 'You just put this medicine in the wound.'

We stayed there for a month, and then he was well. After he had recovered, beer was prepared to take my father out of the house so that everybody might see that although he had almost died he was now well. When he was taken outside, he explained the cause of his injury. He said, 'It was my brother Kamyerungu who bewitched me.' He also said, 'Kumba and my wife Tembo are also involved in this matter. The reason my wife Tembo has bewitched me is that she has a lover. Tembo has been saying, "If I don't kill this man, Gambeki, I won't be able to marry my lover Bambuki." Also this man Bambuki sent a leopard, which killed the wife of one of the Bandinyama. What are you trying to do to me? You made a trap which recently injured me and you have sent a leopard to kill that woman. I will give you the poison ordeal.'

Six people took the poison. Three people vomited and three witches died (lost consciousness). The three witches were given another

155

medicine and came back to life. When they came back to life, each of them gave my father a goat and asked my father to forgive him.

One of them was very angry. He was a member of the Babukwanga lineage. He told the Babukwanga, 'Come, let us kill Gambeki. He has done a very bad thing to us.'

The Babukwanga and the pygmies came to attack us. When my father heard news of this, he beat the drum, collected together all the Bandinyama and then went to meet them on the path. Our people began to fight them. The Babukwanga speared one of our men. While our people were fighting, this man, Agbiye, died. Then the people on our side killed one of their men. During the fighting my father was struck in the back of the neck with an arrow. The arrow broke and the head stayed inside my father. He was carried home. The arrow-head was taken out with a knife, and my father recovered.

Later the Bandimulako lineage attacked my father. While they were still in Bundimulako the mother of Jungiye tried to prevent him from joining the party. She told her son, 'You must not go there to fight.'

Her son didn't listen to her; he jumped over her.

His father, who was an old man, said, 'You must not go there to fight.' Jungiye did not listen to him.

My father had built a fence and had some Toro with him who had rifles. One of the Toro shot Jungiye in the chest, and he fell down and died. The Bandimulako ran away. They did not go home, but stayed in the bush for three days.

When the war took place, two of my father's friends, Nyabases and Kwebuniera, from the Congo were with him. They used to eat human flesh. My father told his two friends to take the dead body and skin it and then they could eat the flesh. They brought the head and it was hung on the fence, and they carried away the flesh in their baskets. My father also put on the fence all the spears and shields which the Bandimulako had dropped when they ran away.

Because of the hatred between my father and the Bandimulako, my father said, 'It would be better for me to live farther away from these people, because they may try to kill me.'

Then he moved up near Bumadu and stayed there. Many of his children were born there. Once he came back to Bundinyama. Then a fire started and burned down all the huts, so my father decided to move back again.

When I was young I started to hunt, a thing I continue to this day. I got two spears and went out in the bush and I killed two pigs. While other people were cutting the meat, I went on and found another pig. It was a female and it had a young one with it. I speared the young one. Then the mother charged, and I climbed a tree. The tree tore the barkcloth off my body, but I was safe in the branches. When the pig went away I came down from the tree and went home. I told the people, 'I wounded a pig, but it escaped.'

The next morning I went with other people to look for it. We found it. Then it turned to fight. Before it turned to fight, it changed into an elephant. When we saw what had happened, we had to hide in the grass.

I made blood-brotherhood for the first time when I was still a young boy. I made it with Petero, a Toro. I met him at the county headquarters when I was there with my father. After Petero had seen me, he said to my father, 'I like your child. I would like him to become my brother.'

My father told me that it would be a very good thing to do this. He said, 'Sometime you will go into another country and you will find him there, and he will treat you properly. When you are in difficulty, he will help you.'

I told my father, 'I would like to have him as my blood-brother, but what am I going to give him? I have nothing.'

My father told me, 'Don't worry. I will give you anything he asks.'

Then we went to our home and made the blood-brotherhood. My father gave him a goat and said, 'This has been given to you by your brother.' Petero took a half shilling piece and tied it on my wrist.

Another Toro also came to my father's house. His name was Kikakuli. When he came down here he said to my father, 'I like your lineage and I wish I could make blood-brotherhood with someone in your lineage.'

My father replied, 'I, myself, am an old man and I do not think that I will ever go outside of Bwamba, but I would advise you to make blood-brotherhood with one of these young men who are able to visit different places.' Then my father mentioned my name; 'You should make blood-brotherhood with Kihara.'

We became blood-brothers. He gave me a bundle of salt, and I gave him a goat in return. After that he went to Muhokya in Toro. There is malaria at Muhokya, so I was afraid to visit him there. After a long time I heard that he had died.

Another person with whom (at a much later period) I became a blood-brother was Kapele, a Nyoro. That man made beds. Once my father asked him to sell him a bed. He refused to sell it, but told my father, 'I will give you one bed for nothing because you are an old man.' Then he made two more beds and he also gave them to my father for nothing. After he had made those beds my father thought it would be a good idea to make blood-brotherhood with him. He asked me to do it, and I agreed. My father gave me two goats, a female and a male goat, to give to him.

157

One day my mother took baskets of dried plantain flour to the market. When she passed Kapele's house, she saw him there in front of it. She greeted him and said to him, 'Are you not Kapele, who made blood-brotherhood with my son?'

He said, 'I don't know you and I don't know your son.' Kapele took those two baskets of dried plantain flour from my mother by force.

My mother said, 'Don't you remember that one day you drank my son's blood? Now you want to take my two baskets for nothing. If you really drank my son's blood, you can take those two baskets for nothing and eat the dried banana flour.'

My mother returned home. When she arrived, she explained to my father what had happened. After he had heard this, on the next day, very early in the morning, at the first cock-crow, my father went out and collected some medicines and brought them home. My mother put a pot with some water in it on the fire. It was the same pot in which maize flour had been cooked on the day the blood-brotherhood with Kapele had been made. My father put the medicine in the pot. Then he said, 'Kapele, if you made blood-brotherhood with my son, you will not live through this year. Your stomach must swell.'

Two months later we heard that Kapele's stomach had swollen like that of a leper. At his death his stomach burst. On that day I realized that the things that my father told me were true. He told me, 'If you make blood-brotherhood with someone, and if you try to cheat him, you will die and all your lineage will be destroyed.'

One day a friend of my father who was staying with him was drinking beer at a nearby house. He saw a man passing by. He got a spear and tried to spear him. A Toro who was also at the beer party prevented him from doing that. The Toro said to my father's friend, 'Why should you kill that man? He is only passing by; he has done nothing to you.'

The man replied, 'Never interfere in matters you do not understand.'

They continued drinking. Later the man threw the spear at the Toro and killed him. The man ran away and hid in the bush. The affair was reported to the county chief, and he told the people to go and look for the man. My father was arrested because the man was his friend. The county chief told my father to bring the man to him. My father went home, got out his drum and beat it. The people came together and then went into the bush. We found the man hiding in a tree. We caught him and brought him back to my father's house. My father killed three chickens for him. Then he took him to the county chief. The chief dug a hole, put the man in it and piled sand up to his neck. He stayed there for four days, and then he was taken out.

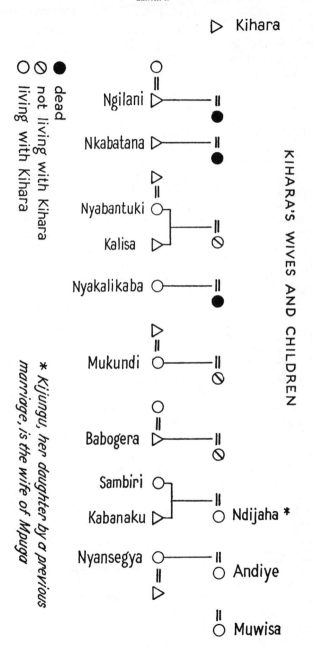

KIHARA'S WIVES AND CHILDREN

● dead
⊘ not living with Kihara
○ living with Kihara

* Kijungu, her daughter by a previous marriage, is the wife of Mpuga

159

The county chief sent him to Fort Portal with two policemen. All the Bandinyama accompanied him to Fort Portal. He was charged with murder and sentenced to death. The District Commissioner told us, 'This is a warning to all you Amba. You must not kill each other. You must know from this day that the one who kills his neighbour will die himself.'

My first wife was Bagilahini of the Bagarama.[1] I got her by exchanging my sister with her brother, Abasigo. I lived with her about a month before we had intercourse. She did not refuse me, but my penis could not penetrate her vagina. I tried my best to penetrate her, but I failed. I told her, 'You must go back to your home.'

She returned to her home. After she left me she stayed there for three years, and then she was married by another man. She produced a child but at the time of the birth she nearly died.

As soon as she had left my home I married another girl, the daughter of Makakeyo, a Muhundu. I eloped with her from her home when she was a young girl. I gave the Muhundu five chickens because I had captured her, and later I paid them brideprice. After I had stayed with her a while, I learned many things: she was not clean and also she was something of a witch. She was the first woman to produce a child for me. She produced Ngilani. I wasn't satisfied with her habits, so I got rid of her. After she left my house, she went home where she stayed until she died.

Since that time I have had very many wives; I do not remember all of them. Once my father cultivated a very large garden of sweet potatoes, but some pigs came and ate them, so my father asked the people to help him kill those pigs. As they were going through some elephant grass, my father saw a movement in it. He thought that the movement had been caused by one of the pigs. The movement was not caused by a pig, but by my brother. My father speared my brother in the right shoulder. The spear went through his body. I took it out, and he died as he was holding on to my legs.

My father thought it best to send for a doctor, who would tell him what was happening in our lineage. The doctor came and prepared poison for the poison ordeal. We put it in three big pots, cooked it and gave it to the people. All of us had to drink it in order that those who were putting out medicine to kill the people of our lineage might die. Two women and two men from outside the lineage were caught. My father said to them, 'These are the people who bewitched me so that my son would be killed.'

One of his wives was related to the people who were sending the medicine. During the night she went out and ran away with those people. When my father went out to look for them, he could not find

[1] Kihara claims to have had more than thirty wives.

160

them. Then he knew that they were the ones who were making trouble and sending medicine to destroy the lineage. He decided to make war against those people who had killed his son. Two members of that lineage were wounded, but none of them died.

Then my father decided to consult the diviners in order to find out which people were trying to destroy his lineage, so that he could fight them. The two diviners advised him to go to Bumati and fight the Bamati, because they were causing all the trouble.

At that time I was a young man and had never been in such a great fight. My father asked me to go to my mother's brother to get spears and shields, so that we could go and fight those people who were trying to destroy our lineage. After I had collected spears and shields from my mother's brother, my father called all the members of our lineage to come and join him in the war.

My father gave me a new spear which he had had made for me. We started our journey and passed the people of Bundibugyo. They stopped my father and told him that he had no right to pass through their village. They said, 'If you are trying to pass here by force, we will fight with you.'

My father preceded most of our people; only my brother Kamohanda and I were with him. Then we heard a great noise behind us. I said to my father, 'Our people are fighting back there.'

He replied, 'No, you are telling lies. Nobody is fighting back there.'

The three of us went back and found some of the Bandibugyo and some of our people fighting. Two of the Bandibugyo had been wounded. We tried to get to our people to help them, but we found that they were surrounded by the Bandibugyo. After we had forced our way through the Bandibugyo and stood with our people, my father said that the wounded should be taken home. When they had been taken away, one man came and threw a spear at my shield, and a second one came and did the same thing and then a third and a fourth. What I did was to stand in front of my father and catch the spears on my shield. While my father was standing smoking a pipe, a man came and speared him in his side. My father was lying on the ground, and I wanted to go and spear the one who had wounded him, but a man called Ruganda who was with us came behind me and caught my arm. He said, 'Don't spear that man. He may not be as healthy as your father.' So I did not spear him and he ran away.

Later, in the middle of the night, we followed the enemy and found them sitting beside a fire. When we prepared to spear them, an old man who was with us, Makina, said, 'Don't spear them.'

We said, 'Why should you stop us from killing them, since they have already wounded some of our people?'

He dissuaded us from spearing them, so we returned home. When

161

we arrived home, my father was lying on the ground, and some of our people were making noise. I said, 'I will blow a trumpet so the people will know that some of the men of our lineage have been seriously wounded. Then they will come and they can take the wounded men somewhere to be treated.'

A man called Kulibatanga was treating my father. Someone shouted, 'The man is dying.'

We were very upset. There were nine of us, and we got spears and shields in order to attack the enemy again. On the way I fell down, and the others told me that it would be better for me to go back, so I returned home. Later they returned, and we planned another attack. On the way we found a man, Kahigwa, talking to his wife. They were talking about my father. He said, 'People have done a bad thing to spear that man, since he is a ruler of a country. They should have speared another man instead.'

Some of the people of my lineage were afraid to spear Kahigwa, but I was angry because my father had been wounded, so I rushed in and speared him. He tried to get up and run away, but he fell down again in a maize garden. I was unable to pull my spear out of his body, but other people helped me and we got it out. While we were carrying the dead man, we met two of his relatives. We hid in the bush and then threw the corpse away.

We returned home and later made still another attack. A woman called Nakibonda was killed by a man called Batoga. People were not pleased with him. They told him, 'You should not have killed that woman. You should have killed a man instead. The woman was not involved in the war.'

We then planned to make an attack with many people on the Amba at Bundibugyo, at the county chief's headquarters. When we attacked, there were Toro with rifles fighting on the side of the Amba of Bundibugyo. The Toro shot two members of our lineage, and all the rest of our men ran away, leaving their spears and shields behind. After running a short distance they stopped. One of our men, who had been wounded in the knee, lay in the grass. He had his bow and arrows with him. When the enemy came near the place where he was lying, he tried to shoot one of them with his bow, but he could not manage to hit the man. Another man rushed by and shot that enemy with his arrow.

When that man was struck with an arrow, the rest of the enemy ran away. They said, 'There's a man back there who is wounded, but he has his bow and arrows with him and he has killed a Toro.' Then they came back in a group and killed him.

After that great battle everyone stayed in his house. No one went out to visit. The king of Toro sent a chief, Hamu Rumili, and another man, Nakadimo Kakulora, to Bwamba. They brought an army armed with rifles. In this battle I was not able to kill a person, but I did kill fifty-two hens, and while our army was retreating I killed three more.

We camped at a place called Ngamba. There my father was arrested and accused of having killed his son. He was sent to Fort Portal, where he was tried and sentenced to jail for two years. He was also told to repay people for the damage he had done during the course of the fighting. I was also arrested and charged with having killed the man whom I had speared. I pleaded guilty and said that I had killed him in revenge, because my father had been speared. I was released and allowed to go home.

While my father was in jail circumcision took place. Our mothers had to go down to the Semliki flats to get fish and meat for us so that we could be circumcised. While I was being cut, I stood with my spear in one hand and a trumpet in the other hand. Shortly after the ceremony a small animal was seen, and we were told to go and kill it. We were told to go with the pygmies. There were many of us in that group, but all of the others failed to kill it; I was the one who shot it. People tied grass together, and we wore one bunch in front and one behind. Then two large huts were built in the bush, and we lived in those until we were well. We used to go out hunting and kill snakes, rats and other kinds of small animals. People prepared two pots of hot water, and two pots of cold water and this water was put on us every day before we had our meals. While we were in those huts, the people who were living at home were not supposed to argue with each other. If they did, we took all of their goats, hens and other things. Many unusual things had to be done. When a person had been to the latrine, he did not use leaves, but had to clean himself on his leg. The old man who was looking after the boys used to take out his penis and say, 'Come, blow it like a whistle', and if the boy did not blow it, he was beaten.

When a boy became well, he was given a spear and told not to stand in one place but to walk around the village until evening. When we left the huts, we were told that the old man would burn them and that we were to walk away looking down at the ground; we were not to look at the sun. After we had been taken out of the huts, they held a big dance which lasted throughout the night. We were painted with red and white paint, and we were taken into the village. We were covered with dried plantain leaves. Our mothers were told to go and identify their sons. If a mother failed to identify her son, she was fined. Some of the mothers found a way to know their sons. Someone who had seen the boys before they were covered with leaves would tell the mother, 'Your son is the fourth one from the right.'

For a month afterward the boy was not supposed to speak. Whenever a relative came and greeted him, the relative had to pay him fifty cents. If the person were a member of his lineage he had to pay him a shilling. Then we were allowed to do so. At first the wives had to pay us two shillings. For another four months we were not allowed to eat any meat or to eat any chickens, but we were allowed to eat fish.

Not long after my circumcision, some women saw two elephants when they were going to fetch water from the river. When they came back, they told us about it. We found the two elephants. They had dug a hole and there was water in it. They were bathing there. We made plans to go and kill them. There were eight of us. We took our spears and went to kill the elephants. One of them was injured. We got very close to them. Then I told the men who were with me, 'You wait here. I will go and spear the one which is injured.'

As I approached, the elephant saw me and charged. I fell down, and it passed over me. It looked for me but could not find me. I was lying on the ground stretched out and thinking, 'Perhaps I may die today.' After it had tried to find me and failed, it turned away. I got up and ran, leaving my spears behind. When I got up, it saw me and it charged again. As it charged it broke a branch of a tree, which cracked with a sound like a gun. I managed to get away and after the elephants had gone away, I went back and collected my two spears. But I didn't want to follow them again.

We all went home. When I reached my house, I killed a chicken and ate it, because I had been about to die. Ever since then, whenever I see an elephant, I never try to attack it.

On one occasion my father's brother was told to select a man to go to work at the county chief's headquarters, but the man refused to go. Then two parish chiefs came and they took a sheep belonging to my father's brother. After it had been taken, my father's brother went and asked the man whom he had selected, 'Why did you refuse to go? Now my sheep has been taken because of you.' He tried to force the man to go, but the man absolutely refused. They started to fight. The county chief and sub-county chief said that he should be shot. But fortunately they missed him when they fired. He ran away and went into the bush. After a while he came back to my father and told him, 'You take me to the county chief's headquarters.' My father took him there and he was arrested. He was sentenced to three months of hard labour. After that my father's brother's sheep was given back to him.

What I noticed about that brother of my father was that when he used to drink beer with other people he would try to spear someone. That was his habit. He might even spear his wife. Before he died he had changed into a wild animal as far as his habits were concerned.

Kihara

A Traditional Elder

One night we had a very heavy rain. At the time I was living in one of my father's houses. My father's lineage brother, Kibita, and some other people were also staying there. The house leaked, but there was no leak over the place where I was sleeping. As a result, although other people moved here and there, I kept quiet. I saw Kibita moving about so I asked him to come and sleep with me in my bed. He replied, 'My boy, it is very bad for you to call me to come and sleep in the same bed with you, because you look upon me as a father. Now you are grown up and you have your wife. It is not our custom to sleep in one bed with a person who is full grown.'

While it was raining, Kibita came near my bed while I was asleep and he touched me. When he had touched me, I awoke and asked, 'Who is that?'

He replied, 'It is I. I am merely trying to find a place to sleep.' I remained quiet. He had already bewitched me with his medicine.

The next day my father killed a chicken, and food was prepared and served to us in our dining hall. My father started to distribute chicken to us. When I began to eat I found that I had lost my appetite. My father asked me, 'What is the matter with you?'

I told him, 'My stomach does not feel right.'

While I was holding a piece of meat in my hand, Kibita took it from me. They asked him, 'Why did you do that?'

He told them, 'I did that because it was I who circumcized this boy, but since that time he has never given me a chicken.'

My mother told him, 'You have done a bad thing. Although he is now married, he has not built his house. When he has built it, you should go to it and ask him to give you a chicken.'

My father told him, 'Well, you take that piece of meat and eat it.'

The next day my father asked Katano, Kibita and myself to go to the house of a friend of his in the Congo to get some maize. I did not feel well on the trip there. We spent three days there, but I did not eat anything. When we arrived there, I became ill. The man whom we had gone to see gave us a chicken, but I could not eat any of it. Kibita ate it by himself.

The day we began our journey home, I was very weak, and the others left me and Kibita behind. When we had gone halfway, I felt very ill and thought, 'I may die on the way.'

I said to Kibita, 'It is you who have done this to me. If I am to die on the way home, I will kill you.' He was very frightened; he took one path and I took another. I went through Bubandi, and he went through the forest.

When we arrived home, my father asked us, 'Why did you separate on the way?'

I told him, 'This man was afraid of me because I told him that I

M   165

would have to kill him on the way. It was he who bewitched me.'
Then I told my father what had happened on the night it had rained.

My father looked for medicine, and he brought some and gave it
to me. When I had been given the medicine, a very big creature with
many legs came out of my body. After that I recovered.

Kibita was a younger brother of the father of Abongo. All of the
people of that lineage were witches with the exception of Mosumba,
the father of Mpuga.

One day when I was at home looking after my garden, the chiefs
came to me and told me, 'You have been selected to be a porter for
a Toro prince.'

The prince planned to take us all the way to the salt lake at Katwe.
There is much fever there, and I was afraid that I might die of it.
When we reached Bunyangabo (in Toro), we put our loads down and
ran away. We returned home. When I arrived home, I was asked by
the county chief, 'Where did you leave your load?'

I told him, 'As soon as I reached the Bunyangabo rest camp, I put
the load in the camp and ran away.'

They put me in jail for four days. When they took me out, I was
given twenty-five lashes. There were seven of us, and the county
chief told us, 'You will be sent to Fort Portal and imprisoned
there.'

We went to the Toro government jail there and then we were transferred to the British government jail. We slept there. On the following
day we were taken to the District Commissioner. He asked why we
had been put in jail. My six companions failed to explain properly
what had happened. When the District Commissioner asked me,
I explained the matter to him. I said, 'There was a prince of Toro.
He was on safari in Bwamba. When he was leaving Bwamba, we
were told to carry his things to the Bunyangabo rest camp and then
to come home. We carried the things to the Bunyangabo rest camp,
and when we arrived there we left them in the rest camp. The only
thing is that we didn't tell anybody that we were going back to our
homes. When we came back, we were arrested and put in jail for four
days. After I had been in jail, I was taken out and given twenty-five
lashes. I have already been punished. If you want me to be punished
a second time, my lord, it is up to you.'

The District Commissioner released me, and I came back home.

The first year that we were asked to pay poll tax, I refused to pay
it. There were about seven of us who refused. We got our bows and
arrows and went to stay with Mosumba. We were there for a week.
The matter was reported to the county chief, and he made plans to
come and arrest us. He had two rifles. One night while we were still
at Mosumba's house, I went out to urinate about midnight. When I

came back to the house, I told the other people, 'I have dreamed that people are coming to arrest us.'

A short time later we heard people coming. These people surrounded the house. After they had arrested us, the other six men were tied together with a rope. I absolutely refused to be tied. I caused a great disturbance there till the break of day. They did not put a rope on my neck. They told me to walk with them without a rope. When we arrived at the county chief's headquarters, we found about a hundred and fifty people who had also been caught. They were going to be sent to work on the road between Kampala and Fort Portal. I told the county chief that I was not going to go with that group to work on the road. When he realized that I had refused, he told me to go as a headman. Then I agreed to go with the rest.

When we arrived there, I looked after my people. But one day another headman said to me, 'You are not looking after your people properly. Your men are not carrying full baskets of earth.'

I told him, 'You must realize that these people are human beings like yourself and are not to be given heavy things.' I also told him, 'You yourself cannot carry a full basket of earth, because it is very heavy.'

He said to me, 'Will you put one on my head?'

I said, 'Yes, I can do that.'

I got a basket full of earth and put it on his head. Then we started to fight. After people had separated us, the man went and reported the matter to the European who was in charge. I was summoned, but I did not admit anything in the presence of the European. I told him, 'This man told me that my men have been going very slowly and that they are not carrying full baskets of earth. But I told him that, "those baskets are very heavy." I also told him, "You must look after your men and I will look after my men".' I won the case.

After that quarrel, we lacked only three days in order to complete one month's work. Since I only had to work three more days, I was told that I had better go with a group of porters carrying goods for a European going to Fort Portal. Then I worked for two days in Fort Portal. After I had completed those two days we were paid, and the District Commissioner asked us if we wanted to continue our work and go back to the road camp. We refused. We told him, 'We want to go back to our homes.' After that we returned to Bwamba and paid the poll tax.

I tried to marry many women, but one of my father's wives made some medicine and bewitched me so that I was unable to marry women. I told my father, 'One of your wives has bewitched me so that I may not marry women.'

My father asked, 'Are your sure? Can you tell me which one?'

I said, 'Yes.' I pointed out the wife to my father, and the woman cried for about three days.

Later when I was alone in my house that woman came and said to me, 'You told your father that I have bewitched you so that you may not marry women. Now I ask you to go and bring the woman whom you want to marry.'

That night I went to the woman whom I loved and brought her to my home. After that I married as many other women as I wished.

Later that wife gave birth to a child. The child died soon after because the mother had no milk. I was very disappointed when I lost my child, so I sent the woman away. When I asked her father to return the brideprice, she told him not to return it. After that I accused her brother in court, and he refused to repay it. The chief asked if any man in the court wanted to marry the woman. One man wanted to marry her, so he paid the brother and the brother repaid me. For a while I worked as a policeman under the sub-county chief, Silwano Bakabagani. He was called the 'keeper of Bwamba' because at the time he came to Bwamba he found the people here were very dangerous, but he controlled them. At that time policemen did not receive a salary. When you were sent to arrest someone, before arresting him, you told him, 'I have been sent to take you.' Then he had to pay you two shillings, one shilling for one leg and one shilling for the other leg. A man wanted to do that because, after he had given you money, you had to treat him properly while he was in jail. When he was released from jail, he had to bring you a chicken which was known as 'the jail-breaker'. However, I had many wives, and there was no one to look after them and no one to do my work, so I asked permission to resign from the job.

I worked as an unofficial assistant parish chief for about two years, but it was very hard work. I found that you had to wake up very early in the morning when you were wanted by the sub-county chief at the sub-county headquarters. I realized that I was wasting my time, because I was gaining nothing from that job. When I asked to leave the job, I was told that I would be promoted to be a paid assistant parish chief. I worked at that for about two years. My only job was to collect the poll tax.

One day I had collected about one hundred and fifty shillings and I came to a certain man who refused to pay his poll tax. I caught one of his female goats and brought it down to the sub-county chief's headquarters. After I had handed over the money, the sub-county chief said to me, 'Take the goat with you and keep it at your home.'

I took the goat home with me. It was almost ready to give birth.

At that time there was a young girl at my house. While she was preparing plantains, the goat came near where she was sitting on the ground and ate a piece of plantain. The girl struck the goat with her knife. When I told the sub-county chief that the goat had been injured by a young girl, the chief told me, 'You will have to keep that goat because I doubt whether the owner of the goat will agree to take the goat back once he has paid his tax.'

When I returned home, I thought it would be best to kill the goat and eat it, as the owner was not going to take it back. I killed it and told my wives to cook it. We ate it. Two days later the owner came to my place and asked me for his goat. I told him, 'Your goat died.'

I went with him to the headquarters of the sub-county chief. The chief told me, 'You will have to give the owner two goats.' I gave them to him, but I was very much annoyed about that. As a result I asked permission to leave the job. When I spoke to the sub-county chief, he told me, 'You must not leave the job.'

I told him, 'I'm getting nothing out of this job. I have my coffee plantation, my wives and seven goats. Why should I continue with this job?' I went home.

Once we became involved in a fight with the Bamadu people, and some of them were injured. The parish chief stopped the fight. On the following morning two policemen came to take me to the headquarters of the sub-county chief. They said that I had started the trouble and caused other people to fight. I refused to let those policemen take me, and they went back to the chief. He then sent four policemen to get me. I got two spears and stood in the doorway of my house. After two days I decided that I should present myself to the county chief. I asked my father to accompany me, and when I went there my father stood behind me. When the county chief saw me, he said to me, 'I don't want to look at you. Put him in jail.'

I was put in jail. I stayed there for a week with eight other people. When the case was heard we were fined fifty shillings apiece.

One day my father brewed beer. He told me, 'You must not drink this beer during the daytime.'

I went out looking for women, and, when I came back late in the evening, my father gave me one pot of beer. While we were drinking, my father, who was standing a short distance away, threw a spear at me. It did not hit me but went into the ground near where I was sitting.

I pulled the spear out of the ground and told him, 'I am going to kill you too.' I asked him, 'What is the matter with you? What are you trying to do to me?'

Then his wives hid him in the house. I tried to open the door to get in. One of his wives was pregnant, and, when I pushed her, she fell down and had miscarriage. She was carrying twins. People prevented me from fighting with my father. I asked him, 'Why should you kill me for no reason?'

He replied, 'I have been told that you have been having intercourse with my wife.'

I told him, 'I have never done that.'

My father gave poison to a dog, and he said, 'If it is true that my son is having intercourse with my wife, the dog will die.'

The dog vomited. My father said, 'It is not true that you have been doing such a thing.' He gave me a big ram. I bought some beer and killed the ram. We all ate the meat. From that time until his death, father and I were on good terms.

After his death, the woman with whom they suspected I had had intercourse asked me to marry her. I refused, for if I had accepted, the people would have thought that the accusation of my father had been true.[1]

One night as I was coming home from a beer party I saw a group of garden witches. There were about fifty of them. They told my father, 'If you don't warn your son not to walk during the night-time, we will send an animal to kill him.'

The following day my father came to me and asked me what I had seen during the night. I told him, 'I didn't see anyone, but I heard people hiding in the elephant grass.'

My father told me, 'Whenever you are drinking beer late at night, stay where you are for the whole night. Never go by yourself at night. Those people have an animal which will kill you, because you are disturbing them before they finish their work.'

Since that time I have given up my habit of walking during the night-time. I just stay at home at night. Whenever I pay a visit somewhere, I never try to come home at night, but stay where I am.

I once had a new wife called Mwabolina. At that time my senior wife, Nguleya, had a child. One day Nguleya had to leave her house. She left the new woman in charge of the child. When she had gone, Mwabolina took her knife out and put it on the neck of the child. She said, 'It would be good if I were to cut off your head.'

A swelling developed on the child's neck on the side where the knife had been placed.

When Nguleya returned, she found that her child was not feeling well. I did not see the new wife putting the knife on the neck of the child, but, since other people told me that it had happened, I had to believe it. At first, though, I thought that perhaps my senior wife Nguleya was trying to convince me that the new wife was a witch when she was not really one. The other people, however, told me, 'Your wife is a witch.'

[1] Kihara later married this woman whose name was Kageye. See page 195.

170

One day I realized that they were right. During the night she left me in bed and went and put her head upside down. I could see clearly what she was doing. She was standing at the door putting her head upside down. The next day Nguleya's child died. They told Nguleya, 'It is this woman, Mwabolina, who has killed the child.'

After I had seen what she had done during the night-time, I called my father. The new wife went to her home and called her brothers. Her brothers came to my house. I told them what I had seen her doing.

Her brothers told her, 'Why did you ask us to come here? Do you want to make us ashamed? Now your husband has told us what you have done. You have called us that we might be killed. You have made us ashamed in front of our brother-in-law. If it were not for the fact that Europeans are ruling this country, this man could have killed us today.'

After that I sent that woman away, and she went to her home. When she left, she was pregnant. I never saw her again. When I heard that she had given birth, I bought a shilling's worth of salt and three shillings' worth of dried meat. I gave the salt, the meat, a bunch of plantain and a piece of bark-cloth to my mother, who took them to her. The reason I asked my mother to take these things to her was that I did not want to see that woman again with my own eyes. I did not even want to see the child because, if I had seen the child, it would have reminded me of the child she had killed. In addition, I thought that she was going to kill her own child. My mother came back and told me that the woman had borne a son. Two months later I sent my mother to her again with more things.

Some time later, I heard that the child's little finger had been cut off by its mother. After its finger had been cut off, the child died.

I went to her home for the death ceremony. I told her brothers, 'Now have you seen what this woman has done? She denied that she was a witch when my other child died, but now she has killed this one too by cutting his finger.'

Then we made a case, and her brothers admitted that she was wrong to have done that. After finishing all those matters I came home.

Two months later I heard that the woman herself had died. I said, 'Amen,' and I thanked God. I said, 'She killed those children and she thought that she would not die. Now God has punished her.'

After that child died, I married a Mumbutuku who was light brown in colour, and I caused her to become pregnant. One night, after I had brought her home and while we were in bed, she got up and lighted a fire. After the fire was going she urinated in it. I saw her do it and I thought, 'Why did she light the fire and then urinate in

171

it? She realized that I had awakened so she lit the fire again. She heated water and brought it to me. I refused it. Just before daybreak she got out of bed again. She took a small calabash which we used for drinking water and she urinated in it. When she brought that urine to me, I refused it. I told her, 'Is that the way they do things in your home? Do you urinate in things people use for drinking?'

I had been keeping her in the house of my father. The next day I left her in that house and went to my own house. The day after that she followed me to my house and spent the night there with me. In the morning she asked me to go and gather firewood with her.

I told her, 'It is not my custom to accompany a woman when she is going to collect firewood.'

She insisted on it, so finally I went with her to the forest. When we got there, she summoned a very big snake which chased me. I ran and sounded the alarm. While the snake was chasing me, the woman stood there laughing at me. I thought, 'Why should this woman laugh at me while the snake is chasing me?'

Other people arrived. I told the woman, 'I am going to kill you because you ordered the snake to chase me. You wanted me to be killed by that snake.'

When I told the woman that I was going to kill her, the snake disappeared. Then I told her, 'Let us go home.'

When we arrived at the house, I told her, 'You must not enter my house. If you go in, I will kill you.'

She ran away and went back to her family. I killed two of my chickens to make a feast because I had escaped being killed by that snake.

I married a very beautiful woman called Musongokali. When I brought her home my father told me to stay with her in one of his houses until I could build a house for her. Whenever I slept in the same bed with her, I felt as though I had been struck by stones. I told her that I was not going to sleep in her bed any more, because whenever I slept in it I slept as though I were a dead body.

Musongokali told me, 'No, you wait. You will be all right.'

She was a doctor and she had a very big bag full of medicines. One night she woke me up about midnight and told me, 'Let us go outside.'

'Where are you taking me?'

She said, 'Come out.'

I went out with her. We went among the plantain trees, and she cut four leaves from a type of plantain called *nzira bahuma* and put them on the ground. She told me to stand on them. She brought her bag and put it down and then she started to make many small cuts on my body. She made a small cut on every joint of my body. She had called her brother and he was also there. After they had done this, they took me up on the roof of my house and there they did the same thing again, making cuts in all my joints. Then we came down from the roof, and they took me to the path leading to the latrine, where they did the same thing again there. After that they brought me back home. We slept.

Early in the morning I went to see my father and told him, 'This woman is going to kill me. She has many kinds of medicine. Last night she made many cuts on my body and put medicine into them.'

My father asked me, 'Is she really a witch?'

I told my father, 'Yes, she is a witch, and you are the one who forced me to marry her by telling me that she was a beautiful girl whom I should marry. I don't want to stay here with her. I want to go away to my house.'

My father advised me to wait until he could observe what she was doing. He said that if I were not satisfied, then I could go to my house. I didn't pay any attention to what my father had told me. Instead, I waited until she was about ready to go to bed and then I ran down to my house. About three or four days later, as I was sitting in front of my house, I saw her coming down the hill from my father's house with all her things. I thought, 'Why should this woman follow me?'

I asked my senior wife, 'Why should this woman come here when I left her at my father's home?'

I went to my father and he told me, 'Don't send her away. Let her stay at your home. If you see that she is still doing these things that you complained about, then you can decide what to do.'

My senior wife prepared food for the new woman. While she was preparing the food, the new woman went and collected some medicines. Later the new wife came to me and showed me the medicines. She said, 'See what your wife has cooked for me.'

I told her, 'I have lived with this wife for a long time and I have never seen her mixing medicine in the food which she has cooked. You are telling lies. It is you who gathered the medicine plants.'

The new wife and I argued. Finally I told her, 'You are lying. What you are trying to do is to make me get rid of my old wife. I won't send my old wife away because of you. If you want to, you can go home. But I won't send her away.'

After I told her that, she went away. That woman went from one man to another, staying one night here and one night there. Finally she went away to Toro, where she died.

Before my father died, he taught me how to circumcise. He told me, 'Since I am getting old, you should know how to carry out circumcision.'

I agreed with him, and when circumcision next took place in

Bwamba, I circumcised twenty men in one place, thirty in another and fifty in another. After circumcision had ended in Bwamba, we went up to the Konjo on the mountain. One day there I circumcised sixty people, the next day ninety and on the third day thirty. A month later, one of the people who had been circumcised died. We heard from the chiefs that the ones who had carried out the circumcision were wanted by the government. All the men who had been circumcisers were brought together. But the government did not punish us. The government said it was all the fault of the county chief who allowed circumcision to take place in his county. The county chief was demoted, and we had a new chief. As a result of all this, the government prohibited circumcision, and since that time circumcision has never taken place.

Once my father sent me to get his pipe, which he had left in the house of one of his wives. When I arrived at the house, I found that his wife was not there. I opened the door, went into the house and discovered the pipe under the bed. When I looked at it, I saw that the bowl was full of medicine. I did not take the medicine out, but took the pipe to my father. When he saw the medicine in it, he said, 'Who has done this thing? This wife has put medicine in my pipe. Perhaps she is trying to kill me. Or perhaps she is trying to get me to send away my other wives.'

Later in the day when that woman came home, my father called for her. He gave her twelve strokes. Then the woman told him that she would never do it again. But my father did not keep her with him.

My father had a wife whom he had married when she was a very young girl with small breasts. One day I was in the forest, and this girl also came into the forest to collect firewood. I heard a roar like that of a lion. I thought it might be an animal, so I sounded the alarm. I started to strike out with my stick. Then I heard her cry and she told me, 'Don't kill me, my husband's son,' and I realized that she had made the noise.

My father refused to give me any money. He told me, 'If you kill my wife, then I am going to go to the doctor's and kill yours. When you went to consult the diviner, you went by yourself, but I want other people to go with you again in order to hear what the diviner says.'

My father selected four people to go with me.

I took a shilling and two chickens for the diviner's fee. The diviner had a horn which could dance, and it took a strong man to hold it still. The diviner took the horn and tied it to a pole by a string. Then the horn said, 'Why have you called upon me?'

I said, 'It is I, Kihara, calling. I want you to tell me who has killed my sister.'

The horn told me, 'The one who killed your sister is the one who is cooking for you now.'

I asked, 'Can you tell me the name of the woman?'

'The person is your father's wife, Mohanika. She got the medicine from a lover.'

The four men and I arrived home before night-time. When we arrived, my father asked me, 'What were the results?'

I told him, 'I am not going to explain anything. You sent four men with me; they will tell you everything.'

These men told him everything which had happened in the house of the diviner. The information which they gave him was the same as that which I had given him previously. Because he was living with that woman he did not say anything to other people. He kept the matter a secret. When other people asked him about it, he told them other things, but he did not tell them what the horn had said to us. I told my father that he should let me tell everyone everything about this matter, and then everyone would know what was the cause of my sister's death.

My father's reply to this was: 'You, Kihara, want to be in my place before I die.' Again he told me, 'You will take my position after my death, but you won't take it now, because I am still alive.'

Then I told my father, 'You like this woman because she is beautiful, but one day she will kill you.'

My father kept quiet. One day that woman had intercourse with another man, and when she came back home, she infected her husband with worms. When he was infected, that woman told us nothing. Instead she took my father by herself and carried him on her back to the diviner's. When she was carrying him, she dropped him on some stones. Then we had a message that we had better go and get our father. We heard that he had fallen on stones and had broken some of his bones. We left home, and we found our father and that woman. We asked the woman, Mohanika, 'Why did you take our father and not tell us that you were doing so? Our father has sons, and you should have informed us. Why should you take him away by yourself?'

Mohanika did not answer; she kept quiet. We took up our father and carried him to the house of another doctor. That doctor was unable to cure him. Then my father sent for another doctor called Babisiani. We went to see him and brought him to our father. On that day he collected his medicine, and on the next day we took our father and the doctor back to our home. Soon he began to become better and was able to smoke his pipe and to eat food.

After my father had recovered completely, he killed two goats for the people who had been looking after him throughout his illness.

He told them 'We should eat food and enjoy ourselves. We should not worry any more, because I have been cured.'

Five months later, Mohanika again had intercourse with the same man, and once more my father became ill with worms. When I saw that, I myself went to that man and told him, 'My father paid money to marry this woman and yet he suffers a lot because you have been having intercourse with her.'

I made an accusation against the man at the headquarters of the county chief. I said that he should bring a goat to our house, because it was he who caused all these troubles. The county chief told him to bring a goat to my house.

The man knew that I had threatened to kill him, so when he returned home he refused to bring the goat.

The county chief had him arrested and put him in jail for two days. After that the man agreed to bring the goat, but he told the chief, 'When I deliver this goat, you will have to give me some policemen and some chiefs who will go with me, because Kihara says that whenever I call at his home he will kill me.'

The county chief gave him three policemen, two minor chiefs and two messengers. All these people and the man himself came to our home bringing the goat with them. When they arrived, I told the man to skin the goat, and it was skinned while it was still alive. Then I caught a hen and gave it to him, and he took out all the feathers while it was still alive. Then the goat and the hen were taken into the house where my father was. After the goat and the hen had been killed, their intestines were taken out. Some of the intestines were put on the hands of my father and some on his legs. The whole goat was then put in one pot and it was cooked. After it had been cooked, the man took a gourd and stood in the doorway and said, 'It is I who have been having intercourse with your wife, and now I want to cure you.'

Then the woman, Mohanika, did the same thing. They cooked millet and some plantains, and we ate. After taking food the man left surrounded by the policemen and the chiefs, so that I could not throw a spear at him. Some time after this father recovered.

My father set traps in the forest near our home. An antelope with long horns was caught in one of these traps. After it had been skinned, my father ordered his wives to cook food for us. While we were eating, a piece of the meat stuck in my father's throat. It remained in his throat for a week. We consulted a diviner. He told us that when my father was distributing the meat he gave one of my brother's wives a piece which was not enough for her. As a result she bewitched him. The diviner advised us to get a goat and to tell the woman, 'If the meat goes from our father's throat, this goat will be killed, and you will eat it with us.'

176

Before we were able to carry out these instructions a young girl told us, 'There is a doctor who knows vomiting medicine. If we give this medicine to the old man, he will vomit and the meat will come out of his throat.'

She told me who the doctor was, and I went to him and got the medicine. I brought the medicine home in a small cup and forced my father to drink it. After he drank it all, his intestines started to rumble and then he vomited. Then the meat came out of his throat.

After he had vomited, he called all the people to come, 'Come and see what was killing me.' He showed us the meat. After showing it to us, he ordered us to kill three goats and one chicken. We killed them, and the women cooked food for us. All the people clapped their hands. We ate so much food that nobody could eat anything at all in the evening.

A few months later he began to cough and then he died. Before he died, he called all of us together. He told us, 'Everybody must do his work. I'm not going to die now, but I will die later in the night.'

In the evening I went and called a catechist to come and baptize him. After he had been baptized he died.

Early in the morning we went to the headquarters of the county chief and got some picks and shovels. Then we dug a hole and buried him.

All my brothers went out and collected many things: goats, chickens and about fifty shillings. On the day of the death ceremony all the lineage and all the relatives of my father collected together. They said, 'We should start to discuss the cause of our father's death.'

The old men refused. They said, 'We are not going to do anything about this. We did not live with the man who has died. Therefore we know nothing about it.'

They decided that Batigwa should be the successor. They said that I should look after my young brothers with Batigwa. Then they took the spear of my father from the house and handed it to me, saying, 'Since you are the oldest son, it would be best for you to tell us everything you know about the death of your father. You stayed with him throughout his illness.'

I explained everything to them and I spoke from the middle of the morning until late in the afternoon. I told them that his wife Mohanika had had a lover from outside and that it was she who had brought the worms. I also told them about another wife who was the mother of Atube. I told them, 'These two women caused my father's death because they used to put medicine in his food, and they are the only two people who killed him.'

We also suspected his son Bakankwisa, who lived in Kampala.

When he had come home, he had spent only two days at his house and then he went around Bwamba and finally reached the Congo, looking for medicine which would make him the successor. After he had returned from the Congo not a week had passed before our father died. He put the medicine which he brought from the Congo on his spear and blew it.

We left matters as they were and waited for the second death ceremony. For this ceremony I prepared about eighteen pots of beer, and my brother Batigwa prepared about eight pots. We killed four goats and started to dance.

We decided to get a doctor and have him cast a spell on the grave. We wanted to do this in order that the person who had bewitched our father might also die. Later we realized that if we treated the grave in that way, it would mean that we would be not able to clean it, because no one would be able to go there. We decided not to have the spell put upon the grave. I myself thought that it would be better to take a pot of beer and put it on the grave for a night. Then in the morning we could take the pot of beer and drink it. My younger brothers said that I made this suggestion because I was frightened. They said that I was afraid to have a spell cast upon the grave because if this were done, I would die because I had bewitched my father. I told them, 'If you suspect that it was I who killed my father, it is all right. I also have suffered a loss. However, my idea was that the spell should not be cast upon the grave because we would have to ask our children to go and clean the grave from time to time.' After I had said that, they decided not to have a spell cast upon the grave.

We built a tomb over the grave. Sometimes we have to take beer there. We put the beer in the tomb and let it stay there for a night. In the morning we collect our lineage, and we all go and drink beer inside the tomb. When a member of the lineage is ill, we take a goat and cook it there. All the members of the lineage eat food in there, so that the one who is ill may recover. We have to repair the tomb every once in a while, because if we do not, we have trouble and some of us may become ill. When that happens, we remember that now it is time to kill a chicken or a goat. We take food there and eat it. Then we are all right again.

At the second ceremony there was a great deal of trouble. There was very heavy fighting for about two hours because the people were very drunk. Then later, while I was there, one of the lineage elders took a pot of beer and started to drink. He also began to beat a drum. While the drumming was going on, a parish chief came and caught him. The parish chief said, 'Don't you know that it is illegal to beat a drum during the daytime?'

They could not say anything. The parish chief arrested the elder and some of the other members of the lineage. While he was taking them away, he met me. He said, 'Are you the one who gave these people permission to beat the drum during the daytime?'

I told him that I was not there when the drumming began. The elder was fined twenty-five shillings because he was the leader of the party, and the rest were fined ten shillings each.

On one occasion when I had brewed beer, my father's brother Mosumba came to my house and drank some beer. He was drunk. A little later he went to another place and asked for more beer. While he was at that place drinking, he started to make signs with his eyes to a married woman. While he was doing this, her husband saw him. The husband watched him. Then he got his stick and beat him. Late in the afternoon Mosumba came back to my house, bleeding. I asked him, 'What happened to you?'

He answered, 'Katabwita has killed me.'

I got together his sons, Mpuga, Atoku and Sengi. Nyamanzi also came with us. I was the leader. I got my spear and said, 'Let us go and spear this man.'

When we came in sight of the man, I told him, 'You are a leopard and I am a lion.'

When he heard me say that he ran away into the bush. I started to take all his things and his goats.

We were going to spear the woman, but she said to me, 'I was not involved in the affair, so please don't spear me. The trouble was caused because your father made signs to me with his eyes. That is why he was beaten.'

So I did not trouble the woman. I took the things with me. While I was on the way, I met the sub-county chief and his policemen, who were carrying rifles. I explained to him that I had to take all these things.

The chief told me that I had done wrong to take the property and that I must take it back and try to find the man. He also told me that I should walk in front of him and the policemen, because Katabwita was angry and he would kill me. The chief said, 'It is better that he should kill you first, before he gets us.'

We went back to Katabwita's house, and the chief questioned his sons. He arrested two of them and took them to the headquarters. Early the next morning we went to try to find the man. We looked in all the huts. When we came to one of them, an old man Kyoma was sitting outside. I heard a man inside puffing on a pipe. I asked Kyoma, 'Who is in the house? There must be somebody in there.'

I told the sub-county chief that Katabwita was inside that house. I asked the chief to send his policemen inside the hut to get the man. The chief refused. He said, 'No, that man will spear my policemen.

It would be better for you to go inside; Katabwita is your father's brother and he might not do anything to you.'

I went inside and told Katabwita, 'Never hide when you have made a mistake. You should come out and be accused by the government for what you have done.'

When he heard that, he decided that he should come out so that I could not shame him. I stood on one side of the doorway; two policemen stood on the other side. When Katabwita came to the door, I caught his hand and pulled him out. Then I hit him in the face, but the chief was not pleased with this. He told me that I had done a bad thing in his presence. I replied 'You told us that when we saw him that we should spear him. So why are you angry with me now that I have struck him?'

They arrested Katabwita. They put a rope around him, and he was taken to jail. He stayed there for two months.

When Mosumba recovered, he did not want to accuse Katabwita in the court because he said, 'We are all relatives. We are all of one lineage. He beat me, but I must forgive him.'

While Mosumba was alive, he used to say, 'My sons, this man Katabwita has killed me. Although I am alive, I am not well.'

Mosumba was always tired and he suffered from that beating throughout his life, and later he died because of it.

After Mosumba had died, I once drank beer with Katabwita. After I had finished my beer, I told the people, 'I want to go home.'

My spear was outside. Katabwita took it and broke it into two pieces. When he did that, I said to the people who were there drinking beer, 'Did you see what this man has done? If I fight him will it be my fault?'

Everybody there told me to fight him. I took my stick, got hold of him, pushed him down and beat him with the stick. When I did this, people came and held us apart and told me, 'You leave him alone.'

I took the pieces of my spear and went home The next morning while I was at home, Katabwita sent me a message saying, 'Please send me a hen.'

I caught a chicken to send to him, but before I sent it I changed my mind and took it back from the man to whom I had given it. I told the man, 'You go and tell Katabwita that I am not going to send him a chicken because he broke my spear. He should buy me a new spear and send it to me. Also tell him that I beat him because he started the matter.'

He did not buy a spear for me, and I refused to send him a hen. At the present time there is a feeling of enmity between us. I do not visit his house, and he does not visit mine. He no longer has the use of one eye as a result of one of the blows which I gave him.

Modern Amba Youth

A Pagan Religious Ceremony

Tea at the Anglican Church, Bundibugyo

One day as I was sitting outside my house eating food with my children, Katabwita walked into my courtyard. He was drunk. I offered him a chair, but he refused and instead stood there holding his two spears. For a while we continued eating our food, and he continued to stand there, refusing to sit on the chair. Then he came near two of my wives and started tickling them. I thought, 'This is my (lineage) father, and these wives of mine call him their father-in-law. Why is he doing this?'

One of my wives asked him, 'Why should you play with us like this when we are the wives of your son?'

I told the women, 'Don't pay any attention to what he is doing. He is doing these things because he is drunk. Please forgive him.'

When he heard me say that to my wives, he said, 'Everybody has been telling me that you are a brave man, but today I have come here to beat you and take out your intestines from your big belly.'

When I heard him say that I was very angry. I went in the house and got two of my spears. When he saw me coming out of the house he ran away. I chased him for quite a while, but I could not catch him. Finally I shouted to him, 'You are lucky. God still loves you.' Then I came back home.

One day I went to Fort Portal in order to buy a dog. While I was there I received a message that my son Kalisa was seriously ill. I came home, and I found that he was delirious. I went to a diviner, and he told me that two men and two women had bewitched him. I went to a second diviner, and he told me the same thing. When I had this true information, I reported to the sub-county chief that some people had bewitched my son. The chief asked, 'Can you identify them?'

I said, 'Yes.'

The chief told me that I should go and tell those people that he wanted to see them. During the night I heard some people dancing outside my courtyard. I looked out through the door and saw them dancing. I got my spear and speared one of them.

After it was light, the sub-county chief came to my house and asked, 'Have you collected all of them?'

I replied, 'Yes, but one man is not present. One man is here and two women are here, but I've speared one of the men.'

I showed the chief the blood. The next day the man died; it was my (lineage) brother. I had not recognized him because it had been at night. The sub-county chief arrested the three people I named and told them they must cure Kalisa and that, if the boy died, he would put them in jail. The three people spat on the boy. Late in the evening he began to feel better.

My relatives asked me, 'Why did you spear your brother?' and I explained to them, 'I didn't intend to spear him, but it was at night and I couldn't see who it was.'

Once I visited a girl and had intercourse with her. Three days later I found that she had infected me with venereal disease. The name of that girl was Ndilenobe. I infected all five of my wives. I took them to a doctor, and he said that he would treat them for fifty shillings each. After they had been treated, they all came home together. They said, 'Soon we will be cured, but you will not be well until the day you die.'

I suffered from that disease for eight years. I had it for a long time, and then I was advised to go to Fort Portal for treatment. I walked to Fort Portal, and when I got there I was given two injections. When I came back, I killed some goats. After I had done that, arrangements were made for me to stay in the bush. They took me into the bush and built a hut for me, and I stayed there for some time.

When I started to feel a bit better as a result of killing so many goats, I was advised to go to Oicha in the Congo. I went there with my wife, Kageye, and four children. We went to Oicha, and I was admitted to the hospital, but I was only given pills. When the European doctor examined me, he was unable to find anything wrong because my disease had run into my backbone. When I returned, I went to the doctor and told him that the disease had come back. He examined me and found the disease. He told me to wait for treatment. I stayed there for a week. When it was time for me to go to the hospital, I was unable to find the disc with writing on it. The disc enabled them to find your name in the book. When I reported to the doctor and told him that I had lost the disc, he laughed at me and showed me a place, 'You go and sit there.'

The people prepared hot water, and when it was ready they took me in a room and shaved me all over and bathed me. After that they put me out in the sun till midday. Then they called me to go in to my bed. I talked to the other people there. Late in the afternoon the person next to me was called to go to have his operation. After the operation they brought him back in a net.

While I was standing on the verandah, I saw the doctor motioning to me with his hand. I went to him, and he told me to get on the table. I lay down, and they put ropes on both my hands and crossed the ropes and tied them under the table. They did the same thing to my legs, and then the doctor came and stood on my left. He gave me an injection in my backbone. After that he took a small knife and cut my belly. All the intestines came out. I saw them with my own eyes as they were pushing them back into my belly. They had not injected me with medicine to make me unconscious. He worked on me for about an hour. Then I asked him, 'Haven't you finished with me yet?'

He said, 'Wait, I will be finished in a moment.'

Then he kept quiet while he worked, and I also kept quiet. After another hour had passed, I asked him again, 'Haven't you finished yet?'

He said, 'I'm almost finished.' A little later he poured cold water over me and started to sew me up. When he had finished sewing, he put some medicine on me which burned like fire. It was more painful than the knife with which he had cut me. When he was working on me, the doctor turned into an animal. I could even see that his face was not like that of an ordinary man. He looked like an animal.

After that I could not eat; I lived on cold water. I cried all during the night, but when the day broke I started to feel a bit better. They brought me a cup of tea and after that I was given a pound of rice.

I stayed there for nine days altogether. On the eighth day they took out my stitches. On the ninth day the doctor told me to leave the hospital and go to the camp. I stayed at the camp for a month, but at the end of that time I was not happy. I had been away from home for a long time. The doctor had told me to stay there for two months, but I left. I walked very slowly. It took me four days to reach home. When I got there, I remained quiet, as the doctor had instructed me not to do hard work and not to have intercourse with women.

Then a woman came along, and I knew I would have to break the rule which the doctor had made for me. I had intercourse with that woman, and she became pregnant. She was married, and money had been paid for her. However, she arranged it cleverly so that I could marry her. It was December, when people were catching locusts. She said, 'I will go home to my father's house before people see that I am pregnant. Then you can bring money to my father.'

I asked her how many shillings her husband had already paid, and she told me, 'Only seventy-five.'

Then she told me that I should have someone write a letter for me to her father saying, 'I want to marry your daughter.' I had the letter written, and her father was willing. I went to see him, and he told me to pay him seventy-five shillings and bring him three pots of beer. After I had taken these things, they asked me for a present for the mother. I gave them ten shillings. The whole thing amounted to eighty-five shillings. I had eight people who witnessed the proceedings. Then I came back home. I brewed four pots of beer and went to the market and bought some flour, six bunches of plantain and a goat. Then they brought my wife to me. I arranged everything properly, and the marriage ceremony was a good one.

After she had been here for some time, she asked me to cut grass for her so that she might cultivate. I did so. She asked me to buy her a hoe, and I bought it for her, but she did not go out to prepare the garden. Then she delayed planting the food. I used to get food, rice and other things only by buying them in the market. Then I had an idea. I took a hoe and tied it to her wrist while she was lying down in the house doing nothing. When I was having all this trouble with her, she produced a child, a girl.

When I saw that this wife was very lazy, that she was only eating my money and was not bringing me any gain, I sent her away, and she went back to her home. When she left, she took with her two blankets and three dresses. She also took my hoe with her, and I was very angry about that, since she did not do anything with it when she was with me. I went to her home and got the hoe. After she had been at her home for some time, I asked her relatives to give me my money. They refused to give it back to me. They said, 'We don't have the money to give you.'

Some time later I heard that she had been married by another man. I went to the house where they said that she had been married and I found that it was true. I went to the chief and reported the matter. I went back to the house with the chief, and we caught them. They were brought to the headquarters and after the case had been heard they were taken to jail. The woman was asked to bring her witnesses and she brought her brothers. When they arrived at the sub-county headquarters, they said that they had already repaid my money. I asked them when they had done so and who besides themselves was present. They said that the money had been given to one of my relatives. He was called before the court and asked if the money had been given to him. He had not seen the money with his eyes, and he had not been involved in the affair. I won the case.

She is still living with that man, but I buy things for her because she has my child. Quite recently I brought her a piece of black cloth and one dress, which cost me twenty-five shillings, and a blanket. I do all these things because she has my child. I was told by the government that I must take care of that wife, feed her properly and feed the child, as I have been paid back my brideprice. Now I am about to ask her to bring the child to me so that the child may grow up near me.

When I had five wives, three of them were having affairs with men outside the lineage, and as a result I suffered from worms. I collected some medicine and told all the wives to come together in one house. That night we all slept in the house. In the morning I took my medicine and placed it in the doorway of the house. I told the women, 'All of you must come and jump over the medicine and go outside. If one of you has been having intercourse with outside men, that one will fall sick.' One wife ran away. After that wife, Nyabalegia, had run away, I went to her house and collected all her things and brought them back to the house where we had stayed during the night. She came back to get her things. She said to me, 'I went to my house and found that my things were not there.'

I told her, 'I collected your things and brought them here. They are inside this house.'

She stood outside the door and said, 'I have left you completely, and I want to take my things away.'

I told her, 'You come in and get your things.'

She said, 'I won't come in because, if I do, you will beat me.'

I said, 'Why should I beat you? I am not going to lose anything. If you go home, I will go to your brother and get back my brideprice.' She came into the house, got her things and went away.

After she had gone to her brother's home, I sent a message to him asking him to return my brideprice to me. He refused. One day I met that woman on the road. I caught her and said to her, 'I must take you home because your brother has refused to refund the brideprice.'

I forced her to accompany me, and when we arrived at my house, I kept her there. When her brother heard what I had done, he went to the headquarters of the sub-county chief and reported the matter. The chief sent for me. I told the chief that I had a right to catch the woman on the road because I had previously asked her brother to refund my brideprice, and he had refused to do so. I had a right to take her home by force instead of allowing her to stay at the house of her brother, where she was enjoying herself with other men while my bridewealth had not been returned. I won the case.

I wanted to make a case against this man for having tried to ruin my name. I also told the county chief that this man, her brother, who was a minor chief, was instructing people to kill animals which the government had told us not to kill. I also told him that her brother was always making beer and not paying fifty cents for a licence. The county chief advised me to leave these matters alone, because they might not concern the man alone, and I might find myself in trouble. The chief told her brother to make a statement in writing saying, 'I have been accused by Kihara of ruining his name, but now he has forgiven me.' Her brother signed this statement. Then the chief wrote a letter saying that I agreed to this and that if I tried to trouble this man again, I could be charged by the court and imprisoned for one year. After this had been read to me, I made a mark on the paper. Since that time her brother and I have had no trouble, for I am afraid to say anything bad about him, and he is afraid to say anything bad about me.

Before he was transferred to a position elsewhere, he used to come to my place whenever I brewed beer. I always gave him a calabash of beer, but he would not drink it at my home. Instead he would carry it to his house and drink it there. He did this in order to avoid trouble. He thought that he might get drunk and cause trouble, and then I would accuse him to the higher chiefs and as a result he might have to go to prison.

His sister stayed with me during that time. The medicine which I had made and placed in the doorway had affected her. Unfortunately, she was three months pregnant, and she miscarried. The miscarriage caused her death. After I had buried her, I stayed in my house. I did not even trouble to go to the grave and keep watch over it, because it was she who had infected me with those worms. She deserved to die.

One day I made love to a daughter of the Banyanguli, and I impregnated her. At that time she was living at her father's home. She used to come and visit me, and then finally she came and stayed with me. While she was pregnant, she used to go to her parents' home to pass the time and visit. Whenever she went there, she had intercourse with other men. That is a very bad thing here in Bwamba. Once after she had come from her parents' home, I was told that she had intercourse with about four men. Her mother knew how to prepare herbal medicines. On one occasion while she was visiting her mother, her mother prepared some medicine for her. She made a whistle and put some hairs and some fingernail clippings and other things into it. When the time came for the girl to give birth, both she and her mother had forgotten to unpack the whistle. She was unable to give birth. She died. We didn't bury her in the courtyard; instead she is buried in the bush behind the houses.

On the day of the death ceremony her parents and her other relatives came. They said, 'You must pay for our daughter.'

I told them, 'I am not going to pay for your daughter at all. She was at fault for having intercourse with four men while she was pregnant.'

When I told them that, they, on their part, told me that they were going to try everything they possibly could to kill me and all my lineage.

Then I said to them, 'Even though you are going to do that, I tell you it was your daughter's fault for having done such a thing while she was pregnant. It was the same thing as when a person puts a rope around his neck and hangs himself.' I told them, 'When this woman was at her parents' home, she had many affairs with men. When she came to my house, she was unable to stop that habit. It was also the fault of her mother for preparing a whistle for her and then forgetting to take the things out of it on the day she was giving birth.' I also told them, 'The woman did not follow the rules of our lineage; therefore she died.'

They asked me to pay, and I offered them one goat. They refused it. Finally I gave them another three goats which made four altogether, and they accepted. The four goats which I gave them were a payment for refusing the corpse. (Kihara made this payment because he had buried the body in the bush and not in the courtyard.)

They asked me to give them an additional goat, which would have made five. Her death was not my fault, and no one in my lineage bewitched her. All the trouble was caused by them. I refused to give them that goat.

I married a woman, Njabala, who was very beautiful. I had heard rumours that she was a witch, but I had to marry her because I loved her. After she had come to my house, I bought a leg of goat meat for four shillings, and I also bought a big three-shilling fish. I told my wife to prepare food for us, and then I said, 'Prepare meat for the Toro, because they don't eat fish.'

Njabala prepared the food and while we were eating I saw one of my father's brothers passing by. I called him and invited him in to have some food. He came in, and we ate the meat.

After the meal my father's brother left, and I went somewhere to visit. When I returned home, I was ready to go to bed. Njabala asked me, 'Are you going to have any more food?'

I told her, 'No, but you eat some.'

She told me that she had kept some meat for me. She said to me, 'You should eat some meat and also some soup if you are not going to eat anything else.'

I refused, but I told her to eat some meat, and I also told her to give some to her child. She refused to eat anything, but she insisted that I eat some meat and have some soup. I took a spoonful and was about to taste some of the soup when I smelled medicine. Two other wives of mine were there at the time. I said to one of them, 'Nyabalegia, you taste this soup; it smells as though it has some medicine in it.'

She and the other wife both tasted it, and both of them said there was medicine in it. I put my hand into the soup and took out the meat. I found that it was not meat but the heel of a human foot. I asked Njabala, 'What is this?'

I showed it to everybody in the house and said, 'Do you see this—this human flesh?'

It was a piece from the heel of one of my brother's sons, who had died. Njabala had taken it from the grave. She said, 'Please do not shame me in the presence of all these people. That is what the householders always see.'

187

I threw the piece of flesh away. When she started to serve food to me the next time she cooked a meal for me, I noticed the same piece of flesh again. I asked her, 'How did this get into the pot again? Does it walk like a human being? Does it have feet? If you continue to cook this flesh, I will have to tell everyone in the village that you are cooking human flesh.' And I took that flesh and threw it far away.

This woman, Njabala, also fought with one of my other wives, Nguleya. On the same day the fight took place, Nguleya became ill; her belly became swollen. Njabala told her, 'If you try to fight with me again, you will see the result. Don't think that you are stronger than I am.'

Nguleya was sick for many days. While she was ill, Njabala continued to make medicine in order that I might get rid of Nguleya. When Nguleya realized what Njabala was doing, when she realized that she was trying to kill her, she went away. Since that time she has never returned.

Njabala stayed with me until God took her away. One day she said to me, 'I know a doctor who lives near my parents' home. You have lost many people in your home. Would you like me to bring you that doctor?'

I told her, 'I don't admit that this man is a true doctor, but, if you know that he is true, you bring him here.'

She went home and came back bringing the doctor with her. He said he wanted two chickens. I gave them to him. Before he killed them, he took the seed of a certain plant and put it in the ground. He said to me, 'Before this plant is full-grown, you will know the one who has been bewitching these people. You'll know whether it is one of your wives, your mother, a friend or a relative.' Then he asked me, 'Is anybody in your home sick at the present time?'

'No.'

He said, 'In four days time, if this plant comes up, you will see the person who has harmed your people. That witch will die of dysentery.'

When he left, I gave him five shillings.

Before the man had time to get home, Njabala became ill and began to pass blood. She called me and said, 'You have killed me.'

I told her, 'It is not I who have killed you. You were the one who asked me if you might bring this doctor. You brought him here, and he put the seed in the ground in your presence and now he has left for his home in the Congo. I won't get him back. You had better stay where you are and die.'

She suffered from the passing of blood for three months. She asked me to feed her properly. I killed three goats for her during that illness, but food would not remain in her body for very long. Before she died, all her intestines came out. She said to me, 'Don't tell anybody the cause of my death.'

Her brothers came to my house for the death ceremony. They asked me, 'What was the cause of her death?'

I told them, 'Before she died, your sister asked me not to tell anyone the cause of her death.'

Finally they forced me to speak. I told them how she had behaved; how she had cooked flesh for me and how she had brought the doctor from the Congo. I said, 'It was she who took the spear and put it on her neck.'

We settled everything, and they agreed with my statements. They asked me to give them one goat because they had lost their sister. I had intended to refuse their request, but then I thought, 'She had been my wife, and she has left a child. I had better give them their things.' I gave them five goats. Then they told me that I had been a good brother-in-law and said that they would give me another woman to replace their sister. Although they made this promise, they have never kept it. I am still waiting.

I had a (lineage) brother who married a woman who produced four children, three sons and one daughter. This brother killed another man and was taken away and hanged. He left the wife behind. When the woman heard that her husband had been hanged, she married another man. She produced a child for him and then later she divorced him. She then left and was married by the Banyanwera lineage. She produced another child there. After they were married, her husband, who was a relative of our lineage, left Bunyanwera and came up here to Bundinyama to live.

One night the mother of this woman came to my house. She brought a bunch of plantains with her. She came in the house, and my wife prepared food for her. After she had eaten, she told me, 'I would like it if you were to marry my daughter who was married to your brother. The man with whom she is now living doesn't think of me at all. He doesn't buy me salt. You should marry that girl. The man with whom she is living didn't pay anything for her, so don't be afraid.'

After her mother had told me all this, I bought meat for the girl and sent salt to the mother. A few days later her husband was hired by the Public Works Department and sent to work in Toro. After the husband had left, the girl used to come to my house and bring me food, and I used to go to her house. While I was staying with her there in that place, she was in the moon (i.e. her menstrual period). After that I impregnated her. Her husband was away for five months. When he returned, he found that his wife was pregnant. He asked her, 'Who has made you pregnant? When I left you here, you were not pregnant.'

She said, 'I have been made pregnant by Kihara.'

Then the Munyamwera told the woman, 'You wanted me to die there. You are a witch. You have been making medicine here. Get your things and go home.'

Then the woman left. She went to her father's house.

When I heard this, I went to her father's house and found her there. She said to me, 'You are the one who caused all this trouble. Build a hut for me.'

I built a house for her, and she came to live with me. She gave birth to a daughter. When this happened, I told another wife to get a piece of dried meat and a basket of mushrooms and a bunch of plantains and take them to the new wife who had given birth. When she had been in the house four days after the birth, I bought a piece of meat, some dried fish and some milk and took it to her in order that my child might be taken out of the house. The woman lived there with her child, and I used to take her things from time to time. Later the child became ill. I went to the diviners, and they told me, 'You did not make a sacrifice for your dead brother. You didn't kill a goat and say to him, "Please forgive me for marrying your wife."' I came home and carried out the instructions of the diviners. I sacrificed to my brother and then the child recovered.

After the child had recovered, the woman told me that she was unwilling to stay at my house while the child was small. I gave my consent, and she and the child went to live at her father's house. She told me, 'After your child is well-grown, you can come and take her.'

One day I went to the forest to cut some poles. On the way back I passed the house of my (lineage) father Kabanja, and I saw that people were drinking beer. I thought, 'I will put these poles down and go there and drink beer. Then late in the evening I will collect my poles and go home.'

While I was drinking beer, the Munyamwera man who had been married to that woman came and sat on the same chair with me. He started to push me gradually until I was sitting on the edge of the chair. I left the chair, went out to the dining hall and started to drink my beer there. After I had drunk about three small calabashes of beer, that man came out and sat down behind me.

I said, 'What is the matter with you? What do you want? Let me drink my beer properly.'

When I said that to him, he hit me in the face. I asked the other people who were there, 'Did you see what he has done to me? If I make trouble, you mustn't say that I started this.'

The rest of the people said, 'You fight him.'

I caught him and threw him on the ground. When I had him on the ground, a relative of his came and hit me. Then a relative of mine caught that man and threw him on the ground. Other people came and separated us. After we had been separated, everyone got hold of his spear, and we started to fight again. During the fight they speared two men on our side, Kabanja and Katabwita. We injured four of their people, and they injured a third one on our side. Finally we chased them to the house of the Munyamwera. They ran into the house and closed the door. I thought it would be a good idea to burn the house down, but Mosumba stopped us from doing that. Then we went back and continued to drink beer.

When the beer was finished, I went home. Later that night the Munyamwera came to my house and asked me to open the door. He came into the house and said to me, 'Please leave the matter as it is. Don't make an accusation against us through the sub-county chief. The people who have been injured will be treated in their homes. Don't report it.'

I told him that I would not make an accusation against them. The next day he brought me two chickens, and we ate them together. After we had settled the matter, the people who were injured on his side were taken to the Congo for treatment, and the people who were on our side were treated in small huts which we made for them in the bush.

After the people who were involved had recovered, I met him one day. I said to him, 'Why should you make all this trouble because of that woman? We Bandinyama were the first husbands of that woman, and we produced children from her. If you continue to act the way you have been acting, I will always fight you when we meet.'

He used to go about with two spears, and I also went about with two spears. When we met at beer parties, people would refuse to give us beer. They would say, 'We can't give any beer to either of you when you are both here. You will both have to leave.'

That man and I also had trouble when we were hunting. I found an antelope and chased it the whole day. While I was chasing it, it ran past the house of that man. He saw it and went after it with his dog. When he reached the valley, he shot it with an arrow. His dog caught it. When I arrived, I did not quarrel with him. I told him, 'This is my antelope.' The man cut a piece from one leg and a piece from the back and gave them to me. I went home.

About two weeks later this man and I and other people went hunting. We found a python which nearly killed our dogs. We caught our dogs and began to fight the python. It stood up like a man, and when its head fell on the ground it made a hole in the ground. The people who liked python meat cut it into many pieces. Then we went on with the hunt. We found the track of a forest hog. We released our dogs, and later I speared it. That man told me that it was his animal. I told

191

him, 'I chased this pig with my dog and when I arrived my dog was holding it; I speared it and killed it. If you want to bring trouble as you did in the past, when you took my antelope and said that it was yours, we will have to kill each other. If you are a man, take this meat and let your wife cook it for you. But remember that I will kill you before you are able to eat it.' I left him there while he was skinning it. I said, 'I am going home, but be ready; there will be a fight.'

When I had left the place, other people told him, 'If you take this pig to your house, Kihara is going to kill you. It would be better for you to take it to Kihara's house.'

They brought it to my house. I gave him some meat, but he refused it. I gave the meat to his wives. I ate my animal. I told him, 'You go and kill your animal, and, if you kill it, I will not eat your meat at all.'

People told us, 'As there is hatred between you, you should never hunt together. Each one should hunt by himself.'

One day I said to that man, 'Why don't you return to your home?' Then I took a brand from the fire and handed it to him saying, 'You go to your real home and do not stay here in our village.'

He was very much ashamed and said, 'I will leave this village. Kihara has made me ashamed in the presence of other people.'

After I had told him that, he went away. He went back to his own home at Bunyamwera and stayed there. When I gave him the burning stick, I meant that he could use it as a torch in order to find his way at night back to his real home at Bunyamwera.

One day I went to Kijura near Fort Portal and bought a dog. I brought it down here to my home in Bwamba, and it proved to be a very good hunter. I killed several pigs with that dog, and it became known that I had a very good hunting dog. There is a man called Kihanda, who one day passed by my house and saw the dog.

He asked me, 'Is this your dog?'

I said, 'Yes.'

He said, 'Is that the one people have told me is a very good hunter?'

He asked me to give him the dog. I refused to give it to him, and he went away.

He came to my house a second time. He looked at me and said, 'Perhaps this dog is not yours, because, if it were yours, you would already have brought it to my house and given it to me.'

I thought of fighting that man. I thought, 'Why should he come and insult me at my house?' After he had gone I decided that if he came to my place again, I would have to beat him. Then I thought, 'If I beat him, I may be charged by the government with having insulted and beaten a man who is a traveller.'

The man came to my house once more. He said, 'I will send someone to you who knows where my house is. If you want to bring that dog to my place, he will show you the way.'

I agreed to this because I was somewhat annoyed. I thought, 'I will take the dog to him and see what happens.' The next day the man whom Kihanda had mentioned came to my house, and I and my dog went with him to Kihanda's home. When we arrived, Kihanda killed a chicken. After we had talked for a while, I said, 'I am going home.'

He prevented me from going and said, 'You will leave tomorrow.' I stayed that night, and the next day he asked me to be his blood-brother. We became blood-brothers, and I gave him the dog.

When I was about to leave, he gave me a female goat. I told him, 'Since you have given me this goat, I am going to slaughter it here. But since I haven't brought along my wife, who will carry the meat home?' He kept me from slaughtering the goat there and made me take the goat home with me, because he had no one there to carry the meat. I thought of refusing the goat and I said, 'You have given me this goat to be used for my food, but you haven't given me the goat of blood-brotherhood.'

He told me, 'You take that goat and later I will send you the goat of blood-brotherhood. Or you can send somebody here to collect it.' I took the goat and went home.

A week later I heard that he had killed a pig with that dog. Later I heard that he had killed four large birds. Again I heard that he had killed four animals. I sent someone to collect the goat which he had promised to give me. When that person arrived at Kihanda's house, Kihanda gave him ten shillings. When those ten shillings were brought to me, I refused to take them. I returned the money to him because it did not equal a goat in value. He sent me a message telling me to accept the ten shillings. He said he was looking for more money and that he would send it later. I sent him a message which said, 'When I bought the dog, I didn't pay half price. I paid the full amount. You also must pay the full amount.'

Then he himself came to my house. He told me, 'I am fighting a court case.' I took seven shillings and gave them to him. I also gave him a bundle of salt. He went away.

After some time I realized that he was not going to repay me. I decided to speak with my hunting god so that the dog would not kill any more animals. After that, when Kihanda went out hunting with the dog, the dog would stand in one place and would not chase the animal. Kihanda was very annoyed by this. He brought the dog to my house and asked me to repay the goat; if I would repay the goat, he would return the dog to me. I told him, 'Perhaps you yourself don't know how to hunt.' While he was sitting in the house, I went out with the dog, and I killed an animal. I returned home and demanded, 'What is this?'

He said, 'I will have to take the dog back to my house.'

I cut a piece of meat from the animal and gave it to him. Then he went home with his dog and the piece of meat. When he got home, he tried the dog and it failed to hunt. He made three attempts, but the dog refused to hunt. He came to my house bringing the dog with him. I gave him a goat and ten shillings, and the dog stayed with me.

Later I thought, 'It may not be a good thing for me to keep this dog, since I have taken it from my blood-brother. It may be useless to me.' I exchanged the dog with another man for two goats.

Then Kihanda made an accusation against me at the court of the sub-county chief, saying that I had taken his dog and his ten shillings, and that I had refused to pay him. He paid the two shillings fee to open the case. I was called to the sub-county headquarters and the case was heard. Kihanda won the case. They did not pay any attention to my statements, and they refused to let my witness come in the court. The chief told me, 'You must repay the money.' I told the chief that I wanted to appeal to the county court, but he prevented me from making an appeal.

He said, 'You should not appeal, because this man is your blood-brother. You should settle the matter between yourselves.' As I was taking the money out of my pocket to make an appeal the chief told me, 'You put that money back in your pocket. If you know that this man is your blood-brother, he will suffer through the blood which you cut.'

I put the money back in my pocket and went home. I went and collected some medicine as my father had done. I told my wife to put a pot on the fire and put some water in it. I put the medicine in the pot and said the words in the same way that my father had done on that day. After a while Kihanda's stomach began to swell. He consulted diviners, and nothing could be done. His people carried him to the hospital. While he was in the hospital, he did not improve, so they carried him home again.

They sent someone to ask me to go and see him. I refused. They sent another person, and I refused again. They sent a third person, and I refused. They sent a fourth person, and I went there. When I arrived, I found him in a very bad condition. His stomach was swollen, and he could not breathe properly. The people there said to me, 'Please try to cure your blood-brother. Help him, even though he cheated you.'

I told them, 'You must bring a big female goat. It must be as large as the one I gave to him on that day. If you don't do that, I won't say one word.'

They said, 'We don't have a female goat.' They brought a male goat, and they slaughtered it. I refused completely to say a word. While they were preparing food and cooking the meat, I left the place and came home.

I stayed at home for a week. Then I heard that Kihanda had died. Before he died, he said, 'I have been killed by my blood-brother because I cheated him. When Kihara has a dog, he must never make blood-brotherhood with a man and then give him his dog. If he does there will always be trouble between himself and his blood-brother.' What he said is true, because whenever I give a dog to a blood-brother there is trouble, and we make accusations against each other in the court.

A few years ago the parish chief made a large cassava garden for all the people in his area. One of my wives had to go and work in that garden. When the cassava was full grown, my wife went into the garden and pulled up three tubers. A policeman saw her and arrested her. He took her to the jail. One of the policemen at that jail forced her to have intercourse with him. She reported what the policeman had done to the sub-county chief. The chief told her to go and be examined by the dispenser at the government dispensary. The dispenser said that the policeman had not had intercourse with her. I was there. I said to the dispenser, 'You are not just. If the woman said that she was forced to have intercourse, how can you say that she was not? What I mean is, this policeman is a friend of yours.'

When he heard that, he told me, 'Because you have said that you must never come here to this dispensary. If you do come here, I will inject you with the wrong medicine and you will die.' Since that time I have never gone to the dispensary. When the case was heard I was fined twenty-five shillings.

My wife Kageye asked me to make blood-friendship with her. I talked to some of the Bandinyama elders about this. They gave me advice. They told me, 'When you have married a wife and when you love her very much, you should make blood-friendship with her.' When they asked me about it, I always denied it. Kageye also denied it. I always treated her properly because I was afraid to make her angry, and I feared the blood. When she died, she told me, 'I am dying; everyone has to die. You have not treated me badly while we have been together. One thing I want you to do is to look after my children properly.'

When the last war of the Europeans began we were called to serve in the army. We received instructions that all of us should go and join the army. I decided not to go. I also told all the Bandinyama not to join the army. We left our houses and slept in the forest. I told them, 'If anyone sees a sub-county chief or a minor chief or a policeman, he

195

should kill him.' We stayed in the forest, and our wives cooked food for us and brought it to us there. We stayed there for two weeks without going home once. After two weeks, we began to come home at night, arriving at our homes very late in the night and leaving them again very early in the morning. All during the day we stayed in the forest with our bows and arrows. Then some people reported through the county chief that it was I, Kihara, who had started the rebellion. Those same people also advised the chief to arrest me and send me to Fort Portal where I could be punished in the way that Nyamukehwa, the Konjo, had been punished for rebelling in the past. When I heard that I was going to be punished as Nyamukehwa had been, I said to my people, 'I had better go home and put on my clothes and then go and report to the county chief. If they want to arrest me, let them arrest me. But you stay here.'

When I got near the headquarters of the county chief, I discovered that all the other Bandinyama had followed me. The chief selected five of the Bandinyama men, including myself, and told us that the next day the five of us would be taken to Fort Portal to report for the army. We had a very big dance in Bundinyama. The dance was held under a very large tree, and that tree fell down, not because it had been cut, but because so many people were dancing near it. Many people from all over Bwamba, including doctors and witches, were at the dance. They made medicine for us which they said would prevent us from going to war. They told us, 'When the doctors examine you, they will have to say that you are unfit.'

At Fort Portal there were two European doctors. They asked us to pull out our penises, and when they saw them they said that we had venereal disease. When they saw our feet they said that our feet were no good for the army. They looked at the anus of each of us and they said that they were not right. Even our testicles were not fit for the army. They examined everywhere on our bodies and they said we were completely unfit. After they had examined us, they told us to return to our homes. Everyone of us returned home. We killed goats and we all said thank-you and clapped our hands, and the other people at our homes did the same thing. We called the people who had made medicine for us and killed chickens and gave them beer. We stayed in our homes. Later we were told that everyone in the whole of Bwamba had to give a shilling to help those people who went to the war. After a long time we were told, 'The British Government has won the war.' All of us were very pleased. That was the last of the war. From that time up to now we have just been sitting down and looking for our poll tax.

Kilagule, who is related to our lineage, is a very bad witch. One day some of my lineage brothers and I attended a beer party. Kila-

196

gule was also there. About ten o'clock at night my brothers and I decided to go home. While we were coming down a hill we heard something ahead of us. All of us stood still and said, 'What is it?'

Someone said, 'It may be a witch, but don't throw a spear because it may be somebody hiding from us.'

I told them, 'Let us try to look for him the way we look for grass-hoppers.' I found his leg. I told them, 'I have caught his leg. It isn't an animal; it is a man—Kilagule.' All of us tried to pull him out of the grass where he was hiding and on to the path. But we were unable to do so because he was a witch.

He said, 'Why do you try to pull me out when I don't want to go with your party? Why don't you leave me?'

Finally we left him. We went to his home and told his wife, 'We left your husband in the grass. We tried to pull him out of the grass but were unable to do so. So we left him behind. You had better go and look for him.' We also told her, 'Your husband was going to kill us on the way. He was going to turn into an animal and kill us.'

His wife told us, 'That is his custom. He is always doing that. He is not a human being; he is an animal.'

Since that time we have realized that we have an animal living near us, a witch who is worse than any others of his kind.

Very often he goes around to all the houses in the village and throws stones at them. Sometimes he pushes at the door. Whenever people go outside to see who is throwing the stones, he runs away. One night as I was coming home, I heard a man sound the alarm. Kilagule had been throwing maize cobs at this man's house. I saw Kilagule, who was trying to get away from the people, running down the path toward me. I put my spear down and waited for him. When he came past me, I caught him and threw him on the ground.

When he realized that it was I who had caught him, he said, 'My boy, let me go. Don't make me ashamed in front of other people. If you want anything, just ask me and I will give it to you. If you want women, I will give them to you. I will give you one who will produce twenty children for you.'

When he said this, I decided to let him go. I told him, 'I want to marry many women.' He agreed to get me some women and I let him get away.

The next day he came to my house. He brought three knives and one axe. When he gave me these things, he told me, 'My boy, never tell anyone that you caught me last night. When they ask you about it, don't say anything.'

I said, 'I will never tell other people.'

One night as I was coming home, I saw him climbing a big tree near my house. He was holding branches of the tree with his feet and his head was hanging downward. I told him, 'If you come near my house any more, I will kill you just as I would kill anyone else.' Since that time he has never come near my place at night. He only comes during the day time. When he comes, I have to get a hen and give it to him and I also give him salt.

I once impregnated a woman. Four months later I visited her at her parents' home. I found her cooking medicine in a pot. I asked her, 'What are those medicines for?'

She told me, 'I am troubled by my stomach.'

I told her, 'There is no trouble in your stomach; you are trying to take out my child.' I kicked over the pot in which she was cooking that medicine. Then I came home.

Then the woman considered to whom she would attribute the child. Her sister advised a certain man. When she told the man that it was his child, he agreed. He got a goat, a white hen and some mushrooms and brought them to the parents of the woman. Then he took her to his home. Later she gave birth to a girl. When I heard about this, I thought, 'How can I send anything to help her; I don't know anyone in that place.' So I kept quiet.

Later the woman went back to her father's home. When I heard this, I got an iron bracelet and some beads and took them to her. After I had given these things to her, I started to explain the whole matter to her father. I told him how I had impregnated his daughter, how she had attributed the pregnancy to another man and how this man had brought him a goat, a white hen and other things. After I had explained all this to him, the father said to me, 'The best thing to do would be for you to bring me a goat. Then I can give it to that man in return for the one he brought to me.' I did this, and I also sent the woman some dried meat, a piece of bark-cloth, and some other things.

Later the woman married a man who lived in the Congo. She lived there with that man for a long time. She gave birth to two more children. During all that time I never lost contact with her.

When my daughter, Mukundi, was about ten years old, I met her mother. I asked her, 'Why is it that you don't bring my daughter to my home?'

The woman replied, 'I want to bring Mukundi to your house, but the man to whom I am married will not let me.'

I told her, 'If you don't have any money, I will give you two shillings for the court fees, and you can accuse the man in court. I will also give you money to give to your husband for the expense he has had with my daughter.'

When she visited Bwamba again, I went to the parish chief and reported the matter. She was called before the court. The chief told her, 'You should have brought the daughter to this man.'

The woman told the chief, 'The child is not here.'

The chief advised me to go to the Congo to the place where the woman was living and report the matter to the chief there.

I took his advice and went to the Congo. I went to the chief's headquarters and paid my court fee. The woman and her husband were called to the courthouse. In addition, the chief asked the woman to bring all her children to the court with her.

The woman played a trick. She brought the children of her sister to the courthouse, and she left my daughter at home. I realized what was happening, and I told the court that these children whom she had brought with her were not really her own. The court ordered her to bring her own children. Then she brought my child and the two children who were born in the Congo to the headquarters of the chief. I had a witness who testified that I had sent things to her. The people in the court asked the woman, 'Why should this man send you anything if you did not have his child? Were these things sent to you because he was your lover? Or is he one of your relatives?'

The people in the court decided that she was telling a lie when she said that the child was not mine. I won the case and was allowed to take the child home with me.

Two weeks later the woman, accompanied by her husband, made an appeal to the county chief here in Bwamba. I was asked to bring my children to the courthouse, and she was also asked to bring hers. The case was heard again. The people in the courthouse saw that Mukundi resembled my other children in appearance, so I won the case again. They made still another appeal to the court in Fort Portal, but again I won the case.

After I had won the appeal case, I wanted to start a new case against the man and accuse him of having caused me much trouble and having wasted a great deal of my time. However, the prime minister, who was in the courtroom, said to me, 'You haven't lost anything. You wanted to get your child, and now your child has been given to you; therefore do not make a case against the other man.' I left the matter and came home with my child.

A year or so later Mukundi was married, and I received seven goats. When the sub-county chief was making a tour of inspection, he saw my daughter and he asked the people who were with him, 'Is this not the daughter of Kihara?'

Mukundi said, 'Yes, I am Kihara's daughter.'

The chief asked, 'What is she doing here?'

They told him, 'She is married here in this village.'

The chief brought Mukundi back with him to his headquarters. He sent for me and told me that I had broken a government rule by permitting my daughter to be married when she was not sixteen years old. He told me that I would have to refund the seven goats to the man who had married her. I promised the chief that I would never do it again. He told me to keep my daughter properly until she should reach the legal age for marriage.

I took Mukundi home. About two years later the girl herself came to me and told me the name of the man whom she wished to marry. I have forgotten his name, but he is a Mundimukuma. I asked the man to bring one goat for Mukundi's mother and eight goats for me. He brought nine goats altogether.

For a few months everything went well. Then Mukundi came home and complained to me about her husband. Since I had accepted the goats, I did not want to let her divorce the man. She refused to go back to her husband, so I had to beat her and take her back there by force. She herself had chosen the man, and I had accepted the bride-wealth, so I had a right to take her there by force.

Later she came home again. She told me, 'My husband treats me badly. He has made me move out of the house and has told me to sleep in a tomb over a grave. He won't buy me a blanket and he never buys me any cloth. Sometimes my mother-in-law asks me to go into the garden to get food, but when I bring it back she calls me an elephant. She says that I am taking food from the garden. How can I stay there when my mother-in-law calls me an elephant?'

I told her, 'If you are being badly treated there, you had better stay here at home. I will give back the goats to the man.'

After she had been divorced, I told her, 'Now it is up to you to get another man to marry you.'

Recently Mukundi told me, 'I would like to be married by my first husband.'

I told the man to bring the bridewealth. He brought seven goats. I told him that he could take his wife, but he has not taken her as yet. Mukundi is now visiting her mother in the Congo. I intend to go to the Congo soon and when I do, I will bring her back with me and give her to her husband.

MPUGA'S DIARY

[Mpuga kept a diary for several months at my suggestion. The portion of it which is reproduced here covers the period from the latter part of March, 1951, to the middle of October in the same year. About a month prior to the first entry in the diary Lubangi and Mpuga quarrelled and she went to her father's home in the Congo across the Semliki. She took her youngest child Sogosa with her, but Nkuba remained with Mpuga.]

March 27th: Last night I dreamed that my mother asked me, 'Mpuga, where is your wife Lubangi?'

I replied, 'She went to the Congo with my child Sogosa.'

She told me, 'When she is away things are not right in your home. You must remember what I told you before I died. I told you that, when I died, Lubangi would replace me. Even though you marry a hundred wives, I will consider her the only good one. She is the one whom Mosumba obtained for you and who was seen by him. It is she who will carry all the gods whom I left behind.'

This morning I told this dream to other people, and they said that my mother has now explained to me that it will be Lubangi who will take the goddess Nyakala. They pointed out to me that Nyakala had entered the breast of my sister-in-law, the wife of Bukombi, and had caused a sore which was lasting a long time. My two children, Nkuba and Muganga, also had bad sores.

March 30th: A man called Kinabiro came from the Congo to my house and asked me for a chicken. He said, 'I want my chicken. You must give it to me now.'

As I didn't know anything about this, I laughed. When he saw me laughing he was very angry. He said, 'You are trying to cheat me out of a chicken.' He said that Lubangi had brought a chicken of his to my house.

I said, 'I didn't see that chicken. She never brought it here.' Then I asked, 'When did she bring it?'

He told me that it had happened a long time ago.

I called Abongo and Koke to witness the fact that Lubangi had not brought the chicken to my house.

Kinabiro said, 'The reason I have come is that I saw Lubangi recently, and she told me that she had left a chicken with five of its

201

chicks here. I have come for them so that I can take them to use at a religious ceremony. I have some patients at my home.'

I said that I knew nothing about the chicken. That man was silent for about two minutes and then he said, 'I am going back to the Congo. I will go and ask Lubangi what she did with my chicken.' I told him to go and do that.

March 31st: During the night we heard Kihara's mother crying, and later she began to moan. Early in the morning she said to the wife of her son, 'I am sure that I will die today. This is my last day. I won't have another day in this world because my husband's house is ready. I stayed with him in his house last night.'

Then Kihara came to the house and said, 'How are you, mother?'

She replied, 'I am no longer with you. I have died. I am not staying here with you tonight.'

Kihara said, 'Let me go and get the doctor for you. He will come and take the things out of your body.'

His mother replied, 'You have seen that my body is gone and that all my bones are broken in pieces. Now I am among the dead. Are you going to get the doctor to come and heal me? Where have you been for the last few days? I have been sick for a very long time. Let me die.'

Then Kihara said, 'If I bring the doctor, he will cure you.' He went and borrowed some money from Nyamanzi. Then he told his mother, 'I'm going now to get the doctor. I will bring him today.' At noon-time his mother died. When we saw that she was dead, Kalisa went after Kihara to the place where he had gone to consult the diviners.

April 6th: Last night I dreamed that my wife, Lubangi, bought medicine at a place called Mboga in the Congo. She paid a hundred francs for it. They told her, 'When you go to Mpuga's house, put it on his bed. Then when he sleeps on your bed, he will get a disease, and that disease will kill him.'

Before I had this dream, I had intended to go to the Congo for her, but I won't go there now. I am afraid to go because of this dream. It may be true. I don't know if it is, but I am very worried. If she is going to be married by someone else, let her be married. I will go and have my goats returned to me. I told Kihara about this dream, and he agreed with me. He said the dream was true. He said that I should not go to the Congo. He told me that the people there might catch me and beat me, or that I might meet some other trouble.

April 7th: Abongo quarrelled with Koke. Abongo's wife had planted some maize in her garden, and, at the same time, Koke had also planted maize in hers. Koke's maize was eaten by birds, but they did not go for the maize of Abongo's wife. Koke complained about this, saying, 'Why has my maize been eaten by the birds while the maize of other people is still here?'

Yesterday the maize of Abongo's wife was attacked by the birds. Abongo was very angry when he saw this. When he returned from the garden, he said, 'Koke, you have bewitched my maize and caused it to be eaten by birds.'

She replied, 'It is your habit always to suspect that somebody is bewitching your things. For example, you neglected your potatoes and you didn't get a good harvest. Then you said we had bewitched your potatoes and killed them, whereas it was really your laziness that caused the death of those potatoes.'

April 8th: I was helping Kihara to thatch his house, the one in which his wife, Muwisa, lives. We saw Ruganda and seven other men of the Banditokwe lineage coming along the path.[1] Kihara gave them chairs to sit on. After a while Ruganda stood up and said, 'Kihara, I have come to settle the matter of having intercourse with your wife.'

Kihara replied, 'I can't speak to you when Batigwa is not here.'

Shortly after this Batigwa arrived. Then he was asked to explain what he knew about this matter. He said, 'I was told that the child of Muwisa saw Ruganda passing through the court-yard. The child told the other children, "He is the one who is sleeping in my mother's house." Then I came and asked Muwisa about this, but she said that it was not true. She said that Ruganda had never had intercourse with her. She said, "Even if he were as handsome as the moon, he could not sleep with me."'

Then the people asked Kihara how he had heard this news as he was not present at the time. He said, 'I dreamed about this when I was in Butuku. No one told me about it.'

Muwisa said, 'No, that is not true. You said that Nyamanzi and Batigwa told you.'

Then Batigwa stood up and asked, 'Kihara, when did I tell you this, and who was present?'

Kihara said to his wife, 'I told you all of this when I first entered the house. I had not been at Batigwa's house.'

Kihara stood up and said, 'I accuse Batigwa in the presence of all of you. He always drinks alone the beer which is saved for the day after the beer party. This beer should be drunk by all the men. Why does he do this?'

Batigwa stood up and said, 'Kihara, you have become a witch.

[1] The Banditokwe who live in the village across the road and to the west of Bundinyama consider themselves related to the Bandinyama. The two lineages do not intermarry.

You are one now. Have I ever drunk this beer alone? I always call you, and we drink it together.'

He asked Kihara very many questions, and Kihara was not able to answer. The people told Kihara that he must not kill Batigwa because of the beer.

Batigwa accused Ruganda of having refused food at his home. Ruganda stated his case. He said, 'Once I went to Batigwa's house. I felt very hungry so I asked him to tell his wife to fix some food for me. He said to me, "Why have you come from your house without food?" He said to me, "You should not ask for food." Then he slapped me. People stopped us from fighting, and I went home. When I arrived home I told my mother what had happened. Then I called my wives. I gave instructions to them. I said, "If I see any of you at the house of Batigwa I will beat you. If I see any of my children there, I will beat them, because Batigwa slapped me after I had asked him for food because I was hungry. Therefore I no longer consider him a fellow clansman." '

Then someone told us that one day one of Ruganda's wives went to the house of Batigwa. When Ruganda found out about this, he beat her.

We passed judgment. We said, 'Ruganda, you are guilty. You were wrong to refuse to eat at Batigwa's and to prevent your people from going there.' Batigwa was fined two chickens and one pot of beer for having slapped Ruganda. This food will be eaten at Batigwa's house because he is the elder. We told them, 'If either one of you becomes sick, we will know that the other has bewitched him.' We said, 'This sort of thing should not happen between clansmen. This is one of the bad things, which we must fear. If enemies outside the clan know that two clansmen are having trouble, they can come and bewitch one of them. This causes a lot of trouble, because one man will think that he has been bewitched by his fellow clansmen, whereas he has actually been bewitched by someone else.'

April 11th: I started to go to Bundibugyo. On the way I met a man from Busaru. We greeted each other, and I asked him for the news. He said, 'The child of Abongo's wife (by another husband) died yesterday.'

I went home and told the news to Abongo. Then we started off for the house where the child had died. I fell once and a short distance later I fell down again. Abongo asked me, 'What is wrong with you, Mpuga?'

I said, 'Nothing is wrong with me.' When we reached the Tokwe River, we washed ourselves. As we were washing I slipped on a stone and fell into the water. I told Abongo that I wanted to go back. I had never had such a journey. I had fallen three times, and we had not gone very far. I decided that it meant that, if I had gone with Abongo, I would have met trouble.

April 12th: My wives, Koke and Kijungu, quarrelled. The reason that they quarrelled was that I bought some sugar for Kijungu and not for Koke. I said to Koke, 'Why do you quarrel with Kijungu about this little bit of sugar?'

Koke said, 'It is you who are trying to make trouble between us.'

Then I said, 'I bought only two pounds of sugar. How could I divide it? You are a small wife; I hate small wives. I don't even like to see one here in my courtyard. Why do you hate Kijungu?'

She said, 'I just want Lubangi here. If I were a witch, I would have driven Kijungu away from here.'

I said, 'If my wife, Kijungu, becomes sick, I won't suspect anyone else. I will know that you have bewitched her.'

I know from this that, if Kijungu has even a slight pain, it will be because this woman is after her. Even though Koke says this about Lubangi, they were not good friends. It is true that they ate food together, but they used to quarrel a great deal. But Koke will not even eat food with Kijungu.

I saw Nyamanzi's goats grazing near my house. Later, while Koke was bathing her child, the goats went into her house and ate the food which she was cooking. She heard a noise in her house and sent Muganga to see what was happening. He said to her, 'There are goats in the house and they are eating the food you have in the pot.' When Koke went in the house, she found that the food had been eaten. She caught the goats, picked up the empty pot and went with them to the house of Nyamanzi. She found his wife, Atolu, and she asked her, 'Where is your husband?'

Atolu asked her what had happened. She asked, 'Why do you have the goats and a pot?'

Koke replied, 'Yesterday your husband's goats ate my food. And today they have done it again. I want him to repay me for my loss. Why doesn't he tie his goats? Other people tie theirs.'

His wife said, 'When your goats ate our sweet potatoes, I did not go to Mpuga and ask him to repay me.' Then they started to quarrel. Atolu also said, 'You did not come here to report your loss. You came here to fight.'

Koke said, 'Oh, now you are saying I am a fighter, when I really came here to be repaid for my loss. I want some money for my food.'

Then they started quarrelling. Atolu said, 'You have come and quarrelled with me now while I am pregnant. If I have trouble during my delivery, it will be because you have bewitched me.'

Koke said, 'Why are you saying that I am a witch? Have you even seen me bewitching anyone? Or have I ever come to your house to ask for salt?'

April 13th: Today a Konjo came to my house. He said, 'Who is the householder of this home?'

I said, 'Why do you ask?'

He said, 'I am looking for a man called Mosumba, who ate my father's goat. I am trying to find him.'

Then I said, 'Do you know him when you see him?'

He answered, 'No, I don't know him by his face but my father knew him.'

I asked, 'Who is your father?'

He replied, 'My father's name is Kamogongo of Bukonjo.'

I said to him, 'If you had asked me in a peaceful manner, I could have shown you Mosumba. He is not far away. He may be among us here. The house in which you are sitting now is the house of Mosumba.'

The man said, 'Would you show me him so that I may talk with him?'

Abongo and myself wondered a great deal about this. I called Koke and Kijungu so that they could hear what this Konjo would say. Then I asked him, 'When did my father eat your father's goat?'

He said, 'In 1939.'

I said, 'Have you never heard that Mosumba is dead?'

The Konjo answered, 'I have been in Buganda, so I did not know about that.'

I asked him, 'Did your father lend that goat to my father, or was it given to him because of blood-brotherhood?'

He said, 'It was a blood-brotherhood gift.'

I asked him, 'When did you go to Buganda?'

He said, 'I went to Buganda in 1939.'

Then I said, 'Thank you very much for coming here. I am going to catch you as a thief. Your father ate two of my father's goats, so your father has my goat. Your father took those two goats in 1943, and he died in 1944 before he returned the goats to my father,' I said this in a very rough voice. Then I told Abongo to go and call a chief, but the man said, 'Oh, please don't do that. I didn't come here to spoil our blood-brotherhood.'

I said, 'No, I can't allow you to leave unless you pay me a goat.'

April 14th: My wives Kijungu and Koke quarrelled. They went into the forest to collect firewood together, but Kijungu decided not to collect it. Then Koke asked her, 'Why are you not collecting firewood?'

Kijungu replied, 'If you have yours, you can go home.'

Koke returned home with the firewood. After she had gone, Kijungu collected her own wood. While she was doing this, she struck her leg with the axe. When she came home, she said, 'Koke bewitched me.' When Koke heard this, she rushed out of her house and came to me and asked me if I would allow her to fight with Kijungu. I refused.

An old woman belonging to my mother's clan has been visiting me at my home. Yesterday a man of the Bandikitibo lineage came to my house and asked for me. He called me. I came and greeted him. After we had greeted one another, he said, 'I have come to tell you that I want the woman who is staying here.'

Then I called the old woman. She came and sat down. The man said to her, 'You are a witch. When you left our village, you left something in the belly of my child. My child's belly is swelling. Now he will not eat anything. You wanted to eat some of my goats and, since you have been away, three of my goats have died. I have come to get you so that you may come and eat some of the meat of those goats, which you bewitched. If you want me to kill you another goat, I will kill it for you.'

The old woman said, 'I am not going with you, because I never attend such meals.' The man had to go away by himself. Before he left he told me, 'If that woman stays with you, she will bewitch all your children.'

April 16th: A neighbouring woman, Sindano, met Koke coming from the stream. She saw that Koke was carrying a pot which belonged to Lubangi. She told her, 'You are carrying Lubangi's pot, because you bewitched her so that she would leave the home.'

Koke was angry. She said, 'Show me the medicine which I used to bewitch Lubangi.'

Sindano said, 'The reason I said what I did was that you used to quarrel with Lubangi, because you said she was making Mpuga hate you. Now that she has gone away, Mpuga loves you.'

April 17th: I did not feel well. One of my mother's brothers came to my house and said, 'Mpuga, you are going to die because you didn't listen to what your father told you before he died. I remember that your father told you that you should leave Bundinyama as soon as he had died. Why have you continued to live here? Why don't you remember what your father told you? When you were sick some time ago, I went to a diviner and asked him about you. He told me that the Bandinyama are bewitching you. They want to kill you. He told me that they will kill you unless you leave this village. I have come to tell you if you do not leave this ridge, I am certain that you will die.

You know that you have been sick now and again. Is this not a sign that they are killing you?'

I replied, 'If I should leave Bundinyama, I will follow my brothers to Buganda. I will do that instead of going to live in another village. If the Bandinyama want to kill me, let them kill me. I will be buried with my father and my mother.'

Then he asked me, 'Don't you want to live?'

I said, 'It does not matter. Only God knows what is going to happen.'

April 18th: My sister Nakulinga came to see me. She told me that she is not leading a happy life where she is now living, because the other wife bothers her and tells her that she will not allow her to have any children by the husband. The other wife says, 'You will continue to have intercourse with your husband, but you will not become pregnant.'

Nakulinga told me that if this woman continues to act in this way, she will divorce her husband. I realize that Nakulinga is having trouble in that home.

April 23rd: A man named Kombili from the Congo came to my house. He told me, 'Your son Sogosa is very sick. Your wife Lubangi sent me here. She says that you, Mpuga, have permitted the child to become sick because you are sending your mother's gods to her. Lubangi's father found this out when he consulted the diviners.'

The next day I went to the Congo with Kihara. When I arrived there, I found the child lying on the ground outside the house. I said to my father-in-law, 'Why do you put my child outside when he is ill?'

He said, 'The house in which we were living was washed away by water, so we are living outside.' Then he gave me a palm-tree log for a chair. They prepared some food for me, but I refused to eat it. My father-in-law asked me, 'Why don't you eat?'

I told him, 'I only want to have tea.' I had tea and slept out in the open; I did not sleep with Lubangi. I returned home the next day.

April 26th: One of my mother's brothers, Gemuli, and his two sons, Erisa and Ndileya, came to my house. They have been living outside of Bwamba for a long time. My mother's brother said, 'When your mother died, why did you give a goat to Ngilipi? Why didn't you wait for me? It is I who should have the goat. You were wrong to do that.'

I said, 'I knew that you were living far away, and I didn't know when you would return. My mother died a long time ago. It is over a year now. Could I have waited so long?'

He knew he was wrong so he did not ask any more questions.

April 28th: My wife Kijungu went to Busaru without my permission. She went with another woman from the village. I had gone to drink beer at Batigwa's and discovered that she had gone when I returned. I asked Koke and she said, 'Didn't you give her permission to go?' I will punish her when she comes back. I may beat her or refuse to eat the food which she cooks. A wife should not go away without her husband's permission.

May 1st: In the morning I found Koke and Kijungu plucking their eyelashes. I asked them, 'What are you doing?'

They replied, 'We are trying to make our eyes look beautiful.'

I said, 'If you don't pluck them, will you look ugly?'

I was very angry with them. All the Amba now have turned into Toro. In the past we used to eat without washing our hands, but now the world has grown up. We are leaving our Amba habits. We are doing this of the light. I was very angry with these women because they were plucking their eyelashes the way the Amba did in the past. I took them to Kihara and told him about the matter. He said that I was right.

A man from the Congo came to my house. He gave me a letter from Lubangi. The man said that she wants to return to my house. The child is well, but he is causing much trouble because he beats other children. Lubangi wrote me that I should go with Kijungu so we might bring the child back here. She said that the Congo was troubling her. I said to the man, 'Why doesn't she come back? She went alone, so she should come back alone. Does she need a porter?'

I had been told by the chief to dig a latrine. I went into the forest to get some lianas to tie the poles together. I was frightened by a snake. Later I came across some wasps, and they stung my face. I fell down and cried.

While I was away, the chief visited my house. He said, 'Why hasn't Mpuga finished his latrine? Why is the house of Koke in such bad condition? You should tell Mpuga that he is lucky that he is away. Otherwise I would have taken him away to the road gang.' When I returned Koke told me about this. The work I have done today was like a prisoner's work. I have had no rest.

May 3rd. The chief came to my house. He found me in the latrine. He said, 'Did your wife tell you what I told her yesterday?'

I said, 'Yes, she told me all the things. I am still trying my hardest to get the work finished.'

He said, 'Come to the court on Friday. I will judge your case.'

[An entomologist from the Virus Research Institute came down to Bwamba for two weeks and Mpuga was hired by him for a two-week
209

period to aid in the collection of mosquitoes. Mpuga's brother, Bukombi, came in the car from Entebbe and went back at the end of the period. While in Bwamba Bukombi obtained a new wife and brought her back to Mpuga's home. E.H.W.]

May 19th: When Bukombi left, he said to Abongo, 'Don't bewitch my new wife. I have left her here. If she becomes ill, I will know that you have bewitched her, because you are the one who bewitches my wives and you are the one who bewitched my child who died. Don't bewitch this new wife. You are annoyed because I have paid goats for this wife.'

Abongo's wife said, 'Abongo is said to be a witch because he always says bad things to his neighbours.'

After this an elder of our lineage came to my house. He asked Abongo where I was and where Bukombi was. Abongo replied, 'I am not in your lineage. Why do you ask me? When you come here in the future, don't ask me anything.'

When I returned, I found the elder sitting in the courtyard. He told me what Abongo had done. Then he told me that his child was sick and that he had taken it to the dispensary. On the same day two of my children became ill. I am sure that this has not been caused by another witch; it has been caused by Abongo. If one of them dies today, I will be certain that he has bewitched me. Also my wife Kijungu has no strength today.

Before we talked about Abongo's witchcraft, we did not have much trouble. No snakes came into my house. Now troubles and snakes are coming into my house.

May 20th: In the night I heard something moving in my house. I called Koke. She got up. Then I got up and sat by the fire. As I was about to go back to bed, I saw a snake on the wall. I called to Koke, 'Come and see the snake which has been moving about the house.' Then I got my spear and tried to spear it, but it disappeared. I went back to bed. I didn't go to sleep, and later I heard the chickens making a noise. I got up and found two of the chickens dead, but I didn't see the snake. I was certain that this had been sent by Abongo because I had said that I was going to send him away from my homestead because of his witchcraft. He sent a snake to kill my chickens. We had promised to give him some goats for his wife and when he saw us paying four goats for the new wife of Bukombi, he was angry. For one whole night he did not talk to any of us. He prevented our children from going into our house. He said, 'I don't like to eat your food.'

In the afternoon Kijungu and Koke began to quarrel when Kijungu passed through Koke's garden. Koke said, 'If my food dies, I will know that you killed it.'

As a result of this, Kijungu became angry and said, 'Why do you suspect me of being a witch?'

I tried to stop them and sent for Kihara. He listened to them and said, 'You, Kijungu, must not pass through Koke's garden after this.'

Later Koke's child saw that Kijungu had some ground-nut soup. The child poured the soup on the ground. When Kijungu saw this she said to the child, 'Your mother said that I am a thief and a witch. Because of that she must pay me one shilling for my ground-nut soup.'

Then Kijungu came to me and told me all this. I told her, 'The child who ruined your soup is my child, and I bought the ground-nuts in the market. I don't see any sense in trying to get money from Koke.' I learned from this that my two wives no longer agree with one another, and that they do not like each other.

May 21st: Mambaiye, the mother of Kisasi, came to my house. She said, 'Mpuga, why is my child so weak? Is he not eating, or are your wives not giving him food?'

I said, 'Have you ever seen a father eating food while his child is dying of hunger?'

She said, 'My child eats when you are here, but I know that he does not eat when you are away. That is not good enough. I must take him away today, because your wives do not know how to take care of children. I won't bring my child here again unless Lubangi comes back from the Congo.'

May 22nd: I dreamed that Mugelia came to me and said, 'Tell me if you want to stay in Bundinyama and die on this ridge as your father Mosumba died. I want to take you away from here and have you stay with me.' Before I could reply, I woke up. I awakened Koke and told her the dream. She said, 'You understand now why you become ill.' Later on in the night army ants came into the house and killed some of my chickens.

Koke's father came to my house. I killed a chicken for him, and when the food was ready I told him to eat. He said he did not come to eat. He said, 'I've come here to settle the accusation that my daughter is a witch.'

I said, 'Is your child the one who told you of this?'

He said, 'Your brother's wife says my daughter is a witch. I want you to tell me why she says my daughter is a witch and to name the people whom she has killed in your home.'

I said to him, 'I can't go into this trouble between my wives. You know that when a man has more than one wife the wives are always jealous.'

He understood that all these troubles were caused by jealousy, so he got up and went to eat. After he had eaten, he went home. I knew that he had been very angry when he had arrived. From this I knew that Koke reports all the troubles in my home to her family.

A man came to my house and said, 'When Bukombi was here in Bwamba I brewed beer, and he bought two shillings' worth. He paid me one shilling and he still owes me one.' That man asked me for one shilling.

I told him, 'Go away. I can't pay a debt which I didn't make and of which I am not certain.'

May 23rd: I met a man on the road. He told me, 'I have heard that Ntingia is working with your brother Bukombi in Buganda. You should write to Bukombi and tell him not to have anything to do with that boy. He is a very bad boy and he is a witch. If you don't write to your brother, he will be in danger.' I told the man that if Ntingia causes trouble, he will be discharged.

May 24th: I dreamed that someone told me that my child, Kisasi, had died. When I got up, I felt cold; I shivered. I got some ashes and blew them away. I said, 'Bad things, go over there.' In the morning I heard that a man called Tisenbi of the Bubandi had died. I was certain that this was the dream which I had dreamed. The shivering did not leave me until I heard that my child was still alive.

In the evening I was away. A friend of mine came to the house and found my wives at home. When I returned he was asleep. I went to the bed and woke him, and we started talking. He said, 'I have heard things. I think you should leave Bundinyama. If you refuse to leave, you will die. You see, now they have started to drive away your wives. Where is your Lubangi now? Was she not driven away by someone? That should teach you.'

I said to him, 'I am a man. I can't simply move away.'

The catechist from the chapel at Hakitengya came to my house. He said, 'Why don't you attend church? Do you think that people who marry three wives do not attend church? I do not see you in church every Sunday.'

I told him, 'If I wish to attend church, I can go. If I don't want to go, I remain at home. Do you force people to attend church?'

The catechist said, 'God will punish you.'

I told him, 'You also will become a sinner and lose your religion.' I was very angry and told him, 'Go away, preach at your church and leave me alone.'

Last night while we were sleeping, my son Muganga had a dream. He got out of bed, went to the fire and said, 'My mother, don't leave me behind. We must go together.'

Kijungu heard him and asked him, 'To whom are you talking?'

The child did not reply. Kijungu went to the fire and picked up the child and put him in bed. She asked him, 'What happened to you, and why are you up out of bed?'

Muganga said, 'I don't know what you are talking about. I have been asleep all the time. What do you want?' This was a bad dream, because his mother died a long time ago.

May 28th: I quarrelled with Abongo. I quarrelled with him because he spoke bad things to my wives, things which should not be said, especially by a member of the lineage. Abongo said to Kijungu, 'To prove that you are a real woman, have Mpuga build you a house. When you have your first harvest after you have been in that house, I will call you a woman. Mpuga says that you are a good cultivator. I will see how you get on with Mpuga.'

Then he said to Koke, 'You are the only person who never becomes ill. Other people become ill, but nothing ever happens to you. You always have your strength. Why are you like that? Since you don't become ill, if you ever get even a slight headache, it will finish you.'

Koke said, 'If I die tomorrow, I will know that you have killed me, Abongo.'

He once told Koke that, if he began to bewitch her, she would not last a day and that he could kill her in a very short time.

May 29th: Bukalibona, the husband of Nakulinga, came to me and said, 'Nakulinga is pregnant, but she is not well. I went to the diviner, and he told me that I should get a male goat from you. He told me that I should take it to him and he will deal with the matter. If you do not do this, she will not have a child.'[1]

June 2nd: I went to a beer party. On the way home I met the diviner, Kigboli. He told me, 'You must not drink so much beer. If you drink beer this way, you will die soon. Drink it carefully. Don't drink it daily. I, Kigboli, have said this.' I thought that this man had a reason for saying all he did.

July 5th: Abongo's wife owned four chickens. While she was away from home, he killed one of them and ate it. When his wife came home she asked, what happened to the chicken. He said, that it had been taken by a wild animal. The wife said nothing. Later Abongo struck Muganga and then the child cried. He said, 'You stole your wife's chicken and ate it.'

---

[1] It was thought that the difficulties Nakulinga was having during her pregnancy was due to the god Kwakwamira who incorporates the spirits of all the men who were slain in the past by men of the Bandinyama lineage.

The wife said to Abongo, 'Oh, you said the chicken was stolen, but the truth was that you ate it. You must return my chicken.' Now Abongo is looking for a chicken.

July 6th: Abongo's wife asked Kihara's boy, Nkabatama, to kill some rats for her, but the child refused. Then she asked him again, saying, 'I very much wish to eat a rat. You must kill me one.'

The child said, 'Wait, I will kill you some today.' So Abongo's wife went to the market and left the child with Abongo. Nkabatama asked him, 'Where are the rat holes which your wife told me about this morning? I want to kill some rats for her.'

Abongo showed him the holes, and Nkabatama started widening them with a piece of stick. There was another child with him. After the hole was wide enough, Nkabatama put his hand into the hole. His finger was bitten. He saw his finger bleeding and said, 'Oh, there are many rats in this hole. See, one has bitten me.' Then Nkabatama started digging again. Then he saw the tail and said to the other child, 'Oh, see its tail.'

The other child said, 'No, that is a snake's tail.' That child said, 'You were bitten by a snake. It was not a rat which bit you. Stop what you are doing, because the poison will kill you.'

Then Nkabatama began to feel great pain. Abongo was watching. He did not think of killing the snake or treating the child. Kalisa came and found the child and took him to the dispensary at Bundibugyo. In the afternoon when Kihara came home and heard that his child had been bitten by a snake, he came and took hold of Abongo's wife's arm and said, 'It is you who caused my child to be bitten by a snake. If he dies today, you will also die. Why did you send him to hunt for you?'

Abongo watched them. I came and found them talking about it. I said to Kihara, 'Leave the woman alone.'

He replied, 'No, Abongo and his wife are both witches. They must come to my house.'

They went to his house. Abongo said, 'I have some medicine from my father and I'll put it on this child. If the snake was sent from my house, the child will recover.'

Then Muwisa, Kihara's wife, went into the house, put her finger in her vagina and wiped her finger on the child. She said, 'I have put the "people-producer" on your bite, so it will not kill you.'

The next day, although the arm was swollen, the child felt better. Abongo's wife felt very much ashamed. All the other women were laughing at her. She has a husband who should kill rats for her.

Another man in our village, Eria, came to me to ask my advice as to what he should do about Abongo, because he paid his poll tax and

Abongo has never repaid him. I called Abongo and asked him why he could not repay his neighbour. He said the thing which prevented him from repaying Eria was that, when Eria got the poll-tax receipt, he kept it himself.

Eria said, 'I am certain that you are real witch, Abongo. You just get all the things which belong to your neighbour for nothing. You trust your witchcraft powers to help you.' Then he took the poll-tax ticket and threw it at Abongo and said, 'Let me lose twenty-four shillings instead of losing my life. Take the receipt. I will get some more money.'

Abongo said, 'You refused to bring me the receipt before. Why did you bring it to me today?'

Nkiambi, wife of Bukombi, has eye trouble. Her mother heard that she was ill and came to me today like a mad woman. When she was still at the entrance of the courtyard, she shouted, 'Are you there, Mpuga?'

Kijungu told her that I was in the house. She said, 'Call him for me.' Then I came outside.

She said, 'Why is my child ill?'

I said, 'I don't know. None of my people are staying well.'

She said, 'I know that you have a witch in your home. I know that Abongo is pursuing Bukombi. He doesn't wish him to have peace.' Then she said to Abongo, 'You must leave my child alone. If you want to, bewitch your own child so that you may eat him, but don't bewitch my child. If you kill my child, you can be sure that I am going to kill you.'

After that the mother took Nkiambi away with her back to their house. Before she left, Abongo said that he was going to accuse her before the chiefs because she called him a witch. Nkiambi said, 'You say you are not a witch. Don't you remember that one day you had intercourse with me? Don't you remember that we were sleeping on one bed and you left me on the bed and went outside?' That stopped Abongo. He didn't say anything more.

July 7th: Kasokura, the husband of my sister Bagelia, came to my house looking for his wife. She was not at my house. She had gone to her mother's sister's house because there was a religious ceremony there. Previously this man had complained about my sister. He said that she was not respectful to his mother and his father. He asked me if she acted that way when she was at my house. I told him that she did not act that way. I told him, 'She is acting that way because you are a young boy. If she did that sort of thing in my house, I would beat her.'

Later that day Kasokura met her coming along the road with my sister Ndigombwa. He asked his wife, 'Where have you been?' Bagelia did not answer him, and he beat her with a cane. I am going to tell him that he cannot be married to my sister, because he did a very bad thing to beat her on the road. It is a very bad thing to beat a wife on the road.

July 8th: A man from the Congo who is a relative of Kijungu's former husband, Musegia, came to Kihara's house to see Ndijaha. He said to Ndijaha, 'Musegia has heard that your daughter, Kijungu, is now married. He wonders if the man who has married her is stronger or more handsome than himself. He wonders if the new husband is a better witch than he is. He says that he will see whether or not the new husband lives throughout the year. If he and Kijungu spend the year together, he says that he will know that this man is a very strong witch.'

Ndijaha said, 'That is why my daughter has been sick from time to time. It is Musegia who is bewitching her.' Then Ndijaha told her son Kimbugwe, 'Musegia said that he will kill your sister because she is married. I know now that this man is bewitching Kijungu.'

July 9th: In a dream my mother and my father came to me. My mother said to me, 'Why do you stay here in your house doing nothing, my son? You are allowing your child to stay in the Congo. You should go and get him and bring him home. Leave his mother there, if she wants to stay there with her parents, because she has said that she has left home forever.' When I awoke in the morning, I told Koke about my dream and she advised me to go to the Congo to get Sogosa.

July 10th: I scolded my wife Kijungu for having left the house without permission and for not having prepared the hot water for my bath. She spoke to me boldly and we began to quarrel. Finally I slapped her. Then she went and asked Kihara and her mother to come and judge between us. We both stated our cases, and they judged in my favour. I told her mother that she should tell her daughter not to set herself up against me. Then I gave Kijungu permission to stay at Kihara's house.

In the evening while I was sitting beside the fire, a millipede began to crawl up my leg. I called to Koke and asked her, 'Why has this millipede come into my house? They used to come into my mother's house because she was a priestess of Nyakala, but since her death I have never seen a millipede.' I put it on a stick and threw it outside.

During the middle of the night while we were asleep, Koke felt something crawling on her head. It was the millipede again. I got up and threw it outside. I am certain one of my wives will be a priestess of Nyakala, because I have seen many signs, such as the toads and the millipedes which have come into my house.

July 12th: Kijungu's brother, Kangoro, came to my house and asked me to pay the goats which I owed him. I told him, 'I have only one female goat. If you want to, you can take it.'

He refused to take it, saying, 'I have not come for one goat.'

I asked him, 'Since you have refused to take the goat, what can I give you?'

He said, 'If you don't give me some goats, I will take my girl.'

We continued to argue, and finally he went home.

I have offered three goats to Kijungu's brother, Kimbugwe, but he has refused to take them. I do not know what to do about this matter.

July 16th: A man of the Bubukwanga lineage whom I know has been in the Congo. On his way home he passed my house. He told me, 'Your wife Lubangi fell in the Semliki River again. Her father says that it happens because you are bewitching her. The gods of your mother have followed her and are trying to pull her into the river.'

July 17th: The Bandinyama gathered together to hear two cases. Kihara accused me of having had intercourse with his former wife, Kageye, who is dead, and of having intercourse with his present wife, Muwisa. The people judged the case in my favour. They decided that because I had said to Muwisa, 'You are bewitching my goats,' she planned to harm me by accusing me of having had intercourse with her.

After they had heard my case they listened to the case between Kihara's wife, Andiye, and Abongo. Andiye accused him of having asked her three times to sleep with him. She said that Abongo told her that, if she refused, she would see what would happen to her. He was unable to say anything. The case was decided against him, and the people advised him strongly not to do this again.

July 18th: I received a message from the Congo asking me to go and get my child at Lubangi's home, because he is causing a lot of trouble by beating other children. I said nothing to the messenger.

Koke and I had a quarrel. She was angry with me because I had cleared a cotton plot for Kijungu before I cleared one for her. Koke said she would not plant cotton in her plot, because she is the senior wife, and I should have cleared her plot first. I told her, 'If you don't work in that plot, it will be because you are lazy. If you are lazy, tell me and I will give the plot to another person.'

July 19th: I dreamed that I had gone to a dance with Nyamanzi's wife. On the way home I had intercourse with her. When I woke up, I was worried. I said, 'Why should I dream such a dream?' I did not feel well, so I went to the shop at Bundibugyo and bought a pill. When I got home I took it in some hot water and then I began to feel better.

A man of the Bandisiyoko lineage came to my house and asked me to take him to my mother's brother's village, to the house of Ngilipi. I asked him why he wanted to go there. He told me, 'I want to get some medicine so that I may capture women. Ngilipi likes to capture women. I want him to give me some of the medicine he uses so that I may capture them too.' I told him that I did not have time to take him to Bumati now, but that I would take him later on.

July 21st: Some members of Lubangi's lineage came to my house carrying a patient. They wanted to put the sick person in my home. I told them, 'Your daughter Lubangi has divorced me; who will look after the sick one?'

They said, 'Why do you drive us away with our patient? You are our affinal relative.'

I replied, 'Your child left me. I don't like you any more.'

I went to work in the garden. After I had been working a while my knife broke. Then I used a second knife, and it also broke. Later Kijungu asked me to fix her hoe. While I was fixing it with a stone, a piece of the stone flew off and struck me on the forehead. I lay on the ground for several minutes just looking at the earth. I wanted to weep. Then I borrowed another knife. Just before I was ready to leave the garden, I cut my finger. I decided that I had better stop working and go home. I think someone must have been bewitching me.

In the afternoon, while I was at Kihara's house, my sister Bagelia and her husband came to my home. I was called. I found them sitting inside the house. Bagelia said, 'I won't go back to the house of this man. He treats me badly. He says that I am a witch. He beats me daily. At night he comes to me and tells me that there must not be any other witches in the country because, if there were, they would come and eat me. He says that he wishes the witches would eat me so he could live in peace.'

When I asked her husband about this, he said, 'She is right. I said that.'

I told the husband, 'Go away. You cannot take my "daughter"[1] with you.'

I received another message from Lubangi's father. He wants me to go to the Congo. I told the man, 'Lubangi went away by herself, and I don't see why she shouldn't come back by herself. The path is still open.'

[1] Now that their father is dead, Mpuga has the authority of her father.

A neighbour borrowed my shirt and went away to Bohanda. The morning after he returned, his wife took the shirt and a pair of shorts and burned them in the fire, because he had slept with another woman. When he looked for the shirt, the children told him that their mother had burned it. I am very angry because my shirt has been burned.

July 24th: When I went to work in my garden, I found a child sitting down in it. When he saw me, he was embarrassed and started covering the place where he was sitting. I asked him, 'What are you covering?' I went there and found that he had defecated. I told him to clean the place quickly and when he had done this, I took him to his elder brother. I told his elder brother to advise him not to do this again.

Katugumia sent one of his children to my house to say that he wanted to speak to me. I went to his house and when I arrived there he told me, 'I have called you in order to speak about my sister Bagelia.[1] She does not want to stay with her husband. He has bad habits. I want to repay the bridewealth to that man.'

I told Katugumia, 'You are a member of the Bandibugyo lineage, so how can you repay the bridewealth of a daughter of the Bandinyama? Such things were not done by the elders in the past.'

July 25th: The wife of Abongo has introduced a lot of things into my home. She has trained my children to eat rats. When she arrived, they had never eaten a rat. The other day she cooked a rat with some ground-nuts. When it was ready, she called Abongo to come and eat. My son Nkuba joined them. When he was about to put some food in his mouth, he saw a rat's leg. He said, 'Why are you giving me rat's meat to eat when our father has forbidden us to eat rats?' When I heard about this, I was very angry.

When I was near the river, I saw a man called Sakwendia from a neighbouring village. He was talking with the wife of the Bandinyama, Kalisa. They did not see me. Then I spoke up, 'You are making a proposition to the wife of Kalisa.' When the man heard me speak, he ran away into the forest.

Later he came to my house and said, 'You must not say anything to her husband. I will give you two shillings so that you may not tell him.' I refused to take the money. I have not said anything to Kalisa.

I scolded Koke for allowing the goats to wander and to ruin other people's food. Later when I was walking along a path, I hurt my foot on a stone. I knew that she had sent witchcraft after me.

July 27th: I went into the forest to cut some lianas to use as ropes. I had a knife and a spear with me. I fell in a game pit and in the bot-

[1] Katugumia is a half-brother of Bagelia. They had the same mother but different fathers.

tom of the pit was a sharpened stake. I was not harmed by the knife or the spear or the stake. When I arrived home and told the people what had happened, they were very surprised that I had escaped harm. I killed a chicken and ate it because I had escaped death.

I received a message from my former wife, Bakweziba of Bubomboli. She said, 'I want to return to my home.'

I replied, 'Do not come back here. You allowed people to kill my children because you went from one place to another. I don't think you have given up your habit of wandering. I know that you will continue to act that way until your last day.'

July 28th: My father used to have a small shrine near his house for a thing that used to enter his house. For several years no shrine has been built for it, and we have not seen this thing. This morning Koke called me, and I went to her house. After I had gone in, she asked me, 'What is this?'

When I looked, I saw a black thing which looks like a snake but which is not a snake. I was certain that this was the thing for which my father used to build the shrine. I got a certain type of powder and a flower and put it on the back of this creature. I said, 'Now, I have given you your things. You should go away because I am a Christian, and my father is dead.' Then I closed the door of the house and went outside. When I went back a short time later, it had disappeared. Later I saw a millipede on the wall of the house. When I saw it, I knew that all my father's gods have arrived and want to catch me. I am a Christian, and they are sparing Abongo who is not a Christian. I am very angry because these things are coming to me.

A little while ago Abongo went to consult the diviners and they told him, 'If Mpuga does not treat the gods of his father well, illness will stay with him, and his children will be troubled by illness.' When Abongo told me about this, I knew that what he said was true, because I had heard that my son Kisasi has been burned on his leg. I sent a message to his mother telling her to send me a chicken.

A woman who is a relative of Lubangi came to my house from the Congo. She said, 'Why do you neglect your wife and your child? Your child is acting very badly. He beats other children who live there and as a result of that he will be killed.'

I thought about this matter a great deal.

August 2nd: I decided to go to the Congo and get Lubangi. On the day after the woman visited me I woke up very early in the morning. I awakened Abongo and told him, 'It is time to go.' We gathered our things and started off. As we were going through the forest, we met a herd of elephants. Abongo dropped his bundle, and we ran away. After a while we returned and found our bundles. When we arrived at the Semliki River, we called to the canoe-man. We paid him forty cents, and he took us across the river. When we arrived at my father-in-law's house, he was very glad to see us. He brought us some palm wine, and we started drinking. I became very drunk. The next morning my father-in-law took us to Lubangi. She welcomed us; she was very happy. She cooked some cassava and some fresh fish. We had enough to eat. Then I said to my father-in-law, 'I have come to talk about your daughter. If she has anything to say, she should say it today.'

My father-in-law said, 'I have nothing to say because I ate your bridewealth. You and Lubangi are truly married to one another. It is impossible for your wife to be married here to another man, because she is a Christian wife. It is impossible for me to exchange her again. Since you have come here, you should take your wife and child home with you.'

They do not have much food there. They have a lot of fish, but all their other food comes from the market. When that is finished, they have to stay hungry until the next market. There is only one market a week, and it is far from their home.

August 3rd: Kijungu and Lubangi talked together. Kijungu told her how Koke had been treating her. Lubangi told her, 'Koke brings medicine to use against her fellow wives. I know that she paid two shillings for the medicine which drove me out of my house.' When I heard them talking, I was certain that they would try to bewitch Koke, so that she would go away.

I went to them and said, 'If my wife Koke leaves this home, it will be because you, Lubangi, and you, Kijungu, have bewitched her.'

They said, 'Are you saying we are witches?'

I said, 'It is well known that you women have a great deal of witchcraft, and you are always bewitching people.'

Then Kijungu told Lubangi that Koke had eaten sweet potatoes from her garden. Lubangi began to quarrel with Koke and wanted to fight with her. Kihara came, and we kept them from fighting. I said, 'Lubangi, you went to your father's house without saying farewell. You simply went away, without a reason. You should not quarrel about the potatoes. It was your fault because you went away without permission.'

My sister Leiko came to my house. She said, 'I want to leave my husband. You should pay back the bridewealth which you ate.'

I said, 'I cannot repay the bridewealth. I told you not to marry those Bambutuku, and you told me that that man was the only one you loved in the whole world. When you told me that, I took the goats and ate them. Why do you want to leave your husband's house now? This is your affair. I know nothing about it. Also, I do not have any goats with which to repay the Bambutuku.' I told her to go away and not to stay in my house.

A Toro friend of mine came from Fort Portal and stayed in my house for the night. He told me that he was on his way to the mission hospital at Oicha in the Congo. He said, 'My penis is diseased. I want to go to Oicha for treatment. If I am fortunate, I will be cured.'

I asked him, 'Why didn't you go to the hospital at Fort Portal?'

He said, 'No, they can't cure me there. I went there, and they told me that they wanted to cut off my foreskin. That would be a very bad thing.'

I said, 'Why didn't you allow them to circumcise you? I didn't keep my foreskin; it is a very bad thing; it makes you look like a woman. Also when you have a disease, it may become dangerous if you have a foreskin.'

He said, 'No, having a foreskin is a very good thing in our tribe, because Toro women like it.'

At night Lubangi showed me some letters which had been sent to her while she was living in the Congo. One of these letters was from a man of the Bandinyama lineage and another was written by a man of the Banditokwe lineage. The letter of the Banditokwe man said, 'Lubangi, you should divorce Mpuga. I will pay goats to your father, and he can repay the bridewealth to Mpuga. Then I will marry you.' The letter from the Bandinyama man said, 'I should marry you, Lubangi. Mpuga is not fit to be married to you.'

From all this I learned that the Bandinyama hate me, and they do not wish me well. They bring medicine to try to kill me so that they can marry my wives. They are doing this in vain. It is impossible for them to marry my wives. I will keep these letters and later I will call a meeting of the Bandinyama. I will explain all these matters to them, and I will show them the letters. Then everybody will realize that some people are pursuing me. If I don't show them the letters, they will say that I am lying.

August 4th: A woman who is a member of Lubangi's lineage came and spoke to her. She said, 'Why did you return? Since you have returned, you must be prepared to be killed by the Bandinyama.'

I said to that woman, 'How do you know this? If you know about it, you must be a witch yourself. I know that you are a witch, and I know that you were driven away from your husband's home for that reason. Don't come to my home again. If I find you here again, I will beat you.'

While all my wives were away getting water, I fell asleep. I felt someone shaking me. I put off my blanket and saw that it was a woman whom I know. I said, 'Why have you come to my bed?'

She replied, 'Don't you like people?'

I answered, 'I like women, but you have to talk to a woman before she will come to your bed. I have never talked to you about these matters. I can't sleep with you today.'

She said to me, 'You are saying that you don't have the power to satisfy women.'

I said, 'Are you the one who is taking care of my wives?' I said to her, 'Remember that, if Lubangi finds you here, she is going to beat you. I think you know her habits.' Then the woman went out of the house, and I went back to sleep again.

Later a man came to me and told me, 'Abongo has visited the house of a doctor named Ezimba and asked him to kill you. If you become ill, don't suspect anyone else; it will be Ezimba. He sends witchcraft to your house every day. He climbs on his roof and blows medicine toward your house.'

August 5th: One of my mother's brothers came to my home early in the morning. He said, 'Mpuga, now that your wife Lubangi has returned, what do you think?'

I said, 'I have nothing to say.'

He said, 'You must move away from Bundinyama and take your wives with you. The men of your lineage do not like to have you with them, because you have very beautiful wives, and no one else in the village has such beautiful wives. If you refuse to take my advice, you must realize that you will die or you will lose your wives. In particular, you may lose the wife who has returned. I haven't consulted diviners, but I heard about these things from someone in your village.'

I told him, 'I cannot move away from this village because my father and my mother died here and I will die here.'

Kihara's affinal relatives came to him and said that they wanted some goats. They said that if he did not give them some, they would take their daughter, Muwisa.

Kihara said, 'I cannot pay any goats to you, because your daughter is a witch. Even though she is cultivating for me, you must realize that I know things about which I haven't told. She killed my mother. If I pay bridewealth for her, people will laugh at me.'

We told Kihara, 'If you want this woman, no one will stop you from paying bridewealth for her. If you still say that she killed your mother, you should send her away.'

I gathered all my wives together to talk about the matter of food. I have found that Koke will not eat any food cooked by Kijungu and

Kijungu will not eat any food cooked by Koke. I asked Kijungu why she refused to eat the food cooked by her fellow wife.

Kijungu said, 'I don't eat Koke's food because Koke won't eat mine.'

Then I asked Koke why she refused to eat the food of Kijungu. Koke said, 'The reason I do this is that Kijungu has said that I am lazy and not as good a woman nor as good a cultivator as she is.'

While Muganga was climbing a pawpaw tree, Nkuba pushed him and made him fall. I slapped Nkuba and warned him not to do it again, because he is an older boy and may break Muganga's bones. Lubangi was angry and said that I had done wrong to strike her child for no reason. This made me angry, because Muganga has no mother.

August 6th: Early in the morning Kihara called Batigwa and myself to talk about paying bridewealth for his wife Muwisa. I told him, 'Why do you trouble us about paying for your wife? We told you yesterday that if you want this woman, you should pay for her. We know that you are fond of women who are witches.'

When Muwisa's brothers heard us talking, they became angry and said, 'We won't come back here again because we know that you are not going to pay us.'

A child came to me and told me that one of my kids was lying dead in the garden. I went to the garden and brought it home. When I skinned it, I saw that it had been beaten with a stick. I realized that some of my neighbours are bad people, because they killed my goat. I went to the house of a diviner and consulted him. He told me that I should not eat the meat of this goat, because the person who killed it had put some medicine in its mouth so that I would die when I ate it. He told me to throw the goat away and not to permit any of my wives or children to eat it. He also told me that the medicine which had been put in the goat's mouth had been brought from Busongora in Toro.

I said, 'Can I give this goat to anyone outside of my lineage?'

He said, 'No, throw it away.'

Then I went home and threw the goat into my new latrine. I said nothing. If I see a goat which belongs to another person in my garden, I will kill it.

During the night Lubangi said to me, 'Are you asleep?'

I said, 'No,' and she started to talk about Koke. She said, 'Do you remember that she stole your mother's chicken? Secondly, she stole Bukombi's chicken. Now she has eaten my potatoes, and I did not give her permission to use them. Why did she eat my potatoes? I never ate any of her potatoes. Now she has begun to bring medicine to her fellow wives which causes them to wander. She wants to be alone in this home. Is this a good thing? Has Koke given you some medicine or has she bewitched you so that you are afraid to send her away? In the past you used to hate all women of this type. Your father used to advise you that it is not good to marry a woman who is a thief. Why don't you get rid of this woman and send her to her father's home? She is a thief and she sends medicine to her fellow wives so that they wander. She cannot raise all your children alone. I know that she feeds the children when you are present, but when you are not here the children cannot touch her food. I will advise Kijungu to go away from your home and to leave you with your favourite wife. If Koke brings medicine to me again, I will get stronger medicine which will send her away. Then she will not come here again, and your child will grow in a foreign place. As a result of that Koke will learn that it is not a good thing to bring medicine to other wives.'

I said to Lubangi, 'You are saying that you want to kill me. Someone will give you medicine and tell you that it has the power to send away the other wife, but the person who gives it to you may really intend to kill me. Then when you bring the medicine into the homestead, I will die. I will have to call all the Bandinyama, and when they come together we will settle these matters. They will find out which one of you is the bad woman, and I will send that bad woman away from my home forever.'

August 7th: A man named Mugaza came to my house and asked me for worm medicine. He has had intercourse with a woman in another village, and the worms have caught his child.

I told him, 'You have been foolish. You should have come to me earlier, before you met this woman. Then nothing would have happened to your child. Give me one shilling and fifty cents to open my bag, and I will give you medicine. You will know that the worms have been caused by something else.' He gave me a shilling and fifty cents, and I gave him the medicine.

Abongo and I went to work in our gardens. On the way back we passed the house of Baganiki. His new wife said, 'Wait for food, and after you have eaten you can go home.'

I think that she is a witch and I have never eaten any food at her house. I was clever; I said, 'I will take my knife back to the house and then I will return.' In that way I escaped. I went home and did not go back. A little while later a child from Baganiki's home came to my house with some food prepared by that woman. I took it, but I did not eat it; I gave it to someone else.

August 8th: My sister Leiko ran away from her husband and came to my house, where she stayed for the night. In the morning she went away and said she was going back to her husband's house. Later her husband arrived. He said, 'Yesterday my wife escaped and came here. Where is she now?'

I told him, 'She was here. She spent the night here. But she went back this morning.'

He said, 'She must have gone somewhere else. Leiko is becoming a very bad wife. She runs away from time to time. You should be prepared to pay my bridewealth back to me.'

I took out one of Kijungu's teeth. She was very frightened. Three people—Lubangi, Abongo and the Ganda, Kasu—had to hold her. After it had been taken out, she bled a great deal.

August 9th: I received a letter from Bukombi. He said, 'My job will be finished at the end of this month. Is my wife behaving well or is she behaving badly? If she is behaving badly, you should go and get the bridewealth from her father.' His wife troubles me a great deal. She has very bad habits. I gave her land to cultivate, and she failed to do anything with it. She is lazy and does not like to cultivate. She has been away for a month. She is staying with her parents.

Then Kasu came to my house and told me that Bukombi wanted his poll tax sent to him, because the chiefs of Buganda were troubling him. I knew that he did not leave his ticket here, and he did not leave money with me to pay the tax. What is he trying to do?

Koke went to Bundibugyo to buy some maize to use as seed. She met a woman called Nyabonboli. That woman said to her, 'I want to go with you, Koke, when you go home so that your husband may buy some salt for me. I have no salt at all.'

I saw Koke coming into the courtyard with this woman. Koke explained why she had come with her. I went to Kasu's shop and bought some salt for her, because I knew that salt could not bring a person such a long distance. I knew that that woman was a witch. It was fortunate that I realized this, because, if I had not bought salt for her, she might have killed me. I know that type of person.

A man who had been sent by Koke's father came to my house to ask for the bridewealth. I told the man that I realized that I owed her father two goats, but I had none to give him at present. The one which I did have I paid for another wife.

The man said, 'You are not honest with your affinal relatives. You have had Koke's for several years and you have never completed the bridewealth payments. I never saw a man who took such a long time to finish paying the bridewealth.'

At night when I went to Koke's house, she refused to open the door for me. I kicked the door and opened it. When I went in, she didn't say anything to me but she pushed me. I said, 'Why did you

226

do that? Am I your wife?' Then I slapped her. She began to cry. After she stopped crying, she took her child and went out. When I realized that she had gone, I became very worried, because she had taken my child out during the night-time. I began to look for her, but could not find her. She had hidden herself on the verandah of Kasu's house. I went back to bed. Later I heard her opening the door as she came in. I did not say anything to her.

August 10th: Kijungu has had a sore on her breast for some time. Today she did not feel well. I went to find medicine for her.

While I was on my way to the house of the man who has the medicine, I came upon the wife of a Nubian bathing in the river. She was facing the other way and did not see me. I kept quiet and watched her. After a while she turned and saw me. She was very angry. She picked up a stone and threw it at me. Fortunately the stone did not hit me. She said, 'If we were at home, my husband would kill you today.' I know now that it is dangerous to watch the wife of a Nubian having a bath.

When I arrived at the house of the man who has medicine, he asked me for one shilling and fifty cents to open his bag. I said to him, 'You want a great deal of money. Have you cured her already?'

He said, 'I must make you pay, because once you wanted to beat my brother.'

When I heard him say this, I left his house, because I knew that the medicine would not be any good. I knew from what he said that he was a witch and that he wanted to kill me.

When I returned home, Koke felt ill. She was crying. I went to get firewood and when I came back, I found the child, Bakatwika, crying for his mother's breast. I made some tea for him, and he stopped crying and went to bed. I did not eat because I was busy taking care of my wife.

August 11th: Baganiki came to my house and told me, 'Abongo's wife must not enter my house, because she has been advising my first wife to divorce me. I have lived with that wife for a long time, and I have eight children by her. Now Abongo's wife wants her to divorce me. Tell Abongo's wife to stop giving her advice of that kind.'

Because Koke was in bed, I went to get firewood for her house. I went to Kijungu's garden and got some firewood there. When Kijungu found out about that, she said, 'Why did you get my firewood for Koke when Koke is always saying bad things to me?'

I told Kijungu, 'I have done this thing for the first time. I won't do it again.'

When I made some tea, I found that I had no sugar. I said, 'My sugar is all gone.'

Kasu, the Ganda, who was there, said, 'Send a child to my house, and he can bring some sugar to you.' Kasu is a very good friend.

During the night Koke was very ill, and I went to her and rubbed butter on her body. It did not help her. Koke told me, 'Your wife has bewitched me.'

August 12th: I went to my garden, and when I came back, I found Koke's mother here making a great deal of trouble. She was saying that my wife had bewitched her child. I said to her, 'Don't say that. All women get this disease; she will not die. If God likes your child, she will recover.'

Koke's mother did not agree with this, and when she went away, she was very angry.

The wife of Kwehemukira, who lives in the village, passed by my house. I asked her, 'Where are you going?'

She said, 'My husband beat me, so I'm going to my father's house.'

Then I grabbed the bundle she was carrying. We argued for a long time. She went on saying, 'Let me go. I want to go to my home.'

Finally I took her back to Kwekemukira's house. He said, 'Mpuga is a very helpful man.'

Lubangi had arranged to meet her father in a clearing in the forest. I bought two shillings worth of maize, a bundle of cassava flour and some cassava roots. Lubangi, Kijungu and Abongo went to the clearing, but Lubangi's father never arrived. Finally they gave the food to some people who were going to pass near Lubangi's father's house in the Congo. On the way back they were frightened by an elephant. Abongo was fast and ran past the women and left them far behind. He is a man, and should have stayed behind to fight the animal. He ran all the way to the edge of the forest. When he arrived there, he sat down and waited for the women. They were very angry with him. I thought that, if the elephant had caught one of my wives, Abongo would not have known who had been killed and where she had been killed.

August 13th: My sister Nakulinga has not visited me for a month. I told Kijungu to go to see her to find out if she is ill. When Kijungu reached the house, the children told her not to enter. Nakulinga heard her and came out of the house. She told Kijungu that she had been ill and that a doctor had been brought in and a ceremony held for her. The doctor had told her not to come to her home in Bundinyama and not to eat any food from Bundinyama. The doctor also told her that no one from Bundinyama should enter her house.

When Kijungu returned, she told me about this. I sent a message to Nakulinga's husband telling him, 'Since you have forbidden my sister to come to our house, you should tell your other wife not to eat my sister's children any more. It is your wife who is eating those children.' When the husband received my message, he told his other wife about it, and she was very angry because I had accused her of being a witch and a cannibal.

August 15th: My former wife, Mambaiye, brought my child to me. She slept with me in the same bed for two nights. That pleased me a great deal. This is the first time a former wife of mine has ever done this. The fact that she brought the child to me and stayed with me for two nights convinced me that she is still in my hands.

I went to Bugombwa with the wife of Kasu, to find a woman who is a midwife and who has medicine for women. The children at her house told us that she had gone to gather firewood. On the way back I heard someone calling me, and when I turned around I found that it was the woman whom I had been seeking and who had followed me. Then we sat down, and she asked, 'Why have you come?'

I told her, 'We wanted you to see this woman, the wife of Kasu, because she had her first child about two years ago, and since then she has never had another one. She had gone into her menstrual period before the usual time. After you have dealt with her, I would like you to come to my house sometime to treat my wives, Lubangi and Kijungu.' I gave her thirty cents, because she was very tired from running after me.

During the night Lubangi dreamed that my mother said to her, 'Why did you eat all of the fish you brought from the Congo by yourself?'

August 16th: Sogosa did not feel well, and I think that this illness was caused by my mother, because we ate by ourselves all the fish which Lubangi brought from the Congo, and we did not give (sacrifice) any to her.

Koke went to her garden and found seven goats belonging to Kihara in the garden. She went to him and complained to him that his goats are ruining her rice and maize.

Kihara said, 'I must get you today, because you have troubled me a great deal. Do you want to eat all my goats?'

I heard this and was very angry. I went out of the house and said to Kihara, 'If you are a circumcised man, try to beat Koke.' Because I was angry, he did not say any more. I said, 'Kihara, you are a very bad man. It is you who told your children to kill my goat when it was in your garden. Do you remember that you accused me of having slept with your wife, Muwisa? I know you always depend upon your witchcraft powers.'

August 18th: I left a bar of soap and a shilling in my house. When I returned to the house, I found that my shilling was gone. I asked Lubangi about it and she said, 'Mukundi, the daughter of Kihara was in the house.'

Then I went to Kihara's and said, 'I want to accuse Mukundi. Call her so that you may listen to what we have to say. Your daughter stole my money.'

The girl ran away and stayed away for a night. Kihara said, 'She ran away because she stole your money.'

I called together my wives. I said, 'I have heard rumours, Koke, that you are bringing medicine to your fellow wives. You must not do it again. You have made a lot of mistakes, and I will not forgive this one.'

August 18th: My father came to me in a dream. He said, 'Mpuga, you never go to see Nakulinga. Now her husband has cured her, and she has been told not to come here. Now you are her father. You should send your wives there from time to time so that they may see her.' Then Mosumba became angry with me and said, 'Is this how you are keeping my children?' When I woke up, I shivered.

August 19th: In the morning I heard Kijungu calling me. I went out, and she said, 'Mpuga, come and see how pigs have spoiled my food. They have ruined the whole garden. Where shall I get food? Hunger will kill me!'

When I went to the garden, I found that it had been spoiled. Then Kijungu started to cry. I managed to get her to stop crying, and I said, 'Let us leave the garden. Come home.'

Later I and my three wives and Abongo and his wife went to the gardens to plant cotton. Abongo's wife quarrelled with him. He told her, 'You are a very bad wife. You have long lips.' She took a reed and struck Abongo with it.

Abongo said, 'You are looking for trouble.' He slapped her leg and fell into a hole. My wives stopped the fight. I was very annoyed, because when my wives were stopping the fight, Abongo's wife told them to eat their sexual organs. I was very annoyed also because she told Abongo to eat his testicles. Abongo is a fool; when he went home, he ate her food. If this had happened to me, I would have told the wife to go to her home and get a chicken and a pot of beer.

I found Atindia of the Bandinyama skinning a small antelope. When he had finished skinning it, he tied the meat in a bundle. I said to him, 'You put all of the meat in a bundle. Am I not going to have a piece?'

He said, 'Let us go to my house. When we arrive there, I will give you some meat then.'

I refused. I said, 'I can't go to your house. It is impossible for a piece of meat to lure me all the way to your house.' Then I left him and went home.

August 20th: In the morning Kasu, the Ganda, came to my house because my goats had spoiled his garden. He was very angry and looked like a man who had come for a fight. I did not say anything to him, because I knew that I was guilty. When he saw that I did not reply, he became cooler. If I had answered him, there would have been a fight. In the future I must not let my goats wander about freely.

In the evening when I was bathing near my house, I saw a snake near the water jar. I wondered about it very much. Luckily I had a small lamp with me; otherwise the snake would have bitten me. I continued to think about this thing. I thought, 'These people are killing me. Their witchcraft is increasing from one day to the next. They don't want to hurt me; they want to kill me. In the future I will leave Bundinyama.'

August 22nd: The brother of my former wife, Bakweziba, came to me and told me that if I gave him some goats I could marry his sister. I told him, 'Even if I had many goats I would not give them to you, because I will not marry Bakweziba again. You should go to other people. They will give you goats, but I will not.'

I heard my wife Kijungu saying to another woman, 'Since I have not produced a child here, I don't see any reason why I should cultivate food. It will be eaten by the children of others. I am just helping the people who have children. They should not give my food to these children without my knowledge. It is I who should offer this food to the children.'

I said to her, 'What are you saying, Kijungu? Have I ever shared the food you have produced without your knowledge? Don't you know my children are the children of your husband? Have any of my children ever treated you badly? What did my children do to you? Have they ever troubled you?'

I still love her and want her to continue being a wife in my home. She is a good cultivator and she is very calm. I was very annoyed when I heard her speaking in this way, because she is bringing bad habits to my home.

The wife of Koke's brother stayed in Koke's house overnight on her way back from Butuku. I did not eat any food or drink any water in that house, because the fish smelled very bad. I am not going to allow such people to sleep in my house any more. I was afraid of Koke this time, or I would have refused to allow the woman to stay here overnight. Since she was the wife of Koke's brother, I had to permit it. I kept quiet.

Kihara's dog smelled the fish and went into Koke's house and stole some of it. It ran away with the fish in its mouth. Koke and her brother's wife ran after the dog. They could not catch it. I told the woman, 'Why did you bring fresh fish from Butuku? Why didn't you dry them first? Now you have seen what the dog has done. You have lost your profit. Who's going to buy fish which smell like that? You must be careful, or Makesi [the Toro health inspector] will burn it.'

August 24th: My wives did not cook any food for me yesterday. The reason they refused to cook for me was that they said that I had slept outside with a girl, a daughter of the Basaru. The only thing I had to eat was sugar. They do not want me to marry another wife. I am praying to God to give me a beautiful wife. I will shame them. I was unfortunate when I was with that girl, because as I was lying over her a boy came into the room where we were with a light. I was very embarrassed.

August 27th: I have been troubled by a chicken belonging to Binzali, the Toro. Whenever I have gone down to the garden, I have found it eating the ground-nuts which have been planted among the cotton. Today when my wives and I were working in the gardens, I saw the chicken coming to eat the ground-nuts. We drove it back to Binzali's house, and I told Binzali to tie it up. He did not do that, and later the chicken came back to the garden. I picked up a small stone and threw it at it. The stone struck the chicken on its head and it fell down. It remained on the ground for a few minutes without moving. Then it got up and went away. It would fall down and get up and walk away and then fall down again. It finally reached Binzali's house and died there.

When I came back from the garden, I heard Binzali shouting, 'Come here, Mpuga! Come and take the chicken which you have stolen.'

I said to him, 'Do you have a witness who saw me strike your chicken? If you have a witness, go and accuse me to the chief.'

Then he said, 'I will go and accuse you at the house of the subparish chief.'

I told him to do that and I came back home. A little later I saw him coming with two chiefs and the dead chicken. He told me that I had killed the chicken. After he had spoken, I asked him some questions and he could not answer them. They gave judgment against Binzali.

Binzali took his chicken away and ate it. I said that God had helped me, because this chicken could have brought a big case if it had died in my garden. I was lucky that the chicken died at the house of its owner.

August 28th: I complained to Kihara that all his people are using the new latrine which I built at the order of the chief. I told Kihara that he should build his own latrine.

While I was sitting near the fire talking with some other men, Lubangi and Kijungu began to talk about Koke. They said that Koke is bringing the same sort of medicine to Kijungu which caused Lubangi to leave my home. They said that Koke has a new supply of wandering medicine. They also said that she got it from a Toro woman who lives on the road.

If Koke did not have that child, I would send her back to her home and recover my goats.

Abongo dreamed that he was taken to the sub-county headquarters and beaten there. His dream was true; it was meant for his wife, because during the day Abongo beat her.

August 29th: A man told me that I should marry his sister. I went to see the girl and discovered that she is very young. It will be another two years before she is ready to marry. I refused to marry her. I told her brother, 'I am a mature man and it is not right for me to marry such a young girl.' The father told me that because she is very young he is asking me for only three goats as bridewealth. I still refused.

When I returned, I found that my goats had not been taken out of the house. I asked Koke, 'What have you been doing all this time? Why are my goats still in the house? Are you starving? Why do you let them go hungry?' I was going to beat her, but Kihara prevented me from doing it.

August 30th: I went to the house of a Toro who lives down the road. He was about to have a meal, and he gave me some food on a plate. He said, 'Mpuga, you young people are still eating rats and snakes here in Bwamba.'

I said, 'Yes, we are still eating rats and snakes.'

He said, 'Oh, if I had known that you were still eating those things, I wouldn't have allowed you to eat with me. I would have given you your food on a banana leaf.' He said, 'If you have beautiful plates from the shop at your home, and you are eating rats and snakes, you are as bad as rats and snakes.'

I said, 'Now that I have eaten from your plate, are you going to vomit?'

He said, 'No, I won't vomit, but I will wash the plates with soap and water.'

I said, 'Keep quiet. I have defeated you.' I had deceived him, because I do not eat rats and snakes.

Later I went to the house of a girl whom I know in a neighbouring village. I know that she has been paid for, but because I am a man I went in her house; I was afraid, but I went in there. A child came and said that her husband was returning, so I had to leave.

August 31st: Abongo made a trip to the market in Butuku. Kihara's wife gave him twenty cents to buy some butter. Abongo ate the twenty cents. When he came back, he said, 'The river has overflowed its banks. There were many pools of water along the road. As I was crossing one of those pools, I lost the twenty cents.'

Kihara asked another man who was with Abongo what had happened, and he reported, 'Abongo is lying; he ate your money. It did not fall into the water.' Kihara's wife was very angry.

Nkiambi, the wife of Bukombi, has returned to her home. A woman who is a friend of hers visited her here. This woman said to Nkiambi, 'Why have you stayed here when your husband is not here? Is Bukombi the only man in the whole world? If you are not a woman, stay here. The week after he married you, he went away. He is enjoying himself with another wife in Buganda and has left you with nothing. I will find some man who will capture you. Why do you suffer here? I think perhaps you don't need men.'

Lubangi heard her and came out of her house and said, 'I have heard what you have said. I will tell you, Mpuga, that you have been giving this wife bad advice. If she goes away, are you going to repay Bukombi's goats, the ones which he paid to her father?'

The son of Kilagule, the witch of the Bandimwendi lineage, came to my house. When I was alone with the young boy, I asked him, 'What do you do when you are acting as a witch, or, if you are not a witch, how does your father act?'

The child said, 'When my father is going out to bewitch, first he tells the three stones in the fireplace to go out, and after that he tells the door, "Door, open yourself, so that we may go out." Then the door opens. After he has gone, he tells the door to close itself, and it closes. When he comes back, he comes in like a rat, and you see him around the fireplace.'

I asked him, 'Do you go with your mother and father when they are going to bewitch people?'

He said, 'Yes, when I was very young, they carried me on their backs.'

I asked him, 'When they go out, do they keep their clothes on?'

He said, 'No, they take off all their clothes and put on banana leaves. Sometimes they go naked.' The child told me, 'If you keep a small stone in your armpit when you are walking about at night, that will save you from the witches.'

Later, a man whom I know, who is a member of the Bandikuliya lineage, came to my house and began to talk with me. I told him what the child of Kilagule had told me about the witches.

This man said, 'I know witches. I met them once. The ones who wanted to kill me were my wives. They have killed me. They have closed my eyes. They can do whatever they like since I am blind.'

I said, 'Tell me how they killed you.'

He said, 'I used to live with my wives; I had seven of them. Then I became weak and had only three wives left. One was of the Bagombwa lineage, one of the Bandimbale and one of the Babukwanga. I kept them in one house. I used to sleep in the bed of the woman of the Bagombwa lineage, and the other wives were angry because of that. Once after I had gone to sleep, they came and carried me outside. But I did not meet death. After they had taken me outside, I woke up. I shouted out, "These women are killing me."

'They were frightened and dropped me on the ground. They took hold of my penis and twisted it. They said, "This is the thing which does not give us our share. You will see how you will use this penis again with the woman you love." After twisting my penis, they pulled it.

'I said, "You have killed me. Take me back in the house, so that the people may bury me."

'They carried me back into the house. I made a great deal of noise, because my penis was very painful and swollen. My brothers heard me and came outside my house. They asked why I was crying. I said, "Leave me alone; I have died. Don't try to open the door."

'One of my brothers said to me, "No," and he kicked the door and came in. When my brothers saw that my penis had swollen to an unusual size, they were frightened. I explained to them that my wives had done it. Then my brothers told the women, "Tell the penis to go back to its normal size. If you do not do that, we will take you to the sub-county chief tomorrow."

'The wives told the penis to return to its normal size. After that I sent those women away from my home, but they bewitched my eyes, and now I am blind.'

September 1st: Koke struck her child Bakatwika. The child vomited and cried. Kijungu called me and said, 'When you hear your child crying, why don't you come and help? Your wife wants to kill him. Come and see.'

I slapped Koke and then I slapped her again. I caught her and threw her on the ground. I said, 'I have repaid you.'

Later, when I went to the garden, Koke took her child and ran away. When she had gone about a half mile along the road, she met Batigwa. He caught her and brought her back with him. I explained to Batigwa what had happened, and he gave judgment against her.

During the night, I saw a man called Makata going along the road. He had captured a daughter of the Babukwanga, and she was with him. When he saw me, he was afraid, because it was night, and he thought I was one of the Babukwanga. When he recognized me, he said, 'If you see anybody following me, don't say that you have seen me.'

I told him, 'Would I report you, when I am a thief the way you are? This is what I always do.'

Kijungu's brothers, Kimbugwe and Kangora, came to my house. Kimbugwe said, 'We have come for our three goats; I want to go and buy a new wife with them.'

I said to them, 'The last time I gave you goats, you said that I had made the final payment. Do not look for more goats, because I have finished the payment. I have no goats at all.'

Later Lubangi told me, 'I met your affinal relatives as I was coming along the path. I hid and listened to what they were saying. They said that they are going to come tomorrow and, if you do not give them their goats, they will take Kijungu away from you and return the goats and the eight shillings which you have given them.'

September 2nd: Kihara asked me to come to his house to speak to Kijungu's brothers. They had spent the night with their mother, Kihara's wife. Kijungu's brothers asked me, 'What do you mean by saying that you have finished paying the brideprice?'

I said to them, 'You began this matter. You cursed my wife. You said that she would not have a child until after she was married to me. I told you, Kimbugwe, to come and have a ceremony in order to lift that curse so that Kijungu could have children. Then I told you that I could not pay you any more goats because people pay only six goats for women who do not produce children. In the past only five goats were given for a woman who did not have children. I gave you one more goat and six shillings in addition. I will not pay you anything more unless your daughter has a child.'

They said, 'Our daughter cultivates and works hard in the garden.'

I said, 'That is nothing. The main thing in marriage is the production of children. Even if God takes the children after they have been born, you can still call the woman a producer of children. You can't thank a woman unless she has produced a child for you.'

Abongo bought a rat trap from the Indian shop at Bundibugyo. Today he caught his finger in the trap and was very annoyed. He said, 'I have been injured by the trap and I am very annoyed.' He said, 'I have been injured by the trap, because I have married a rat-eater. All the people here have stopped eating rats except my wife.'

I said to Abongo, 'You are the one who allows her to eat rats. Why don't you tell her not to eat them?'

In the evening we heard Banganiki's wife calling, 'Come and help me! A leopard has taken my goat!'

I ran there with a lamp. She showed me the tracks of the leopard, and Abongo and I followed them down to the valley. We finally came upon the goat and discovered that one leg and part of its neck had been eaten. We brought the goat back to Banganiki's house. His wife asked us to skin it, but I said, 'It is too late; we have not eaten. We will go and eat, and we will skin it tomorrow morning.'

Banganiki is away, and we were afraid that, if we skinned it, his wife would tell him that we had stolen some of the meat. That is why we did not want to skin it.

September 3rd: After I had gone to the gardens, Kimbugwe came and said to Kijungu, 'Your womb is not producing anything. Because you can't produce, you must get out. I will take you away today. I don't want you to stay with Mpuga, because he gave me only six goats and eight shillings.'

Kijungu said, 'Mpuga did not tell me that I would go away today.'

My son Kisasi heard them talking and ran down to the garden to tell me, 'Kimbugwe is taking your wife.'

I ran home, and I found Kimbugwe there. I said to him, 'Are you doing a good thing or a bad thing?'

September 4th: Kijungu's brother talked to her again. Kangoro said to her, 'Tomorrow you, Kijungu, must leave with us. Your husband has refused to pay goats to us. Kimbugwe's wife has been taken away from him, because he did not pay all the goats which he owed, so we will not leave you here. We will take you somewhere else and exchange you for goats which will pay for Kimbugwe's wife. Let Mpuga stay here with his goats.'

When I heard this, I said to Kijungu, 'They must bring my goats here before they take you with them.'

Abongo and I and our wives went to work in the gardens. When we went, Abongo's wife left her child with my son, Muganga. When Muganga saw the other children going out to the road to play, he left the child. The child began to cry, because he was alone. Then a man of the Bandinyama lineage who was passing through the court-yard heard the child crying. He tried to find the person who was taking care of the child, but he could not find anyone, so he took the child to Kihara's house and gave him to Kihara's wife, Andiye. Later Muganga came back and found the child was missing. He began to cry. When we came back from the gardens we said, 'Why are you crying?'

Muganga said, 'The child has been lost.'

We said, 'Where did you leave him?'

He said, 'I left him here. When I came back, he was gone.'

I asked him, 'Who remained here with him when you went away?'
He said, 'No one was there.'

I said, 'You must find him now.' He started to look for him, but could not find him. We went to Kihara's house to report the matter and found him there. He was there with Andiye, who gave him to his mother. Then I caught Muganga and started to beat him for leaving the child alone.

In the evening Lubangi gave me some water for my bath. When I was ready to bathe, I found that there was very little water in the pot. I said to her, 'Why have you given me so little water? This is not enough to wash my whole body. You should add some more water to the pot.'

After I said this, I went into the house. Lubangi went out to the water jar and poured all the water on the ground. When I saw her do that, I was very angry. Fortunately, Koke brought me some more, and I had a good bath. This proves that it is very bad to marry only one wife. If I had had only one wife, I would have had no bath at all after Lubangi had poured the water on the ground. It is very difficult for men who are accustomed to two or three wives to have only one. A single wife troubles you a great deal. She wants to rule you and the house, whereas the man should be the ruler of the home.

September 5th: Lubangi was in Kihara's courtyard and heard Kijungu's mother advising Kimbugwe to bring his goats and give them to me, so that he could take his sister away. She said, 'I didn't want Mpuga to marry Kijungu, but she insisted upon it. Kihara hates me; can I allow my daughter to stay with the Bundinyama?'

When Lubangi told us about this, Abongo said, 'That is true. Kijungu's mother did not want her to marry Mpuga. It is only Kijungu who likes Mpuga. Ntura Kali, the Mugarama, was troubled very much by his mother-in-law. He got a feather from an owl and bewitched her. Two weeks later she died.'

Kijungu heard Abongo say this and she was angry. She said, 'Abongo is advising you, Mpuga, to get a feather of an owl and bewitch your mother-in-law. If my mother dies today, I will know that it is you, Abongo, who told Mpuga how to get medicine to kill my mother.' She was preparing food and when it was ready, she said to Abongo, 'You must not eat my food, because you told Mpuga to kill my mother. If my mother were not married to a man from this lineage, you Bandinyama could not have got me.'

That night I was supposed to sleep with Kijungu, but when I went into the house she drove me out. She said that I wanted to kill her mother. I left her house and went to Koke's house, where I slept for the night. It was very bad of Kijungu to send me out of her house before I finished my days with her. She has four chickens, and I am going to eat one of them before I go back to her bed.

September 6th: I told Lubangi, 'Now that you are pregnant, you should go to the hospital in Fort Portal and be examined.'

She said, 'Before the Europeans came, who examined me? Who examined your mother? You Amba want to spoil the bearing of children. You have seen Europeans and you like their ways. If they don't examine me, will I not have my child? Won't it be strong and healthy?'

I said, 'It is best to trust the Europeans' medicine. I was very sick and, if I had not been treated by the medicine of the Europeans, I would have died. Because of that, I know that the medicine of the Europeans is stronger than ours.'

She said, 'If you want me to go to Fort Portal, I will not climb the mountain. Give me three shillings and thirty cents twice for the bus.' I told her I would give her that amount so that she could go to Fort Portal.

September 7th: I heard that Bukombi is coming to Bwamba and that he is in Fort Portal now.

Lubangi went to see Ndigombwa. Ndigombwa cooked some food for her. Then Ndigombwa said, 'You should tell Mpuga to come and hear what my husband's wife has said to me. She also cooked some food for me and put some medicine in it. Since then I have had pains in my stomach.'

I have heard that my mother's brother, Katwihero of the Bumati, has returned from the hospital at Oicha. He is the uncle who loves me best. When I get a chicken, I will go there and give it to him, because he is the person who loves me.

September 8th: In the evening I went to visit Kasu, the Ganda, at his house. While I was there, Bukombi arrived. We heard him outside Abongo's house shouting, 'Is Abongo still here? I'm going to burn his house.' He took the door of Abongo's house and threw it away. Lubangi and Kijungu went out. They said, 'Why are you doing this? Why don't you sit down?'

Bukombi said, 'Where is Mpuga?'

Koke said, 'I will go and call him.'

Koke came to Kasu's house and said to me, 'Bukombi wants to burn Abongo's house.'

When I arrived, Kihara was already there. He told Bukombi, 'Why don't you sit down? Tell us what is wrong with you.'

Bukombi said, 'What did you do when I was last here and I told you to send Abongo away? He is still here. Does this mean that you have no power over him? Don't you wish me to stay in this village? If I had come and found that Abongo had gone away, I could have said that you are good people and good relatives who want to stay with me. I will have to do what I can. I will try to burn this hut. If you want Abongo to live, you should tell him not to come here. I don't want you to talk to me because, since my mother died, I am a foreigner. I will say that my lineage is foreign. This Abongo, when my father died, was at Atube's house, and all the people who live at Atube's house came to the ceremony except Abongo. When we had the first death ceremony, he was not here. When we had the second death ceremony, he was not here. Now is he going to send me out of my house? Do I fear him? Let him kill me since he ate my children and spoiled my wives.'[1]

September 12th: While I was asleep Abongo and Kihara came and called me and told me to go and see Lubangi. Lubangi had been sleeping, and when she woke up, she found that there was blood on her stomach. When she looked, she found two small cuts there. When I went to her house, I saw the two cuts. She began to cry and said, 'They have shaved me and now they have come to cut me while I am sleeping. I am going to die.' I was very worried. Why are they doing this to her when she is pregnant? This is my home and the home of the Bandinyama. I will thank God if Lubangi produces a child. I thought that this might be Abongo, because he has been sent out of the home. Perhaps he is the one who made these cuts. Later I called Kihara, Abongo and his wives and my wives and I told them, 'You are my people. If my wife has trouble giving birth to the child, it will be one of you who has done this. It is after Bukombi sent you out of this home, Abongo, that we found these cuts. I don't want you to bring any trouble to my home, especially to my wives.'

Banganiki with whom Abongo is staying said, 'Abongo, before Bukombi sent you out of his home, nothing was happening here in my home. You know that if there is any trouble caused here, it will be caused by you. You should take care of your brothers by your father. You should not wish them to die or hate them for their riches or for their children. If you do so, you also shall be killed.'

September 13th: Kijungu took some maize to the market and sold it for one shilling and fifty cents. She returned and told me she had re-

---

[1] When Bukombi visited Bwamba in May, he accused Abongo of bewitching him and of having caused the death of his children. Abongo left the village in order to avoid a fight. In addition to warning Abongo not to bewitch his new wife Bukombi, he made Mpuga promise to drive Abongo away, a promise which Mpuga did not keep. This time Abongo again fled to a nearby house, that of Banganiki, but this time Bukombi himself decided to ask him to return.

ceived one shilling for the maize. Then Muganga said, 'No, she received one shilling and fifty cents for the maize.'

I asked her, 'Why did you tell me you received one shilling?'

Kijungu was very angry and later, when I was in Lubangi's house, she slapped Muganga. I heard him crying so I went out. I asked, 'What is wrong with the child? What have you done?'

The child replied, 'Your wife is beating me, because I told you the truth. That is why she beat me.'

I told Kijungu, 'If you continue to beat my children in this way, I will beat you and you will know how hard a person can be beaten.'

A man named Gakilia from Ntotoro stopped at my house on his way home. We began to talk. He said, 'Mpuga, if I gave you my riddle, could you answer it?'

I said, 'Let me hear it. If I fail to answer it, you explain it to me.'

He said, 'Do you know what the thing is which people never dream about?'

I said, 'No, I don't know what it is.'

He said, 'The thing which people never dream of is drinking at their mother's breast.'

I thought about this for some time, wondering whether he was right or not. I could not remember whether anybody had told me about such a dream, and I had never dreamed such a dream. I thought he must be right.

Then he said, 'What is the thing which you never give up?'

I said, 'Women. A woman is the one thing which you can't give to another man.'

He said that I was wrong.

Then I said, 'The child which you have borne is the one thing which you cannot offer to another person.'

Then he said, 'Oh, Mpuga, you are still a very young man. You don't know the riddles of old people.' Then he explained to me that the thing you cannot give to another person is sleep.

I said, 'No!'

He said, 'If you will oppose me, think of this. If you get up in the morning and your wife tells you, "Oh, I am not feeling well. I have not slept well," will you ever offer her any sleep?'

I said, 'No.'

He said, 'Yes, sleep is the only thing which you can't give to another person.'

I thought about this a great deal, and I decided that this man has very great intelligence and that God has given him a very great gift. It is true that you cannot offer sleep to another person. When this man went on his way, I went to Kihara's house and asked him if he could answer these riddles. He failed to answer any of them. I told

241

him 'Gakilia has very good riddles.' Then I told them to Banganiki, and he also failed to answer any of them.

Bukombi asked me to go to the house of Kingano, one of the Bandinyama to ask him to lend him a male goat. I told Kingano what Bukombi wanted. He said, 'What happens to the money which Bukombi earns?'

I said to him, 'Has Bukombi asked you for money?'

Kingano said, 'No, but he has asked me for a goat. His father left him some goats. Why doesn't he kill one of those?' I left Kingano and returned home.

September 14th: My friend, the school-teacher Serapio, came to my house. When I greeted him, he said, 'Call Abongo for me and your wives, Koke and Kijungu.' When they arrived, he said, 'Who went out of this home and went to Leo Ngisa and told him that I am not fit to marry his daughter, Foresta, because I am a drunkard, a man who always gives money to women to have intercourse with them and a man who buys meat and eats it outside? Leo Ngisa told me that from what he has heard I am not fit to marry his daughter. When I asked him who had told him this, he named Abongo. Abongo has denied that he said this.'

Then Serapio asked Abongo, 'Didn't you tell this to Leo Ngisa on Wednesday when you met him in the market? He was there with his son Miliko.'

My brother said, 'No, I didn't speak to either of them.'

I said, 'Abongo, you must have told them this.'

Later in the day I heard Kihara's wives talking about Nyamanzi, one of the Bandinyama. They said that, when he kills animals in the hunt, he does not give them any meat. Whenever his wife is sick, he comes to them for help. They said that from now on he will have to care for his wife by himself. When they saw me, they became silent. Then one of them said, 'You heard all our gossip. You must not tell that to Nyamanzi or to Kihara.'

I said, 'Why should I tell them? I am an elder now, and I hear many things much more serious than this.'

September 17th: This morning Bukombi came to my house. He said, 'I have something to tell you.'

I said, 'Tell me what you have to say.'

He said, 'I have decided that it would be a good thing to bring Abongo back. You go and tell him to come back, and go into his house, and I will bring my first wife, Voroneka. She will stay here. Then I will tell Abongo to look after her. We will see what happens. If I find that he continues to act badly, we will send him away from this home forever. Do you think that this is a good plan or a bad one?'

I said to him, 'I cannot tell you whether this is a good or a bad plan. You should go and talk with Kihara and Batigwa. We will do whatever they say.'

Then I advised him, 'When you go back to Buganda, you should take your wife, Nkiambi, with you, because she cannot do anything here. Now that Voroneka is here you should take Nkiambi with you so that she can become pregnant.'

He said to me, 'Nkiambi is not good enough to go to Buganda with me, because she looks like a monkey. If you take a wife with you to Buganda, you should take one who looks like a Ganda. If the Ganda ask me, "Where is the wife you brought with you?" can I show them this monkey? They would laugh at me. I will not take her to Buganda with me. If she wants to leave me, let her go. Then her brothers will return my goats to me.'

I said, 'Why don't you buy some clothes for her?'

He said, 'Don't you remember that I told you that my money was stolen? Do you have ears or are you deaf?'

In the afternoon Kihara came and asked me if I would let Kijungu go with him to Butuku. He wanted her to carry some cassava flour. I gave him permission to take her there. He asked me if he could also take Nkiambi. I said, 'I have no authority over that girl. If you see her husband, you can ask him. You know that her husband is very fierce.'

Nbugu, one of the Bandinyama, came to my house. He said he wanted the two plates which his brother, Kilagule, who works with Bukombi in Buganda, sent him. Bukombi gave him the two plates. Bukombi told him that he wanted something for his trouble in bringing the two plates from Buganda. He said, 'I don't want money. Come and work with me in my garden for the whole day.' Nbugu agreed.

After they had worked for a while in the garden, Nbugu went home. Bukombi came to me and said, 'Why is Nbugu giving me trouble in that way? I brought his plates here safely.' Then he said, 'I'm going to Nbugu's house to ask him for money.' I tried to stop him from going, but he would not listen to me.

He went into the house of Nbugu without saying a word and took the plates. He told the people who were there, 'If Nbugu wants his plates, tell him to bring one shilling and fifty cents to me. Does he think I am a fool? I was good enough to bring the plates from Buganda just because he is one of the Bandinyama.' Later Nbugu came and gave Bukombi one shilling and fifty cents.

After he had gone, I said to Bukombi, 'Forgive him.'

Bukombi said, 'Why? Don't you know that his father killed my father when he broke his back?' I said nothing more to him.

243

September 22nd: Bukombi came to my house and he said, 'I have no money to take me back to Buganda. Can you give me some money?'

I said, 'Where can I get money? The money which I had I have spent on blankets for my wives. That was all the money I had. I have no money left to give you.'

I was very worried about that. I thought in my heart, 'This man is getting fifty-eight shillings a month in wages. During all the time that he has been working he has never given me one shilling. Why should I lose my money?' I said, 'I will help you. I will go and see if I can borrow money, and, if I can, I will give it to you.'

September 25th: Nyamanzi and I heard that the Toro sleeping-sickness Inspector had killed an elephant in the forest. When we arrived, we found that all the meat had been taken by the pygmies and by other Amba.

September 26th: Kihara called us to listen to the case of his wife, Andiye. When they were all coming from the market in Butuku, Kihara bought some soap for his wife, Ndijaha, but he bought nothing for Andiye. While they were at the market having some tea, she became very angry and said that she was going to go ahead. Kihara said, 'Why are you angry and why are you leaving us?'

Andiye said, 'Have your tea. You will find me on the road.'

After they had finished their tea, they followed her. They did not overtake her, and when they arrived home, she was not there either. She stayed away for a night. When she arrived, they asked her, 'Where did you spend the night?'

She replied, 'You passed me at Sempaya while I was in the latrine. Later, when it became dark, I spent the night at someone's house.'

Kihara was very angry and said, 'You slept with a man!'

We decided that Kihara was right.

September 25th: Nkiambi complained about her husband Bukombi. She said that he had deceived her by telling her that he would take her to Buganda when he went. When he did go, he left her behind. She complained that he said that he had no money, whereas he has many goats here. She said, 'If he thinks that I am not good enough for him, why did he marry me?'

Koke has a swelling on her back. She came to me and said, 'I heard your wife Kijungu talking about me with Abongo's wife. Kijungu said, "I am working for Koke because she is the one who has children. Since I do not have children, all my food will be eaten by other wives." You see now that I have a swelling on my back. I know that Kijungu has bewitched me.'

Abongo came to me while I was eating. I said to him, 'Come and eat with me.'

He said, 'I can't eat your food. Your wife told me that when I eat here my food will be her sexual organs.'

I said, 'Which wife said she would cook her genitals for you?'

He replied, 'It was Koke who insulted me in that way.'

I called Koke. She and Abongo told me what had happened. I asked Abongo, 'How long ago did Koke say this to you?'

Abongo replied, 'It happened three days ago.'

I said, 'Why didn't you come and tell me this on the day she insulted you?'

He said, 'I have come here from time to time, but I have not found you here.' I did not decide the case in favour of either of them; each had insulted the other.

September 28th: I was sitting in the house with Lubangi, and we quarrelled with each other, so I decided to go to Koke's house. As I was leaving, Lubangi pushed me. When I tried to go back in the house, she closed the door and caught my fingers in it. I said to her, 'You are squeezing my fingers,' but she refused to leave the door; instead she pushed harder. She nearly broke my fingers. I was very angry and in pain. I was so angry that I would have fought with her if a Toro who lives nearby, Butambaki, had not stopped me.

September 29th: The sub-county chief and some of his people came to my house. He said, 'Mpuga, when I walked around the village, I found that your plantains were not being taken care of. Do you weed them or not?'

I said, 'Sir, I am going to weed them. I won't try to deceive you and tell you that I have weeded them, because you have seen them.'

He said, 'If you don't weed them, I will give them to someone else.'

While Lubangi was cooking food, she said to Nkuba, 'You will die just because you are dirty; you don't wash; you have a lot of jiggers.'

I said to Lubangi, 'It is your fault that he is dirty, because you don't wash him, and you don't take out his jiggers.'

Lubangi and I went with Nkuba to the hospital to get some medicine for him. The dispenser asked me, 'Whose child is this? He looks like Bukombi.'

I said, 'He is my child.'

He said, 'In the past this child was very clean, but now he is very dirty. His sores are almost killing him.'

I said, 'Nobody takes care of him, because his mother picked up bad habits while she was away.'

When Lubangi heard me say this, she became very angry. She said, 'Nkuba, you must not eat with Mpuga any more, because he says that you are very dirty. When you see him eating, hide. If I see you eating

R 245

food with his other wives, I will beat you to death. You will eat only my food. Even when it is my food and Mpuga is eating it on his table, don't go there, or, if you do go to the table, don't eat with him from the same plate.'

I wondered about this a great deal. Lubangi has been organizing my home, and she is not a man. Later, when she has cooled down, I will ask Kihara and other elders to come to my home. If she wins the case, I will leave her. If I win, I will beat her to death. The elders will tell me if a woman can organize a home. This is the first time in my whole life I have seen this happen.

September 30th: Both Koke and Kijungu told me that they wanted to go away and visit their relatives. I told them, 'When there are two or three wives in one home, and they want to visit other places, they should go in turn. You, Koke, will go tomorrow and return the day after. Then after you have returned, Kijungu will go away.'

Kijungu replied, 'You can't stop me. I'll go away tomorrow, and I will see what you will do.'

I said, 'You can go without permission, but remember that I have forbidden you to go.' I went to bed, and Kijungu went and slept at the house of her mother, the wife of Kihara. She will leave from there in the morning. This has taught me that Kijungu is a bad woman. She will not listen to me; she is very disobedient.

October 1st: While I was eating some elephant meat and cassava, Baliabuga, the son of Katabwita of the Bandinyama, came to my house. He said, 'I have come to you to ask you to help us to carry Sikinga, who has a swollen belly. If we don't get him away from here and take him to Butama, he will die.'

I said to him, 'Don't you know that I have a very bad chest? I can't carry anything heavy. If I did this, it would be the key which would open my illness. I can't go there with you, or, if I do go with you, I can't help you carry the man. Oh, oh, oh—all the way to Butama.' (Butama is several miles from Bundinyama.) 'I can't carry a man to Butama. Even if the Government forced me to carry the man, I would die.' I said to Baliabuga, 'Go away, I have no strength.' He went away. The Amba don't know a sick man when they see one.

As I was sitting on the side of the road talking to Sabakaki, a Toro, Odaliko came along on his bicycle. Sabakaki said, 'Stop!' and Odaliko stopped. Sabakaki said, 'Odaliko, you are using the bicycle now, but you haven't paid the ninety shillings which you still owe me for it.'

Odaliko said, 'If you are a man, try to take this bicycle to your home. If you want this bicycle, give me back the two hundred shillings which I have already paid you. Also you should bring the written agreement which we have.' Sabakaki went to his house and came back

246

later with the paper. He called Kasu, the Ganda, to read the agreement for him, 'Because' he said, 'if Mpuga reads this for me, he will not read the truth, because Odaliko is another Amba and his friend.'

Kasu came and read the agreement. Then another man, Babute, read it, and I read it. We found that the agreement said, 'Odaliko will pay the remaining money on September second.' But there was no year written on the paper. We told Sabakaki, 'There's nothing you can do about this. You have to wait until Odaliko pays you, because there is no date on the agreement.'

October 4th: Lubangi said that she wanted to take a knife and cut her co-wives into small pieces. I said to her, 'If you cut anyone with that knife, I will tie you with ropes and carry you to the sub-county headquarters. They will arrest you and put you in jail, so that you will get over your madness. The Government stopped warfare, and you still want to kill people with knives. Where do you get such ideas?'

She replied, 'Those women told me to drink their urine. Then they told me to eat their sexual organs. I am very angry about that. Then you gave palm leaves to your wives and you gave some to my enemy, Koke. I want the mat which she made from those palm leaves.'

I went and got the mat and gave it to Lubangi. I said, 'Here is the mat which she made from your palm leaves. You should take Koke some money for having made the mat. Give it to me, and when she comes, I will give it to her.'

Lubangi announced, 'I'm not going to give anything to Koke.'

I said, 'If you won't give me any money for Koke, I will take the mat. I will give you the mat when you give me some money.'

She replied, 'I will know that you are a man, if you give this mat to her.'

I said, 'I will give it to her.'

Then Lubangi said, 'I will tear her into pieces if she takes that mat.'

I asked, 'Why are you fierce with me today? I paid my own goats for you. I didn't bring you here to be my king. The goats which I have paid for my other wives were my own goats. Did I take a goat belonging to you and use it as bridewealth for one of the other wives?' I took my spear, threw it on the ground, jumped over it and then I said, 'If you touch your co-wife, you will see. I won't kill you, since you are the person who bears children for me, but you will not sleep in my house. You will go to the houses of the other men who advise you with such cunning. Do you think I will die if I don't have you? I know you. It is your habit to wander about. You don't cultivate here, and you don't stay here. You simply wander about. I almost died the last time you went away, and you were not here. You were in the Congo, enjoying men and eating fish. Now you have come back and you want to drive all my other wives away so that I must remain alone. I know that you won't stay here. So you must not spoil my other wives.'

Many people heard us and they came to the house to see what was happening. Kihara said, 'Explain to us how the quarrel came about.' Lubangi explained first and then I explained what had happened. After this I asked Lubangi many questions and she lost the case. Afterwards I said, 'Even though you have listened to the case, I am not going to eat your food. If you want me to eat your food, you must pay me a chicken. If you don't pay me a chicken, I won't eat your food. I won't change my mind.'

October 5th: Some people were at our house, and Lubangi and I started to talk about her case, how she had insulted me and I had insulted her. She spoke and then I spoke and then I began to ask her questions. She lost the case again. These people questioned the witnesses who had been present yesterday, and they all supported me. These people said Lubangi should be fined three shillings. Then they turned to me and said, 'You should pay two shillings also, because you should not have jumped over your spear. You have the right to beat Lubangi or do whatever you like with her, but you should not take your spear and jump over it. That is why we fined you.'

I said to them, 'You have given judgment this way. Have you ever seen the accuser and the accused both lose the case? How can I be sure that I have won?'

Then the Toro, Salin Mukisa, came in and I explained to him all about the case. He said, 'Oh, they are quite wrong. You can't have both the accuser and the accused losing the case, or both of them winning it.'

Kilolo and his wife Sindano came to my house. They asked me, 'Where is our child, Nkiambi?'

I said, 'She has gone to get firewood.'

They said, 'We have come for her. She is no longer your wife.'[1] Kilolo said, 'My son gave the twenty-five shillings to Bukombi which you have given me for my poll tax.'

I asked, 'When did you give this money to Bukombi?'

'When he came and stayed at our house.'

I said to them, 'Why didn't he tell me he received that money? Why did he ask me for money to get back to Buganda if he had that money? If you did give him the twenty-five shillings, did you also give him the goat?'

They said, 'No.'

I said, 'You have no right to take Nkiambi. I will write to Bu-

---

[1] That is, she is no longer a wife of a member of Mpuga's lineage.

248

kombi, and he will tell me whether or not he received money from you, and I will also ask him about the goat. You cannot take your daughter while you still have the bridewealth.' They asked me to write to Bukombi and went away.

October 6th: I called together my wives and told them that for three days I have been unable to have intercourse. My penis is dead. I asked them, 'Are you trying to kill my manhood? If you are doing this, you must stop.'

Women are very bad. They know how to kill the power of a man. I had this trouble with some of my wives in the past. For a long time my wives have not done this, but now it has begun again. I told them I will find out who is doing it.

In the morning Kihara, Nyamanzi and another man went hunting. When they returned, Nyamanzi had been injured. I asked what had happened, and Kihara told me that Nyamanzi was fortunate, because they might have brought only his body home. A pig charged him, and Nyamanzi jumped and caught a branch. His spear went into the ground with its head pointing upward. As the pig ran, it struck the spear, and the spear struck Nyamanzi's leg and cut it. Nyamanzi called, 'Kihara, Kihara, Kihara!' Kihara ran to him and found Nyamanzi holding the branch of the tree and kicking his legs. He was bleeding. Kihara helped him down from the tree and asked, 'Did the pig catch you with its tusk?'

Nyamanzi replied, 'No, it speared me.'

October 7th: During the night Kijungu vomited, and today she is very ill.

When Kihara was inside the house talking to his wife, Muwisa, his wife, Andiye, stood outside the house and listened to him. Kihara said to Muwisa, 'If my other wives continue to trouble me, I will send them away from here.'

When Andiye heard this, she went and called Ndijaha. She said to Kihara, 'How can you gossip about us to your wife, Muwisa? Do you want to bewitch us? You are both witches. This is why the Bandinyama say that you are a witch, and it is the reason they say you kill your wives. You want to bewitch us. Is this the reason you allowed this woman Muwisa to bewitch your mother? Did that make you happy?' Kihara knew he was wrong, and when the women talked to him, he said nothing. He said nothing at all. Then he went to bed.

October 8th: My wife is not any better. She is very ill. I told my son, Kisasi, to take the goats outside. Lubangi said to me, 'You should not trouble the children when you are sitting there.'

Then I said, 'Who is teaching the children the customs of this home, you or I? You want to organize this home. Whenever I tell

249

somebody to do something, you rush up and begin to quarrel with me.' Lubangi wants to take the position of the householder. If she had no breasts, she would be a man. I said to her, 'You must do this work from now on, because you are the man. I will be your wife, because the home is always organized by the true husband.'

I went to Abongo and talked to him. Abongo said, 'All of you say that I am a witch. Now I have gone out of your home. Nobody should be sick there now.'

I said to him, 'Allow my wife to recover.'

Abongo replied, 'You say that I am the only witch. You say that no one eats your children except me. If I am the witch, your wife will recover.'

I wanted to take Kijungu to the dispensary, but she did not want to go, and her mother did not want me to take her there.

October 9th: In the morning Kihara and his wife, the mother of Kijungu, came to see Kijungu. Kihara said, 'Mpuga, why do you keep quiet? Why don't you talk to the people in your home? You know that your wives are witches. Kijungu has told us many things that your wives have said to her. Lubangi said bad things to her, and Koke fought with her and said bad things to her every day. Koke once said that she would kill her. Now see, Kijungu has become ill. If Kijungu dies, her mother and I will know that Koke has killed her. What have the diviners told you?'

I said, 'I have not been to a diviner.'

October 10th: In the morning Kihara came to me and told me, 'I have heard that Kijungu's former husband took the pot which she used for washing herself when she was living with him and put some medicine in it. He put two whistles in it, and then he put the pot upside down underneath the bed where Kijungu used to sleep. He said, "Kijungu must not remain long at the house where she is now married. She will have no peace there. I am sending her only illness." '

I went to look for medicine for Kijungu. I went to the house of a man who has medicine in the neighbouring village. He said to me, 'Since you know that the disease was brought from her former husband's home, why don't you send her back there? In the future you should not marry a woman who has left her husband. You should marry unmarried girls.'

When I returned home, I went to Kihara and said, 'Because Kijungu's former husband has put whistles and medicine in the pot under her bed, he is the one who is bewitching her. If Kijungu dies, I will know that her former husband has killed her. Her mother should call Kimbugwe and Kangoro to come here, and I will tell them about this before their sister dies.'

250

October 11th: Kijungu's brothers came to Kihara's house. Lubangi saw them and told me they had arrived. I went to Kihara's house and greeted them. They refused to greet me. Then they said, 'Mpuga, if Kijungu dies, we will destroy you and all your people.'

I said, 'Kimbugwe, why do you accuse me? Where have you been? Your sister has been sick for seven days. She is almost dying, and you have not come here until just now. I have done everything I could to cure her, but I have failed. I wanted to take her to the hospital at Fort Portal, but her mother said that I should not take her there.'

Kimbugwe said, 'I went to a diviner, and he says that Abongo and his wife and your wives, Lubangi and Koke, are the ones who are trying to kill Kijungu.'

I said, 'She has been bewitched by her former husband.'

Her brother Kangoro denied this. He said, 'Her former husband is not the one who is bewitching her.'

Finally we agreed to carry her to Kimbugwe's home. Then they would send for her former husband. Her two brothers, Kihara, myself and four other people from Bundinyama, carried her all the way to their home. Her mother went with her. It was a very difficult journey, because we were caught by the rain.

October 13th: In the morning a man told me, 'I have heard that your sister Nakulinga is having trouble.'

I asked, 'What is wong?'

'I don't know.'

I said, 'Maybe she is giving birth?'

'I don't know.'

I went into the house and told Lubangi to prepare some cassava for me. I said that I would eat it and then would go and see what was wrong with Nakulinga.

As I was sitting in the house, the son of Nakulinga's husband came to the door. He said, 'I have come to tell you that Nakulinga has been in labour for three days.'

I asked the child, 'Why didn't your father tell me this before? Do you think that she is an animal? A person is not an animal!' I said to Lubangi, 'Give me my spear so that I may go. It is late.'

Lubangi said, 'I will go with you so that I can help her.'

Abongo also said, 'I am going.' The three of us went there. When we arrived, we found her lying behind the houses in a sugar-cane garden. I sat down, and Lubangi went to see her. Lubangi came back and said to me, 'They called us too late. She is already becoming cold; she is tired. Don't just sit there. Go and try to find a midwife.'

Abongo and I went to Bugombwa to find a midwife. The woman was not at her home. The people there said she might be visiting some of the neighbours. I went from one house to another, but I did not find her. Then we asked the woman there to try to find a midwife. We went back to see Nakulinga.

When we arrived, we found that her husband had brought a Toro doctor. The doctor took a bowl of water and put some twigs in it. He asked many questions, but the twigs did not move. When he asked if it were the god, the twigs moved. He said, 'This is what is going to kill Nakulinga.' I was not convinced that this was it, because I had already given her husband a goat for the god, Kwakwamira. Then the doctor took some sugar-cane leaves and broke them in some water and gave them to Nakulinga to drink. He said, 'Wait for a while. She will give birth.'

I went home and put my goats in the house and then I returned. I found that she had not given birth to the child. Then I became certain that she would not. Lubangi said, 'Nakulinga is dying.' My heart broke.

The Toro doctor came back late at night and said, 'I brought my horns. If there is any witch here, this horn will catch him. Let one of the women sit on a stool, and I will give her my horn. Then the god will catch her, and the god will say who the witch is who is killing this woman.'

They put a girl on the stool, but nothing happened. Then they put a boy on the stool and again nothing happened. Then the doctor himself took the horn and began to sing, and then he began to make a noise like a cow. He put his head near the fire.

While this was happening, I found that my sister was getting weaker. As the first cock crowed, she called me to come near her. I went to her and she said, 'My husband's wife is the one who has killed me. That woman said to me, "The womb which you now have is the one which will be the heir of our husband Bakaliboni!" Where is the heir now? Then that woman said to me, "I am the senior wife of this home, and I eat meat without salt, while you, Nakulinga, eat salt with your meat. If you continue to eat salt, I am not a human being." You see, Mpuga, that I am dying. Also she told me that my house is not a house, that it is the courthouse of a chief. She said that this courthouse will break. You see, now, is not the house broken? Again she said to me, "My husband hates me because of you, Nakulinga. I will see if he continues to love you." Then she said, "I am eating wild vegetables while Nakulinga eats meat. Let her eat meat, since she is the first woman in the world. I will be a beautiful woman one day." I could tell you many other things, but that is enough.'

Then she died, and I began to weep.

CONCLUSION

In this concluding section certain aspects of the role of the woman in Amba society will be analysed for their own interest and in order to demonstrate how personal documents of the sort presented here can help us to understand the social structure. This will be followed by a few observations concerning social change, since Amba society, like all societies in Africa, is at present changing rapidly under outside influences.

Koke's life history forms a very convenient basis for a consideration of certain facets of the life of a woman in Bwamba, because it throws them into high relief. When Koke was quite young, her father tried to exchange her for a wife for himself. The worst feature of this plan was that the man to whom her father wished to give her was a leper. Koke pleaded with her father to no avail. She was joined in her protests by her brother. In Bwamba, a father, when his sons are young, often uses a daughter in order to obtain another wife for himself. Nevertheless, this daughter should ultimately be used to obtain a wife for one of the sons, and when a father acts as Koke's did, the sons naturally see it as a threat to their future marital plans. In this case, Koke's brother was not old enough to offer sufficiently strong opposition to the father. Koke was taken to the leper against her will.

Placed in this intolerable situation, she decided to run away. Obviously she could not return to her father's home. Because her parents were divorced, her mother's home appeared to offer a refuge. Her mother, however, was a weak ally at best because, although she sympathized with Koke's refusal to live with the leper, she wanted Koke to be exchanged for a wife for her son, Koke's brother. Thus she, too, thought that Koke should return to the home of her father and brother. Koke was unwilling to do this, because she knew that her father had not changed his plans. Her mother was not able to offer her any real protection since her father had the right to come there and take her away at any time. Koke's mother did help her to a certain extent by not recognizing the leper as her son-in-law when he visited her. By so doing, she denied him any right to take Koke with him.

Koke then sought the protection of another man. By eloping with a man, she gained a position of safety and circumvented her father's plan. When this happened her father reconciled himself to the futility of trying to force her to stay with the leper against her will, and decided to obtain a wife for his son, Makoso, with her help. He did not attempt to take Koke away from the man with whom she had eloped; instead he merely asked for bridewealth. At this point, Koke, having gained her objective, was forced to ask her father for a favour. She was not really certain that the man with whom she had eloped was the one to whom she would like to be permanently married. Consequently, she asked her father to defer his bridewealth demands to give her time to arrive at a decision.

When Koke returned to her parental home for the first time, her father and brother, gaining confidence from this, took a stronger line and declared that they were unwilling to accept bridewealth. They said they wanted a girl in exchange. When the man was unable to supply a woman, they refused to allow him to take Koke with him. It is obvious that Koke was not infatuated with the man; if she had been, she would have managed to escape to his village. It seems that once she realized that her father would no longer try to take her to the leper's home, she was willing to obey him and her brother. Soon after this, she was exchanged for a wife for Makoso. At first all went well and she, her father, her brother and her husband were on good terms with one another. This ideal state of affairs did not last very long. Trouble developed because her husband would not permit her to leave his village to visit her relatives. She was beaten for attempting to visit them despite his prohibition. Koke managed to escape from her husband and run to her father's home. Her father, now that he was no longer directly affected by her marital fortunes as he had been when he was attempting to obtain a wife for himself, was sympathetic to her complaints and he told her husband to take his sister and to leave Koke with him. Makoso, though, was satisfactorily married and he did not want to see Koke's marriage dissolved, because this might also have meant the end of his own marriage. Therefore, he wanted her to return to her husband. The problem was finally solved by the offer of Koke's father to pay goats to her husband, thus freeing Koke and at the same time maintaining Makoso's marriage.

Makoso exchanged her for another wife for himself. Again she was unhappy. She went to her father's home, but she was told to return to her husband because of her pregnancy. Finally, after her child had been born, she left her husband for the second time and her father did not force her to return, although her brother was as unwilling as he had been before that she should obtain a divorce. This time he was determined that Koke should remain with her husband. She fled to her mother, but this afforded her only a temporary respite, because she was followed and taken back to her father's home. Before she was returned to her husband, she fled to the home of her mother's father. This also was only a temporary measure, because her grandfather would not have provided her with protection against her brother. Again, as in the case of her first marriage, she tried to solve the problem by seeking the protection of a man, this time Mpuga. Her brother tried to force Mpuga to return Koke to him by laying an accusation against him in court. By this time exchange marriage had been banned and the court, in view of Mpuga's stated willingness to pay bridewealth, would not return Koke to Makoso so that he might take her to the man to whom he had given her.

At the present time, Koke, although far from being completely happy with Mpuga, wants to stay with him. Her brother is absolutely opposed to the marriage and as a result she and Makoso are very hostile towards one another. Koke is on safe enough ground, because her father approves her marriage and she can go to him for aid when she has trouble with Mpuga.

Koke has found herself in a number of serious predicaments during the course of her brief marital career. Not all Amba women become involved in so many difficulties. For example, Lubangi's marital history has been much simpler, as has been that of Mpuga's sister, Ndigombwa. However, Koke's experiences have been more typical than those of Lubangi, as can be seen from those of other women referred to in the narratives, such as Mpuga's other sisters, Kijungu, and the wives of Kihara. Of course, few women have had exactly similar experiences; probably very few women have been forced into marriage with lepers by their fathers. On the other hand vast numbers of Amba women have been forced to marry men whom they would not have chosen for themselves. But the particular dilemmas which have confronted Koke have been made possible by the nature of the Amba social structure.[1]

Koke found herself the wife of a leper because in Bwamba a father has the right to give his daughter in marriage to anyone whom he may choose. Her solution to the problem was dictated by the relevant characteristics of the system. At first she attempted to solve it by appealing to her father's interest in her happiness and welfare. When this failed her only real remedy lay in seeking another husband. A woman in Bwamba cannot expect the protection of her relatives against her father, nor can she live as an independent single woman;

[1] For a more extended discussion of this and related matter see: David F. Aberle, *The Psychosocial Analysis of a Hopi Life-History*, Univ. of Calif. Press, 1951, especially pp. 1–5, 118–126.

this solution, such a common one in similar situations in our society, does not exist as an alternative for an Amba woman.

Not only is a particular type of solution for the problem of a distasteful marriage dictated by the social structure, but its success is also assured by other features of the system. Polygny is not only permitted but is the desirable state of affairs, at least from the point of view of the man. It is a source of prestige to him, and a matter of envy for others, if he has more than one woman living with him at a time. Thus the demand for women is, for all practical purposes, infinite, and consequently women are scarce and sought-after objects. There are never surplus women, as has sometimes been the case in European countries after catastrophic wars. All of this means that a woman is assured that she will be able to find a man who wants her, and who is willing to offer her protection, with little difficulty.

In spite of the fact that women have little legitimate power, their scarcity gives them considerable actual power. A woman can frustrate the plans and desires of the men in her life. By running away with another man and repudiating the leper, Koke upset her father's scheme for the acquisition of an additional wife for himself. Then, she disappointed the hopes of the man with whom she eloped by returning to her father and remaining with him when he demanded a girl in exchange for her, a girl whom the man was unable to supply.

Although she has the power to prevent her father or her brother from forcing her into an unpleasant marriage, despite their right to do so, her use of this power is inhibited by her desire for security. The problems in this sphere are much more complicated. They are given their characteristic form in Bwamba by the complex position of the woman in the social system in contrast with that of the man. Ideally, every man is born into one lineage group and grows to maturity in its village, marries and fathers children there and finally dies and is buried there. By contrast, the woman is born and grows up in one village among one lineage group and then, at marriage, she goes to live with her husband in his village, a man to whom certain rights have been transferred by her lineage in the persons of her father or her brother, and a man for whom she bears children. For one group of men she is a daughter and a sister while for another group she is a daughter-in-law and a wife, and perhaps for one or more men she may ultimately be a mother. Complications do not end there, for although, according to the rules of exogamy, a woman cannot be married to a man of her lineage, she is nevertheless the means whereby one of them, usually her brother, may obtain a wife for himself either directly under the exchange system or indirectly under the bridewealth system.

Her ties with her own lineage are permanent, while those with her husband are fragile; they can always be broken by divorce. It might be said that her lineage furnishes her with a permanent base of operations, while her husband's home may be only a temporary encampment. When a marriage ends in failure a woman returns to her parental home. Marriage by no means implies that her ties are severed with her father and her brother, and they should maintain a lively interest in her affairs. Koke's father was justly angry when his son lied to him and said that Koke was happy and contented when he saw her at Mpuga's home, when in actual fact she was ill. The same thing is shown by Mpuga's dream in which his father, personifying his conscience, rebuked him for neglecting his sister. The woman relies upon the aid of her father and her brother to defend her in any trouble she may have with her husband. She feels that she can always run to them if she feels herself mistreated, and that they will see that justice is done. Finally, she expects them to extricate her from a marriage which she considers intolerable by repaying the bridewealth.

When a woman takes matters into her own hands by eloping with a man she risks losing the support of her lineage. Once she has lost this she is almost completely under the control of the man with whom she is living, although, of course, she can flee to the house of another man. In certain ways, however, she is absolutely dependent upon the men of her lineage. For instance a goat may be required for the ritual protection of her child, or in order to prevent a miscarriage. In the normal course of events her father or her brother will supply the goat which is required for this purpose, as Mpuga did when one was requested by the husband of Nakulinga. However, if a woman were repudiated by her lineage no animal would be forthcoming. There is no doubt that Koke's brother, Makoso, would refuse such a request.

The loss of the support of her father and brothers would not be so important for a woman if she were absolutely certain that she could depend completely upon her husband; if she were certain that she could live with him for the rest of her life in a satisfying relationship. But her husband may acquire another wife, who may make the situation unbearable for her. Even though the odds are against a woman being sent away by her husband, because of the scarcity of women, nevertheless it does occur from time to time. In the particular case of Mpuga there is always the fear that, as happened once before, he may 'return to his religion' and send away all of his wives with the exception of Lubangi, whom he married by Christian rites.

An Amba woman may come to the conclusion that she is merely a pawn being manipulated and exploited by the men in her life—her father, her brothers and her husband. Her basic dilemma is caused by the fact that she must rely upon the protection of one man or another. A woman only escapes this basic dilemma and achieves a sense of security when she has an adult son. Then the woman has a man who is bound to her by indestructible ties and who will not try to use her to further his own ends. Lubangi and Koke will not reach this stage for a good many years. The sense of freedom which a woman attains at that stage of life can be illustrated, however, by Mpuga's mother, who after the death of Mosumba refused to marry one of the Bandinyama who proposed marriage to her. She told him, 'I am quite old and I have old sons who will act as my husband.' Mpuga and Bukombi were both adults and she was assured of food, clothing and shelter and other necessities, and thus she did not need a husband, nor on the other hand was she forced to rely upon the protection of her brothers, who might have wanted her to marry again for their sakes. In short, she had escaped the basic dilemma of the Amba woman.

Today, the most important fact about the social system of the Amba is that it is no longer a closed entity. It is true, of course, that Bwamba was never completely isolated. There was always contact with surrounding peoples. Nevertheless, the situation which exists today is profoundly different from that which existed fifty years ago. At that time, if by some magical procedure the area and its people had been placed in the middle of an ocean, the social system could have continued to operate, almost unaffected by the move. If this were to happen now, the system, as it is now organized, could not continue to operate. Radical readjustments would have to be made, as a result of severing contacts with the outside world.

While the physical boundaries of the area have remained the same, the mountains, for instance, still rising like a great wall to the east, the social boundaries have not remained constant. The social system no longer has the sharp and distinct limits which it had in the past. Amba society has been absorbed by a far larger one, consisting of the Kingdom of Toro, the Uganda Protectorate, the British Empire and indeed the world. In the past, an Amba village was part of the Amba social system; a Konjo village, only a mile or two away, was not part of the system, and certainly the king and his officials and chiefs in Toro, and before them, the kings of Bunyoro, were not part of this system. By contrast, today we see the catechist working in a little one-room building. Although his daily contacts are almost entirely with his neighbours and their children, he is, nevertheless, a part of a world-wide organization. Again, Balikengo, the person who collects Mpuga's taxes, is an Amba engaged in many of the same activities as are Kihara and Mpuga. Yet, on the other hand, he is merely the smallest cog in an enormous bureaucracy which stretches to the sub-county headquarters, to the county, to the Toro Native Authority, to the District Commissioner, to the Provincial Commissioner, to the Government at Entebbe, and even to far-off London. Mpuga and Kihara are citizens of a vast Commonwealth, and although this fact may not always be as readily apparent to them as it was during the last war, when Kihara was asked to take up arms in defence of king and country, it, nevertheless, exerts a continuous and all-pervasive effect upon them. Is Balikengo in his role of chief a part of the Amba social system, or is he rather a part of quite a different system? Is the catechist inside or outside the Amba social system? There are no correct answers to these questions. All one can say is that the ab-original system has been incorporated into this larger whole and where one wants to draw the line is purely a matter of convenience. For some purposes, the chief may be taken as part of the internal system; for other purposes, his position may be taken as external to the system. However one defines the social system of the Amba, no great understanding of its operation can be achieved unless the fact of its involvement in this greater unit is constantly kept in mind.

Of primary importance is the fact that this new political system has reserved for itself the legitimate use of force. When Kihara and the other Bandinyama accompanied the man who had committed a murder to Fort Portal, the District Commissioner told them, 'This is a warning to all you Amba. You must not kill each other. You must know from this day that the one who kills his neighbour will die himself.' This was a blunt statement of fact which the Amba had to accept. Their attitude toward this new policy, whether they con-sidered it right or wrong, was irrelevant. What they received was a warning of what would happen given certain occurrences. In short, their situation of action had changed and this resulted in changes in actual behaviour. At the present time, even though a person like Kihara may be tempted now and then to take force into his own hands and to lead a war party, he does not. He, and the others whom he might wish to enlist in such an undertaking, know that if they kill someone they may be arrested, forced to stand trial for murder and executed. Such a change in the situation and the resultant suppression of certain types of behaviour have far-reaching implications. The village and lineage systems have undoubtedly been weakened to a very considerable extent. It is apparent throughout the life histories, especially in Mpuga's, that many of a man's most significant con-tacts are with people who are not members of his lineage. To a con-siderable extent Mpuga relies upon and seeks aid from people who are his friends rather than upon people who are his lineage mates. Bukombi's very unpleasant behaviour towards another member of his lineage in the matter of the plates which he brought from Buganda is another illustration of this same point. The truth of the matter is that Mpuga and Bukombi are no longer wholly dependent upon the goodwill of the other members of the lineage. In cases of serious difficulties they no longer depend upon the armed force of the village; instead they can appeal for aid to the chiefs with their policemen and courts.

This matter of the courts also demonstrates the way in which the new political system has not remained external to the Amba system, but instead has become inextricably interwoven with it. We have seen how both Mpuga and Kihara make ready use of the courts in order to further their own ends when they believe it will be to their advantage. Mechanisms for settling disputes between members of different villages were very weakly developed in the aboriginal system. Therefore, it is quite clear that a person like Kihara should be willing to make use of the courts when he has a dispute with someone living beyond the boundaries of his own village. Within the village, it is still considered that disputes should be settled by the local group itself. To a large extent, as is apparent, this continues to be true in fact as well as in theory. Even within the village, however, in certain serious circumstances, there is a temptation to make use of the new political agents. For example, when Mpuga's father was severely beaten by Katabwita, Mpuga and Kihara called upon the chief and his policemen for aid. Finally, lineage sentiments prevailed, and Mosumba, after he had recovered, refused to press charges against Katabwita in the courts.

This increasing involvement of the chiefs and their courts in the fabric of the older system tends to be handled situationally rather than in terms of broad political principles. When Kihara is a defendant in a case in which it is fairly certain that the decision will go against him, he may wish that the courts did not exist, but when he himself has a case which he believes will be successful, he appreciates the fact that the court is there. On one level, this means that the chief does not work in a hostile situation in which all of the people perceive his acts as tyrannical and as a curtailment of their own power and freedom in abstract terms. Instead, he is assured of the whole-hearted support of those in whose favour he judges, and the tacit approval of the great majority who recognize the usefulness of the courts in the settlement of inter-village disputes.

A political system which depends merely upon its effective control of force and appeal to the self-interest of individuals is in a rather precarious position. In order to be based upon a firm foundation there must be a positive sense of loyalty towards it on the part of at least a significant number of the people concerned, and a feeling that it is a legitimate system, in the sense that the chiefs, for example, have not only the power to arrest people for certain offences but the right to do so. In other words it must go beyond situational changes and attempt to bring new values into being.

As far as the Amba are concerned this whole matter is closely connected with their desire to become Toro. Broadly speaking, contemporary conditions in Bwamba and in Uganda result from the impact of European society upon the local people. However, the processes by which change occurs are far more complex than this simple formulation would seem to indicate. In the political sphere, for example, Bwamba has not only been incorporated into the British Empire but has also been incorporated into the Kingdom of Toro. In terms of personal face-to-face contact Kihara, and especially Mpuga, have had a great amount of contact with Europeans, as compared with the average Amba. However, even in Mpuga's case, most of the new influences with ultimate European origins have been transmitted to him through the mediation of other Africans. For example, when he worked for the church his immediate superior was a Toro, as was the case when he was employed by the Yellow Fever Research Institute. When considering the changes which are brought about in the behaviour and viewpoint of individuals in a society such as the Amba, the sheer quantity of personal relationships is not the vital factor. Of greater importance is the group which the individual selects as his reference group. Despite the fact that Mpuga has had excellent opportunities for observing the behaviour of Europeans, and despite the fact that, through conversations with them, he has some understanding of their beliefs and values, he has been relatively unaffected by them. Instead, he has attempted to make himself a Toro and in so doing he has become sensitized to cues and sanctions emanating from them. Both groups are admitted to be superior to the Amba, and Europeans are admitted to be superior to the Toro, but the European is far too strange, far too alien, far too wealthy to serve as a model for behaviour. The differences between the behaviour and the beliefs of a traditional Amba and a Toro, while they are great, are not unbridgeable. Mpuga's desire to become a Toro is brought out clearly in the matter of eating rats: the Toro consider it disgusting to eat rats and Mpuga is not willing to have any of the members of his family eat them. It can be seen, too, in his attitude toward the plucking of eyebrows on the part of his wives: Amba women have always plucked their eyebrows, Toro women do not. Mpuga's is an extreme case, but all of the Amba are shifting in the direction of Toro patterns of behaviour and belief. In the political sphere the implication of this is that if one is to become a Toro one must submit to the Toro political system and this, in turn, gives it legitimacy.

The new administrative system is a bureaucratic organization which implies among other things that the people chosen to occupy roles within it should be selected on the basis of their qualifications. In the past, of course, almost all social roles were filled by ascription on the basis of kinship. Today individuals may try to get appointed to various posts and gain status and prestige in ways which were not possible previously. While new opportunities are created, new problems also arise. It is clear that Mpuga has been much more successful in the political sphere than Kihara has been. Kihara appears to have modelled himself upon his father and to have looked forward to a career in the government. In the earlier years of this century when the Toro were trying to establish their political system in Bwamba, Kihara's father was a valuable person. By all accounts, he appears to have been strong willed, forceful and brave in the face of personal danger. He was not the man to be squeamish about the methods he used in introducing a new system of law and order. Kihara appears to share many of his father's traits. He worked for the government, first as a policeman in the service of a Toro chief, which was a very good form of apprenticeship for government service, and then he became an unpaid local chief. However, he finally realized that his way was blocked. For one thing he was illiterate and it has long been impossible for anyone to obtain the position of parish chief without the ability to read and write. For another, the very character traits of ruthlessness and violence which served his father so well in earlier times were no longer thought desirable. Even his father appears to have outlived his usefulness. In the course of its development, a political system of this type requires different kinds of men at different periods.

Christianity is the second very powerful force now at work in Bwamba. As yet but a small minority of the Amba are Christians, but, as I have mentioned, there seems little doubt that the majority of them will be converted to one or another of the forms available to them. Although very often the aims of the administrator and those of the missionary are broadly similar in terms of the type of behaviour which they wish to encourage and the type of society which they wish to see developed there is, nevertheless, a very strong contrast between them in so far as they act as agents of change. The government's effectiveness in bringing about various changes lies in its control of force. The government merely had to say, 'Now you have been incorporated into the Uganda Protectorate,' and once the Amba realized that the government had the force to back up this statement the problem of order was solved. By contrast, the missionary or his agents try to bring about changes in behaviour by persuading the Amba to adopt new beliefs and standards of morality. He gains a measure of control over them only when they voluntarily become members of the church.

The missionary programme, the conversion of the pagan Amba, giving them a new understanding of their relation to the supernatural world and creating within them new ideals which will enable them to lead good Christian lives, is quite straightforward. However, as in all such endeavours there are unanticipated consequences.

Mpuga's commitment to Christianity is genuine. As far as beliefs are concerned there is little doubt but that he accepts the positive teaching of the Church as being true. For example, he accepts the Biblical account of the creation of the world as a historical fact. Furthermore he believes heaven and hell to have actual geographical locations.

The missionary realizes that the Amba have a set of beliefs about the supernatural. He would like to destroy these older beliefs and substitute new ones for them. However, while the creation of new beliefs is a relatively easy task, the destruction of old ones is very difficult indeed. All of this is quite clearly demonstrated by Mpuga. In his mind the old beliefs continue to exist beside those he has acquired as a Christian. The spirits which possessed his mother are as real to him as they are to a pagan such as Kihara. These spirits exist in the supernatural world and they can influence his life. This persistence of the pagan belief in the existence of the spirits does not cause Mpuga a great deal of intellectual difficulty. He assimilates the pagan spirits with the Christian devil. He has been taught that the devil can lead him into temptation and sin: to this belief he adds the idea that the devil and his cohorts, the pagan gods, can actively harm people, for instance by causing them to be ill.

On the level of action the problem is far more serious. Given the fact that these spirits exist and given the fact that they are dangerous what should a person like Mpuga do? The answer of the Church is to pray to God for strength and protection. This does not appear to be a completely satisfactory course of action for the reduction of the stress under which the individual is placed. Mpuga, for example, knows that the Amba for generations have had ritual prescriptions for dealing with these supernatural beings and he believes them to have been quite effective. Mpuga believes that if he prays to God, God may give him aid, but then again He may not, especially in view of the fact that, with his three wives, Mpuga lives in a continual state of sin. Thus a serious dilemma is posed. He may carry out the pagan ceremony and thus deliver himself from an immediate difficulty or avert an impending one. However, if he does this he will commit a sin and thus worsen his relations with God. But then again, if he does not carry out the ceremony, he may receive no aid from God. Obviously neither solution is entirely satisfactory, since each may lead to further difficulties. The course of action to be pursued in any particular case appears often to be decided by features of the external situation. When the snake-like creature, which Mpuga believed to be a manifestation of a spirit for which his father had previously built a shrine, appeared in his home, Mpuga followed the traditional ritual prescriptions. Fortunately for Mpuga the ritual was a very simple one which could be carried out privately without the knowledge of other people. The problem presented by the goddess Nyakala who possessed his mother and who, Mpuga believes, is trying to possess one of his wives is more complicated. If the proper ceremony is not carried out for her, she may cause misfortunes to descend upon Mpuga's house; in fact many of his current misfortunes may be due to her. The ceremony for her would be a very elaborate affair involving a large number of people, drumming and general publicity. Mpuga has always refused to carry out any conspicuous pagan ceremonies at his house. To do so, he says, would offend not only God but also the Christians.

As long as the society remains partly pagan there are means by which some of these difficulties may be overcome. Thus, although Mpuga and Bukombi are Christians it is possible for a pagan to carry out rites which will benefit his Christian kinsmen. Mpuga expressed this when he said that the goddess of his mother should not trouble him, but his pagan brother, Abongo. If only Nyakala would possess the wife of Abongo, Mpuga's anxiety would be lessened. The goddess could then be cared for properly and she would cease to trouble any of them. I have no doubt that should Abongo's wife show any symptoms which could be interpreted as resulting from the fact that she had been 'caught' by the goddess, Mpuga would do all he could to encourage this interpretation and would aid Abongo liberally in carrying out the rather expensive ceremony which would be entailed.

Although the Amba woman who becomes a Christian is caught in as many dilemmas in dealing with the supernatural world as a man, she escapes the danger of a major deviation in Christian practice. The most serious apparent difficulty with which the churches find themselves faced in Bwamba is the tendency for Christian men to acquire additional wives. Women, of course, cannot err in this way. Thus, at the present time, Lubangi can consider herself a good Christian woman, while Mpuga is constantly aware that he has sinned by acquiring additional wives.

An Amba who becomes a Christian finds himself placed in situations of great stress. The man, such as Kihara, who remains a pagan avoids them. This would seem to imply that few people would wish to become Christians and that those who did become converted would revert to paganism. However, becoming a Christian means much more to an Amba than merely joining a religious group and accepting its tenets. In Bwamba it is the gateway to the modern world. A clue to this attitude is given by the fact that the term used for Christians has no religious connotations, but instead means 'reader'. Literacy and education of a European type are seen as the keys which unlock the doors to new positions of prestige and influence. Kihara has lost much and Mpuga has gained much in the modern world because the latter is literate while the former is not. The possession of an education, roughly speaking two or more years of school, gives a person a special status in Amba society. An educated person is almost a Toro. Even as it would be unseemly for an educated person to go about in a loincloth, so also would it be unfitting for such a person to express a disbelief in Christianity. Education and Christianity are inextricably interwoven in the minds of the Amba. To be educated and to be a pagan is a contradiction in terms as far as they are concerned. As a result of the fact that Christianity confers benefits far beyond purely religious realms it appears to offer people such as Mpuga a net gain in spite of the stresses to which it subjects them.

Mpuga's adherence to Christianity does not lead to much trouble between himself and his pagan kinsmen and associates, although this sometimes occurs, but it does lead to severe internal conflict. Although this whole problem is but incompletely understood, evidence from other parts of Africa, as well as from other areas of the world, suggests that people subject to such internal conflict attempt to resolve them through the formation of new cults. Sometimes the anxiety generated by these conflicts has been released with sudden and explosive force.

THE CIRCUMSTANCES UNDER WHICH THE LIFE HISTORIES WERE COLLECTED

The first life history, that of Mpuga, was recorded after my wife and I had been in Bwamba for only four months. By that time a broad general outline of the social structure of the Amba had begun to take shape in my mind, although, of course, after such a short period a vast amount had yet to be learned. These first few months had been spent largely in visiting various parts of Bwamba in order to familiarize myself with the entire area, asking people to tell me such things as the sequence of events which occurred when a man died, attending burials and death ceremonies, taking censuses, and trying to learn to speak Kwamba.

At the time we were living in the Yellow Fever Research Institute's camp. The headquarters of the Institute, now known as the Virus Research Institute, is in Entebbe, the capital of Uganda. The camp, consisting of two living quarters and a laboratory, had served as a field station. Prior to our arrival research work at the Bwamba station had ceased and only a skeleton staff, consisting of a few local people employed to maintain the camp, remained. Dr. Horgan, the Director of the Institute, very kindly offered us the use of the facilities of the camp during the course of our field work. Mpuga was one of the Amba whom we found on the staff of the camp. A few months later the camp was closed and all the salaried positions, including that held by Mpuga, were abolished.

Thus it came about that Mpuga was one of the first Amba with whom we became acquainted. His home is less than a quarter of a mile away from the camp, and we became acquainted with other members of his family in the course of visits to his home. A number of long conversations were held with him concerning various aspects of life in Bwamba. In these discussions he showed a great deal of intelligence and furthermore he was quite willing to admit his ignorance when the conversation entered a sphere beyond his knowledge, a not inconsiderable virtue, as many fieldworkers will testify. Mpuga, as a result of his prolonged personal contact with Europeans, was much more at ease with them than was the ordinary Amba.

When in the initial period of fieldwork, I decided to record a life history, Mpuga appeared to be a sensible choice. I was interested in discovering whether or not it would be possible to obtain a fairly lengthy life history from an Amba and whether or not such a document would provide valuable material for the study of the social structure. When the life history had been collected, I felt amply rewarded for the time which I had spent upon it.

Once Mpuga's life history had been obtained, we decided to obtain those of his wives, in order to obtain similar data from a woman's point of view and in order to see how much light they would throw on the material contained in Mpuga's life history. Of his three wives, the life histories of two, Lubangi and Koke, were obtained. When we were ready to work with Kijungu, she was away visiting relatives. Later, when we had another opportunity to work with her, she was ill. We then recorded the life history of Kihara and also those of another family in the village. Finally, Mpuga was asked to keep a diary for a period of several months.

When I decided to work with Mpuga, I told him that the recording of his life history would probably take a considerable time, and I offered him a pair of gray flannel trousers for his co-operation. In fact, a period of some fifty-five hours was spent with him during a two-week period. The trousers became the most prized item in his wardrobe, and he only wore them on special occasions. By this time, Mpuga was well aware of my interest in the customs of the Amba. He was rather surprised, however, by my request for his life history, because he could see but little sense in such a project. I assured him, however, that some people in Europe and America would be interested in the story of his life. He began willingly enough, and he appeared to enjoy relating his experiences.

When we decided to record the life histories of Mpuga's wives, we asked him if he would give his permission, which he did, and then we asked him to obtain his wives' consent. After these preliminaries we talked to them ourselves and explained what we wanted them to do. Mpuga's wives and Kihara were offered a shilling a day. We then worked with them for two hours each day. Kihara, whose life history was collected after those of Lubangi and Koke, said that his stories were worth much more than those of any woman, so we paid him two shillings a day. These wages were very high, since non-skilled labourers in Bwamba at that time received about twenty shillings a month. This meant that all of them, and especially Kihara, could earn more than a labourer could for only two hours work a day. The wages were put on this high scale in the hope that they would be more strongly motivated to keep their appointments. This was successful with Kihara and with the other men with whom we worked, but the women proved to be more difficult. They were much busier than were the men, cooking, caring for children and doing the bulk of the agricultural work. Subsequently we thought that it would have been better if we had offered the women say a pound of meat on every day on which an interview was held. Very often they arrived several hours later than the time we had agreed upon, or after having sent a message saying that they would come, they would then fail to appear. All of this means, of course, that the collection of life histories can be extremely time-consuming. However, when the women did appear, they were quite easy to work with and talked very freely.

The facilities of the Yellow Fever Camp, or something like it, were absolutely essential to work of this nature. Privacy was a necessity and in their own homes this was impossible to obtain, because anybody who was

267

passing by would always stop and listen to any conversation in progress. Again privacy was unobtainable when we lived in a tent, because people would have been very offended had we said that we wished to interview certain of them privately. When we lived in a tent in a village we felt free to walk into anyone's house to participate in what was going on there. They quite rightly felt equally entitled to make free use of our tent. In the Yellow Fever Camp it was possible to have an office in which conditions of privacy could be obtained. The Amba were accustomed to respect the privacy of the European research workers who had lived there.

Furthermore, the use of a camp made it possible to offer them wages without complicating other aspects of the field situation. The camp was looked upon as a place where people worked and received wages. Thus, it was natural that if they came to us there at stated times for our purposes, they should be paid. On the other hand the Amba did not receive the impression that we were people who were prepared to pay for information. Had this impression got abroad, it would have been well-nigh impossible to conduct fieldwork. The dangers of this possibility were clear to us from the situation in regard to photography. A band of pygmies is often to be found in an encampment along the road. The few pygmies who live in Bwamba are the only ones found in British East Africa. As a result they are often photographed. Most people who have photographed them over the years have given them money, a course of action which today is suggested to them by the pygmies themselves who set up an incessant chatter of, 'Shillingi! Senti!' The Amba realize that this occurs and as a result they are most unwilling to have their pictures taken without financial reward. They feel that a European who takes their photograph and who does not pay them for the privilege is a thief. As a result of this attitude we found it necessary for the most part to give up all attempts at photography. In the present context, however, no harm was done, since the collection of life histories under these special circumstances and the payment for the work involved did not become associated in the eyes of the Amba with more general aspects of my work.

An interpreter was used throughout. At the time I could not have gathered life histories in Kwamba. However, even when a certain knowledge of Kwamba had been acquired, this was irrelevant as far as this particular group of people was concerned, since all of them speak Lubwezi. It might have been preferable, of course, once the trial autobiography of Mpuga had been taken, to have waited and to have obtained life histories from Kwamba-speaking people at a later date. The fact remains, however, that any accounts of this sort would have to have been originally spoken in a local language and then translated into English. Felix Rwambarali, the interpreter, is to my mind a very extraordinary person. He has now become quite an influential person in the Uganda political scene. For instance, he is a member of the Uganda Coffee Board. At the time when the life histories were recorded he was the overseer of the Yellow Fever Camp. When the camp was closed, he remained in Bwamba in order to work as my research assistant and to tend his coffee groves. He had lived in Bwamba for several years when I first met him, and he knew Mpuga and

Kihara and their families quite intimately. Lubwezi is very closely related to Lutoro, his native language, and in the course of the years he had gained a very full command of the former. By the time the life histories were recorded, I had discussed anthropology in general and my work in particular with him at considerable length, and he had acquired quite a clear idea of what I was trying to do. He has had a secondary-school education, and his command of English is very good indeed, mainly as a result of having spent a considerable amount of time in the company of English-speaking people. In short, I feel that even had I known Lubwezi, his translations would have been preferable to mine.

In collecting the life histories we tried to give as little direction as possible. We merely asked the informants to tell us what they had done and what had happened to them during their lives and left the decision as to what aspects of their lives should be commented upon to them. They found this quite easy. They are accustomed, in the numerous disputes which they have with one another, to lay their cases before other people and on these occasions they give long coherent accounts of the sequence of events. Again, if a husband has been away for a few days his wife will give him a detailed account of what has transpired in his absence. Furthermore, they give their accounts, by and large, in the correct temporal sequence. Thus the idea of starting the account from their earliest memories and proceeding to the present made sense to them. This does not mean that they gave their accounts in a strictly chronological order. Very often in a later interview they would remember incidents which had occurred earlier and they would then recount them. However, the point is that they did make an attempt to relate the events of their lives in a chronological order.

When they were talking, we made no effort to question them or to divert them to other topics. The only occasions when we did this occurred with Lubangi and Kihara when they became involved in long tales which they had heard at second-hand and which had no relevance to their own affairs. In each case after this had gone on for two sessions and they showed no tendency to return to their own careers, we stopped them and asked them if they would return to their own lives after they had completed the episodes they were relating at the moment. When they themselves had completed their own accounts, we did ask them some supplementary questions. Kihara, for instance, had recounted to us his career as a policeman and as a chief. We asked him to tell us about any other experiences of employment which he might have had during his lifetime. Again, both Mpuga and Kihara were asked whether or not they had had any bloodbrothers, and their accounts of blood-brotherhood followed as a result of this. Finally, we asked them some minor and specific questions. For instance, upon reading our notes we found that in a certain place we would not be certain to whom a certain pronoun referred, or again it might be unclear from the text whether or not the word 'father' referred to the person's actual father or to a classificatory father in the same lineage. In retrospect we wished that we had suggested more topics to them. We would have liked, of course, to have asked them about specific events in which they were involved and which came to light in the accounts of other people.

This was quite out of the question, for each of them trusted us not to betray their confidences to the others with whom they were living. Their relations with one another are filled with enough tension as it is without fuel being added to the flames by an outsider.

The interview situation always contained three people, the person whose life history was being recorded, Felix Rwambarali, the interpreter, and my wife or myself. Although only one of us (E. H. W.) recorded Mpuga's autobiography, in the other cases we alternated. We could discover no difference in the type of material which was produced according to which of us was recording it. The Amba in general are so impressed by the difference between Europeans and themselves that the difference in sex between us was unimportant. Furthermore, we often found that unsophisticated Amba were not sure of the sex of European women they encountered. Mr. Rwambarali was well known to them. Furthermore they were well aware that he was a devout Anglican, and that he did not share many of their beliefs and attitudes. On the other hand, it was also known to them that he was very tolerant towards them, an attitude which he possessed long before I explained its importance in anthropological fieldwork to him.

They knew that we were interested in their whole way of life, and they had been told that we approved of their customs and beliefs. Nevertheless, I do not think that they believed this, at least at the time when the autobiographies were taken. Mpuga and Lubangi were most self-conscious of their Amba background. Lubangi, I think, tried to picture herself as a modern Christian woman. She could not believe that we did not, in our hearts, have contempt for the older pattern of Amba life. Kihara, on the other hand, took pride in the fact that he was to a large extent an Amba of the old school. Koke, by contrast, seemed less concerned with the impression she gave and used the interview situation as one in which she could give vent to some of her complaints about the mistreatment she believes she has received during her life and her present-day difficulties. Mpuga realized that we did not take the attitude of, say, a missionary towards their way of life. However, he does see himself as a modern, advanced type of Amba man. I think his acceptance of our role and our attitude was eased by his contacts with the medical research workers, who had taken a lively interest in native customs and who had, if anything, a predilection for the older as against the newer patterns. Nevertheless the fact that he had some reservations is demonstrated by the fact that the amount of material dealing with witchcraft and pagan religious beliefs in the autobiography is very slight compared to that in the diary, which was written later when he knew us better.

As for the diary, Mpuga was hired as an assistant whose only duty was to write it. He thought this a most extraordinary type of job and was very pleased to accept it. His surprise was tempered, however, by the fact that he himself had known Europeans who had hired people to sit high in the branches of trees in order to catch mosquitoes. He made entries in the diary at night in his own house, and each week Felix Rwambarali read a translation of it to me, which I typed.

In preparing the material for publication changes have been made when they have been necessary for clarity. Personal names and the relationship of particular people to the narrator have sometimes been added in preference to pronouns, in order to increase intelligibility. Some incidents have been rearranged in a more strictly chronological sequence. A certain amount of material has been deleted. At times, knowing where our interests lay, our informants would embark upon lengthy accounts of purely ethnographic interests. For example, Lubangi at one point started to tell me about the different types of fish and their names. Material of this type has been discarded, as have accounts of events which had no relevance to their own lives. Perhaps the changes made reduce the value of the texts to psychologists, but they do not do violence to the pattern of Amba thought and expression. I have changed the names of the people principally involved, and also the names of certain lineages and villages. Otherwise nothing of a factual nature has been altered.

Index